D. J. WEST

---—◎—---

The Young Offender

GERALD DUCKWORTH & CO. LTD.
3 Henrietta Street, London, W.C.2.

First published 1967
simultaneously by Penguin Books Ltd. and Duckworth

Printed in Great Britain by
Cox & Wyman Ltd., London, Fakenham and Reading

Contents

1 The Youthful Record of Crime
What is meant by the 'young offender'   11
The general outlook   14
The favourite crimes of youth   19
The expectations of a delinquent career   24
Summing up the situation   29

2 The True Extent of Youthful Crime
The crime wave   33
The deterioration in morals   36
The extent of unrecorded delinquency   39
Honesty non-existent?   42
The delinquency problem in perspective   47

3 The Social Background of Offenders
Criminals as creatures of circumstance   51
Low social class   55
Financial hardship   61
Bad neighbourhood   64
Race and colour   67
Broken homes   69
Too big a family   73
Combinations of adversity   74
Social pressures not the final answer   78

4 Some Social Theories
Schools of crime   83
Social protest theories   87
Second thoughts on the delinquent sub-culture   95
Choosing between the theories   99

5 The 'Bad' Seed?
The born criminal   105
The dim-witted delinquent   109
Physical defects   118
The criminal physique   124
Inherited criminality   129

6 Some Psychological Theories about the Development of Criminals
A behaviouristic view of criminal traits   137
Psychoanalytic theories about the origins of the anti-social
    character   147
The 'neurotic' criminal   152

7 Verifying the Psychological Factors in Delinquency
Maternal deprivation and criminality   157
'Prediction studies' and their relevance to the psychology of
    delinquents   163
Personality measures applied to delinquents   167
Classifying delinquents on a psychological basis   173
Classifying delinquents by their moral development   178

8 Girls, Sex, Drugs and Violence
Drugs   185
Young sex offenders   192
Girl delinquents   196
Youthful violence   200

9 The Penal System
Sentences for the young   207
Courts for the young   214
Penal régimes   219
Detention centres   223
Borstals   225
Approved schools   229

10 Delinquency Control and Prevention
Protection, detection and deterrence   233
Welfare   240
Education   242
Capturing the audience   246
Evaluation of schemes for delinquency prevention   252

11 The Treatment of Apprehended Delinquents
From psychotherapy to therapeutic community   261
Therapeutic communities in action   267
Behaviour therapy   276
Demonstrating results   278

12 Some Cautionary Afterthoughts
   Our state of ignorance   289
   The phenomena of youthful crime   291
   Delinquency theories   293
   Delinquency prevention and treatment   296

List of References   301

General Index   325

Index of Persons   331

1 The Youthful Record of Crime

Crime today covers everything from the housewife who shakes her doormat in the street after 8.0 a.m. . . . to the robber who hits an old woman with a length of iron pipe.

Barbara Wootton (quoting Glanville Williams), *Social Science and Social Pathology* (1959). Allen & Unwin. p. 305.

All one really needs to start with is a first approximation sufficient to indicate what one is talking about; the fuller and more exact description should emerge later as the investigation progresses.

T.H.Marshall, *Class, Citizenship and Social Development* (1964). New York, Doubleday. p. 174.

What is meant by the 'young offender'

Defining offenders

The offences committed by young people differ in kind and in motive from the typical crimes of adults. Infants may steal things not knowing this is forbidden, older children may do so because they have not yet learned the self-restraint which normally develops with increasing years, and adolescents may break the law to show off their daring or to annoy their parents. Adults are more often credited with taking calculated risks for the sake of dishonest gains. The relevance of age to culpability and to methods of control is recognized in the statutes of every modern legal system, although the precise chronology differs from one country to another.

In England, criminal responsibility begins at the age of ten. (Before 1964 it used to be eight.) A child of this age is held to be capable of deliberate criminal intent, and liable to legal punishment, but up to the age of seventeen he is dealt with by special juvenile courts and protected from the full rigours of the criminal law. Even after that, and up to the age of twenty-one, the young offender receives some consideration for not having attained full adult status. Recent legislation, not yet in force, envisages that in future persons under twenty-one years of age will not normally be sent to prison, but will serve all custodial sentences separately from adults, in borstal institutions or detention centres.* In this book, the term young offenders covers all who are under twenty-one, which includes juveniles, who are those under seventeen, and children, who are those under fourteen [91].

Text-books of criminology sometimes begin by emphasizing the limitation of their subject-matter to behaviour defined as criminal by the legal code of the day. Unfortunately nature takes no heed of academic or legal convenience, and to find out about the causes of delinquency one has to go further than court

---

* Except for re-convictions following release from borstals, or for long sentences of three years or more for serious crimes. Criminal Justice Act, 1961, s.3.

procedures. For instance, one cannot hope to elucidate how absence of a father, or mental dullness, may contribute to delinquent behaviour without also examining fatherless and mentally dull children who do not break the law.

Even where discussion is limited to persons convicted by the courts, it is not so easy to define precisely and comprehensively what is meant by a delinquent, especially in the case of juveniles. The familiar tags – 'a crime is what the law says it is' and 'a criminal is a person convicted of a crime' – are not such infallible guides as the text-books make out. For instance, how does one categorize the condition of being beyond the control of one's parents, or being 'in moral danger', or of failing to attend school – an offence under the Education Act of 1944 for which the parents may be convicted rather than the child? These matters have no parallel in the criminal code relating to adults. Official statistics often simplify matters by equating 'criminal' with 'convicted of an indictable offence' or an offence which would be indictable if committed by a person of seventeen or over.

The predominance of thieves

Generalizations about delinquents are subject to serious limitations. The legal process by which the group is defined produces a strange hotch-potch of characters, including anything from rapists to children who keep running away. Clearly they need to be sub-divided somehow, otherwise the search for common factors and predisposing causes is doomed to failure, and yet a great deal of research and comment refers to delinquency in the abstract, with never a hint that this label covers a multitude of things.

Fortunately, observations about delinquency in general, and statistical trends based upon the sum total of law-breakers, need not be written off completely. Although the Home Office classification of indictable offences lists ninety-nine separate categories, some with as many as twenty to thirty sub-divisions, in practice nearly nine out of ten convictions are for crimes of dishonesty – stealing, burglary or fraud – and among young persons the proportion is even greater. For 1965 the distribution of convictions was as in Table 1.

Table 1. Numbers of persons of all ages found guilty of indictable offences (England and Wales, 1965)*

Offence	Number (in thousands)	Percentage
Larceny	128.6	59
Breaking and entering	44.6	20
Receiving, frauds, false pretences	17.2	8
Violence against the person	15.5	7
Sexual offences	5.5	3
Unclassified	7.0	3
Total	218.4	100

In England (as in all the developed countries) 'crime', roughly speaking, means thieving. The persons who go in for crimes against property may be a somewhat heterogeneous collection of individuals, but at least their activities have something in common, and as a group they differ distinctly from the average of the population in age, sex distribution, social-class membership, and probably in temperament. Among persons convicted of indictable offences, they preponderate to such a degree that their activities determine all the statistical trends of crime, and their characteristics are reflected in all the statistical observations on offenders. And this is true for both young and old offenders. Therefore, when statements are made in this book or elsewhere about delinquents or criminals without further qualification, the reader must remember that to all intents and purposes this means thieves. All other types of offender must be isolated from the general mass and considered separately.

The use of statistics

Much of the raw material of researches into criminal behaviour at any age consists of figures of convictions and re-convictions, figures for the varying incidence of different kinds of crimes as reported by police and courts, and the break-down of these figures according to age, sex or social class of the offender, and the type of punishment or treatment awarded. Although many people interested in the individual criminal's motives find such figures boring, they provide a fund of background information essential to serious discussion.

* *Criminal Statistics, England and Wales, 1965*, Appendix I.

Owing to the difficulties in classifying crimes, in obtaining accurate records set out in comparable form, and in knowing whether all sections of the community have been subjected to the same degree of scrutiny, deductions from official statistics have to be made with great reserve. Whereas the number of officially recorded house-breakings or shootings to kill may give a reasonable picture of the incidence of these crimes, the frequency with which naughty boys are brought to court is likely to reflect the policy of parents, teachers and police in dealing with juvenile misconduct as much as the actual incidence of delinquency. The need for caution in this regard will appear more clearly in the next chapter in relation to actual instances in which figures have proved misleading. Comparisons between one country and another are particularly difficult because numbers of convictions take no account of the vastly different levels of defining, reporting, detecting and recording crimes which exist in different parts of the world.

Apart from the statistical complexities of cross-cultural comparisons, it is probably best, in the first instance, to study delinquency in one particular country (in this case England), since the offences committed and the motives involved are very closely tied to the social setting. It would be nonsensical to compare juvenile law-breakers in the East End of London with the activities of youth in the wild tribes of Borneo, and almost as unwise to equate the delinquency of an American city that has a large Negro and immigrant population and a national tradition of criminal gangs and firearms with the delinquency of an English provincial town, or with the delinquency of a country like Algeria which has recently undergone the upheaval of war and revolution.

The general outlook

The ages of convicted offenders

In England, about fifty per cent of the persons found guilty of indictable offences are in the age range ten to twenty-one, which is more than double the proportion of this age group in the population. (In 1965 approximately twenty per cent of males over ten were under twenty-one – *Criminal Statistics*, Appendix II.)

The incidence of convictions at various ages is shown in Table 2. Among males there is a steep rise in the frequency of convictions from the minimum age of ten years to a peak at fourteen, with a swift dwindling thereafter, so that at twenty-five it is only a half what it was at fourteen, and after sixty it is very small indeed. The trend among females, shown in the same table, is rather similar, and also shows a peak at fourteen, although the decline with age is less swift. The table also shows plainly that boys constitute the main problem in England, as in other countries. At the younger age levels the incidence of convictions of females is only about a tenth that of males. It has been pointed out with justification that troublesome boys go in for crime, whereas troublesome girls merely go with boys. At one time, when the school-leaving age was fourteen, the peak incidence of convictions for both sexes was at age thirteen. Some authorities confidently predict that the peak will occur at age fifteen when the school-leaving age is raised again.

Table 2. Numbers of persons of various ages convicted of indictable offences per thousand of population of the same age (England and Wales, 1965)*

Age	Males	Females
10	6.7	0.5
11	12.5	1.0
12	20.5	2.8
13	27.5	4.2
14	35.4	5.9
15	30.8	5.1
16	26.5	3.8
17	28.2	3.4
18	27.3	2.8
19	26.8	3.0
20	23.9	2.5
21–4	20.2	2.0
25–9	14.3	1.9
30–39	7.8	1.5
40–49	4.2	1.3
50–59	1.9	1.0
60 +	0.7	0.4
All ages	9.7	1.5

* *Criminal Statistics, England and Wales, 1965,* Appendix III (a).

Many people seem to have got the idea that the *Criminal Statistics, England and Wales*, show an ever-increasing proportion of young people among convicted persons, but this is incorrect. The total number of convictions has increased, but even before the war, in the year 1938, the same proportion of convicted offenders, about a half, were under twenty-one. The Home Office *Report of the Committee on Children and Young Persons* (1960, Appendix 1) gives graphs of the numbers per 100,000 of population of males in the age groups eight to thirteen inclusive, fourteen to sixteen inclusive, and seventeen to twenty inclusive who were found guilty of indictable offences in each year since 1938. In each age group, up to 1953, the general trend was towards a rise in incidence year by year, with the groups maintaining roughly the same position relative to each other, the highest incidence being in the fourteen to sixteen age range, the lowest in the seventeen to twenty range. Since 1953, there has been a noticeable change. In the youngest age group, the incidence has increased only slightly. In the other age groups it has increased more sharply, but especially so in the seventeen to twenty group, which now has much the biggest incidence of convictions, even though the actual peak still remains at age fourteen. The significant statistical change in recent years, therefore, has been in the redistribution of offenders within the youthful category, those in the seventeen to twenty range having increased much more than those under fourteen.

'*Non-indictable*' offences

The practice of dividing the *Criminal Statistics* into indictable crimes and non-indictable offences, the latter being considered in principle less serious and often ignored in discussions on crime trends, has the effect of exaggerating the contribution made by juveniles to the crime problem. The non-indictable offences are in fact more numerous, include some very serious infringements of the social code, and probably have more relevance to the behaviour of the average person than the more dramatic indictable offences. They include common assaults; drunkenness; malicious damage; taking away motor vehicles without the owner's consent; reckless, dangerous, and drunken driving; offences by prostitutes; and two of the largest categories of sexual offences, exhibitionism and homosexual importuning. Compared with their numbers in the population, young people are actually under-represented among those convicted of non-indictable crimes. This is because the enormous numbers of motoring offences which make up the bulk of this category are committed pre-dominantly by adults. Even excluding these, some of the other common offences in the non-indictable category, such as drunkenness or failure to take out licences for dogs, cars or wirelesses, are at least as frequent after twenty-one as before, if only because juveniles, at least, have so little opportunity to commit them.

In an article in *The Times** Michael Power, who was engaged in a survey of juvenile delinquency in east London, made the point that the practice of equating crime with indictable offences may lead to dubious conclusions, since some of the activities of the young which arouse most public concern, such as malicious damage, insulting behaviour, and taking away motor cars, are charged as non-indictable. Whereas younger children are respon-sible for large numbers of minor larcenies, which account for the peak of indictable offences at age fourteen, these other kinds of offences are commoner in youths, and account for the fact that more youths of sixteen than boys of fourteen actually appear before juvenile courts, although not necessarily charged with indictable crimes.

In this book, because of the lack of research studies on non-indictable offences, the usual practice has been followed, and, except where the contrary is stated, 'crimes' and 'convictions' refer to the indictable category only.

The situation in other countries

Although comparisons between the criminal statistics of different countries are open to fallacy, it is worth noting some apparent contrasts in the trends of convictions of young persons reported from a variety of places. In some countries, such as Japan, the United States and Sweden, criminal convictions, and especially convictions of young offenders, have been increasing rapidly ever

* 9 August 1962.

since the end of the last world war. The increase has been particularly noticeable in the more prosperous countries. In other countries, such as England, there has been a decline in convictions of juveniles, either immediately after the war or in the early 1950s, only to be followed by a sharp increase since. In many countries which have recently experienced rapid socio-economic changes (such as West Africa and Latin American states) published statistics suggest that a serious delinquency problem has arisen where it never existed before. In some cases this may be due simply to the introduction of official record keeping; but at least in those under-developed countries undergoing rapid urban growth, social observers confirm the appearance of new forms of delinquency in the new towns [39]. Areas in which delinquency statistics have remained at a negligibly low level seem to be limited to remote agricultural regions and island communities, such as St Helena or some of the Pacific Islands [160; 165].

Exceptions to the general trends are Denmark, where the juvenile delinquency figures have been going down ever since the war, and Italy, where they have also been going down until very recently. Since both these countries have enjoyed increasing prosperity, the association between this factor and rising juvenile crime statistics cannot be invariable.

Cross-cultural studies to discover the nature and possible causes of these different trends might well yield valuable insights; but the difficulty of carrying out such projects, and still more the difficulty of obtaining finance for them, has held back research. In my opinion, it is one of the drawbacks of the way modern social research is organized that the more important and fundamental issues tend to be neglected in favour of easy, short-term projects that satisfy the academic demand for quick results.

The expectation of becoming a criminal

On the fundamental question of how far the increasing volume of youthful crime results from a greater persistence on the part of established offenders, or a wider recruitment of first offenders, the statistics give no immediate answer. Although the number of convictions of young persons has increased dramatically, the high proportion of first offenders among all young persons found guilty has changed only slightly, from seventy-four per cent in 1952 to seventy per cent in 1962. An ingenious calculation by Alan Little of the London School of Economics [156], comparing the statistics of indictable crimes by young persons in the age range eight years up to twenty-one in the years 1952 and 1962, suggests that over this decade twenty-eight per cent of the increase was due to growth of population, forty-two per cent to increased numbers of first offenders, and only thirty per cent to increased recidivism – including recidivism of the additional first offenders. It seems clear that a wider recruitment of new offenders has made the major contribution to the increase in youthful convictions. In a sense this is an optimistic conclusion, since it is the recidivist who represents the real menace, whereas the first offender usually disappears from the statistics after either his initial or his second appearance.

Nevertheless, the stubborn fact remains that these days a very substantial section of the young male population have the experience of being convicted at some time. Taking as a base the statistics of year 1961 for convictions of males aged fourteen to twenty inclusive, and counting convictions for theft, sex offences, violence, drinking and disorderly behaviour (whether classed as indictable or non-indictable), G. Prys Williams [212] has made the following estimate. In England and Wales, of all boys aged fourteen in 1961, 'in the absence of spectacular improvement, about one boy in every five will be convicted before he is twenty-one'. A rather similar estimate, made by Rose and Avison [215], based upon the statistics of 1962, concluded that the risk for males of being convicted for an indictable offence was 12.4 per cent by the eighteenth birthday, and 29.5 per cent for a total life span.

The favourite crimes of youth

The substance of youthful offences

Figure 1, taken from the *Criminal Statistics, 1964*, shows how the convictions of males in different age groups are distributed according to type of (indictable) offence. The under-fourteen group has the highest proportion of convictions for larceny, the

fourteen to sixteen group has the highest proportion of breaking
and entering, the seventeen to twenty group has the highest
proportion of violence, while the twenty-one and over group has
the highest proportions of convictions in the sex and fraud
categories. The picture fits in with the general impression that
young men are responsible for most criminal violence, adolescents
for the cruder types of offences against property involving breaking into premises, and older persons for the more sophisticated
types of dishonesty. It is safe to say that, in England, although
young persons go in for crimes legally classified as serious, notably
breaking and entering, compared with older offenders their scale
of operations is usually more limited, their techniques more
primitive and their organization less professional, especially so
in the case of juveniles.

Former approved-school boys, being mostly recidivists, might
be expected to commit more serious crimes, but a recent follow-
up study of one such group showed that the bulk of the offences
they committed in the three years after release were rather
trivial. Three quarters consisted of minor thefts, traffic offences,
loitering, and similar charges [234]. One boy had been convicted
of the classic offence of cycling without a rear lamp, and another,
who was wearing a studded belt when the police raided a café,
was for this convicted of carrying an offensive weapon. There
were no crimes of violence in which the victim was killed or
detained in hospital, no firearms were carried, and there were no
offences involving narcotics. Only eight per cent of the offences
were distinctly serious, the worst being the rape of an unwilling
girl by a group of boys, and some skilful shop-breaking for
expensive goods.*

Youthful crimes of violence arouse particular concern. An
analysis by Charlotte Banks [13] of the substance of the violent
offences of a sample of over 900 young men under twenty-one
sentenced to imprisonment, detention, or borstal showed that
violence constituted no more than ten per cent of the total of
offences. Among these offences of violence, no more than six
per cent led to serious injury or death. The circumstances of the
offences divided into three groups of roughly equal number:
youngsters brawling among themselves, fights with the police in

* See also p. 26.

Figure 1. Males found guilty of indictable offences in the year 1964, by age and class of offence*

Type of offence	Males under 14 years	Males 14 – 16 years	Males 17 – 20 years	Males of all ages
Miscellaneous	2.4	2.1	3.0	3.2
Sex	0.8	2.2	2.7	3.1
Violence, robbery	1.5	5.4	11.9	8.3
Receiving, frauds	5.3	5.6	5.3	8.0
Breaking and entering	32.9	33.1	25.8	23.5
Larceny	57.1	51.6	51.3	53.9
Total of all offences	100%	100%	100%	100%

* *Criminal Statistics, England and Wales, 1964*, p. xiii.

the course of arrests, and attacks made on others in the course of thefts. In addition there were a few cases of family squabbles. In the bulk of offences the violence consisted of punching or pushing aside, and the injury was trivial or technical.

At the same time one must never lose sight of the fact that, though the majority of young offenders may not commit very serious crimes, a small minority are as dangerous as anyone can ever be, and are responsible for some of the most atrocious and brutal crimes on record. Robbery with violence is most frequent among young men in their late teens or very early twenties. In the case of murder, it is often pointed out that the majority of offenders are over thirty years of age and that most of them are ordinarily law-abiding citizens who have attacked one of their own family under the influence of insanity or severe mental stress. However, among predatory murderers, those who kill strangers in the furtherance of robbery or other crimes, some are boys of sixteen and seventeen, and altogether something like a half are under twenty-one, and a large majority have a previous criminal record [277].

In the female sex, the trends of indictable crime are rather different. For all ages, breaking and entering is unusual, representing only 3.9 per cent of the total convictions of females. Sexual offences are very rare (0.1 per cent), but larceny is particularly common (83.1 per cent). The difference in the distribution of female crimes at different age levels is relatively slight. Soliciting for prostitution is a common type of female offence, but being non-indictable it is not included in the above percentages.

Where the increases have been greatest

In recent years in England, as in most countries, there has been a substantial increase in numbers of convictions, but it has been by no means uniform for all categories of offences. Certain crimes, which are predominantly the work of youthful offenders, have increased more than most. Convictions for breaking and entering, for example, have actually doubled over the last ten years. About the steepest rise of all, however, has been in convictions for drinking offences by juveniles of fourteen to sixteen, both boys and girls, which more than trebled between 1955 and

1962, largely due to the number of reported transgressions of the licensing laws by people under age trying to obtain drinks in public houses.

Convictions for crimes of violence have been increasing for all age groups more rapidly than most crimes, but especially so among youths. In recent years, however, convictions for indictable offences of violence against the person have tended to stabilize as far as the age distribution is concerned, with about fifteen per cent of those convicted in the juvenile age range, and another twenty-seven per cent of young persons over sixteen but under twenty-one.

A significant part of the increase in crimes of violence is only apparent, and due to the policy of charging as indictable offences acts which used to be dealt with as non-indictable common assaults. Between 1938 and 1960 the increase in non-indictable assaults was less than the increase in the size of the population. If, instead of considering, as is customary, convictions for indictable crimes of violence only, the non-indictable convictions are added, then the increase in total incidence of crimes of violence is no more than the general increase for indictable crimes of all kinds [13].

F. H. McClintock [163] made an interesting analysis of the circumstances associated with indictable crimes of violence in London in the years 1950, 1957 and 1960. The annual number of convictions of persons under twenty-one almost trebled from 1950 to 1960, but the types of offence remained much the same. Violent sex offences formed 10.1 per cent of the total in 1950, 13.5 per cent in 1960. Domestic disputes were 11.8 per cent of the total in 1950, 8.3 per cent in 1960. The most noteworthy change was a relative decrease in attacks on the police (from 32.9 per cent to 15.4 per cent) but a corresponding increase in attacks committed in streets, public houses, cafés, etc. (from forty-five per cent to sixty-three per cent). The figures for convictions of adults differed from these most conspicuously in the much larger proportion of attacks arising from family disputes (about forty-one per cent), and the much smaller proportion of attacks occurring in public places. This provides some confirmation of the common observation that violence committed by young persons often takes the form of rowdyism and fighting around cafés, dance-halls and similar resorts frequented by teenagers. In order to see whether preference for this type of violent hooliganism has been increasing more than other kinds, McClintock used data from the years 1950 to 1957 to compare the following categories of indictable crimes of violence: (1) unprovoked attacks; (2) attacks on strangers following some slight dispute; (3) attacks on bystanders who had tried to remonstrate; (4) gang battles. Altogether, these four categories, corresponding to what most people would regard as hooliganism, formed in 1950 27.6 per cent, and in 1957 29.9 per cent, of the violent crimes for which persons under twenty-one were convicted. So during that period, at least, young hooliganism had not increased appreciably more than other types of violence.

Although convictions of young offenders for larceny have not been increasing so rapidly as convictions for drunkenness or violence, nevertheless certain types of theft have shown a particularly sharp increase, notably pilfering from motor vehicles and larceny from shops. These types of theft are the ones likely to be most influenced by the temptations presented by more and more cars without garages, and more and more goods displayed on open shelves in shops and supermarkets. Leslie Wilkins [282] has plotted on a graph the numbers of offences of larceny from motor vehicles in the years 1938 to 1961, and the numbers of private vehicles registered in the same years, and demonstrated a close correlation between the two curves.

The expectations of a delinquent career

The chances of re-conviction

The majority of offenders are never re-convicted after the first time, but, other things being equal, the younger the offender when first he is convicted, the greater the likelihood that he will be re-convicted. Home Office research [132] has shown that of all criminal first offenders only thirty-six per cent are re-convicted within five years, but for children under fourteen years of age the re-conviction rate is fifty-two per cent. The figure decreases sharply with increasing age: for first offenders aged fourteen to twenty years it is forty-two per cent, for those who have reached twenty-one but are still under thirty it is thirty per cent, for those of thirty to thirty-nine it is fifteen per cent, and for those of forty and over it is only nine per cent. Naturally the chances of re-conviction are proportionately greater for offenders who have been previously convicted, but the general rule still holds true that, for any given number of previous convictions, the expected re-conviction rate is greater the younger the offender. For instance, with three previous convictions, the approximate re-conviction rates of national samples are ninety per cent for juvenile offenders, seventy-five per cent for those aged seventeen to twenty-nine, and fifty per cent for those aged thirty and over. Incidentally, the use of a standard five-year period for the calculation of re-conviction rates is justified by the observation that, at all ages, only a small proportion of offenders are re-convicted after a lapse of more than five years free from convictions. Follow-up studies of borstal boys confirm that re-conviction rates are definitely worse for boys first convicted at an early age. In the famous Mannheim and Wilkins study [168] it was forty-six per cent for those first convicted at sixteen or later, but sixty-five per cent for those first convicted at eleven or earlier.

In case these figures present a too gloomy impression of the criminal tendencies of young people, it is only fair to look at the other side of the coin. The fact that the peak age for criminal convictions is fourteen, and that each successive age group thereafter contains a smaller and smaller number of persons convicted for current offences, can only mean that the general trend is towards greater social conformity as the young offender matures. The very young offender, although likely to be re-convicted in the short run, is also very likely to cease being convicted by twenty-one or soon after. In other words, delinquency is typically a youthful characteristic which may be expected to clear up in later years. For example, in a recent search of the criminal records of a group of married men, average age forty-two, living in London, I found that of those with any kind of criminal record only fourteen per cent had convictions both as juveniles and since reaching the age of twenty-one.

A somewhat similar observation was made in a well-known survey of the after-careers of a sample of Glasgow schoolboys which was reported by Ferguson and Cunnison [72]. Of a total sample of 568 males who were followed up to age twenty-two, seventy (or twelve per cent) were convicted before they were eighteen years of age. However, of these seventy, only twelve, or approximately one sixth, were re-convicted during the four years following their eighteenth birthday.

The long-term prospects

A recent study of the subsequent careers of borstal youths, by Gibbens and Prince [88], has shown that even though many of them had large numbers of previous convictions, or had passed through approved schools before coming to borstal, and even though the majority were re-convicted not long after release, still the fact remained that the delinquent careers of these persistent offenders mostly came to an end in their early twenties. Ten years or more after discharge from borstal, only one fifth of the group were persistent serious offenders, convicted for robbery, burglary and similar crimes. Forty-five per cent had had no convictions, or only minor convictions, since discharge. A further fifteen per cent, although re-convicted soon after discharge, had had no further convictions over the last five years or more. Five per cent were persistent petty offenders, mostly associated with alcoholism. The remaining fifteen per cent had sporadic convictions with very long intervals in between, but some of these were probably persistent offenders who had been relatively successful at evading capture.

A rather similar result emerged from the study by P. D. Scott [234], who followed the careers of 149 boys released at ages from fourteen to sixteen from an English approved school. Although sixty-seven per cent had a further court conviction within three years of release, there was clear evidence of some improvement with time. The frequency of convictions for the year following release was only about a third what it had been for the same group of boys during the year preceding their committal to the school. Furthermore, a large majority of the re-convicted boys committed more offences in the first eighteen months than in the second eighteen months of their period of release. The discouraging statistic of sixty-seven per cent re-convictions masks the tendency for delinquent behaviour to decrease with time, even among recidivists. Evidently youthful crime in England, notwithstanding the publicity it attracts, has not reached anything like the level of seriousness or persistency reported in some of the great cities of North America, where narcotic addiction and lethal violence among adolescents are relatively commonplace.

It is in fact the exception rather than the rule for a juvenile offender to become a persistent recidivist. Indeed, really persistent offenders, although they may be held responsible for a high proportion of recorded crimes, are relatively unusual among the population of convicted offenders. In England and Wales, less than two per cent of all adult males found guilty of indictable offences have a record of twenty or more previous convictions. Of all offenders with a previous record, a substantial majority have less than five previous convictions.

Similar findings have been reported elsewhere. Bovet [22], in a report for the World Health Organization, suggested that in most countries only about twenty per cent of those convicted as juveniles are later convicted as adults. Nils Christie [36] in Oslo, who surveyed the records of all males born in Norway in the year 1933, found that by the age of twenty-five, out of a total of 20,000 still alive and in Norway, about a thousand had been convicted of an offence sufficiently serious for their name to have been placed on the Central Criminal Register, but of these only twenty-two per cent had been re-convicted. In this Norwegian survey, as in England and American studies, it was those first convicted at an early age who carried the greatest risk of re-conviction, and in these cases the risk persisted for many years afterwards.

In the United States also, a number of large-scale follow-up studies have shown that only a minority of juvenile delinquents go on to become persistent adult criminals, although the chances of this outcome are higher in that country than in England. William and Joan McCord [164] studied a sample of Boston delinquents. These were boys from a working-class area (average age eleven in 1939) mostly selected by teachers as being potential delinquents, who were enrolled in the Cambridge–Somerville youth project, an experiment designed to test the efficiency of a programme of big-brother guidance in the prevention of delinquency.* Their criminal records were followed up to 1955, when their average age was twenty-seven.

Of the total of 104 convicted at some time during this period for an offence other than traffic violation, sixty-six per cent were convicted by the age of seventeen, a further twenty-four per cent from age eighteen to twenty-two, and only ten per cent were convicted for the first time after twenty-two years of age. Of the ninety-four cases first convicted under twenty-three years of age, three quarters were not re-convicted after attaining that age. The self-limiting character of the delinquent careers of most young offenders was clearly demonstrated.

In the famous studies of Sheldon and Eleanor Glueck [96], who also worked in Boston, the prospects of young delinquents were found to be much worse than this, but they were dealing with more serious cases. Nevertheless they noted the same tendency to reform on growing older. They began with a sample of 1,000 boys from the Boston Juvenile Court during the years 1917 to 1922. Followed up for five years after completion of their penal sentences, only 14.6 per cent were found to have been free from delinquent behaviour during this period. Since the delinquents chosen for the study were those whom the court had referred to the Judge Baker Guidance Center for a report, and since the clinic recommended removal from the parental home of more than half the children, the sample probably included many of the worst types of cases. Although of an average age only thirteen and a half, their average number of previous arrests was over two per boy. In eighty per cent of cases one or other parent was born outside the United States, in seventy-four per cent of the cases both parents were Catholic† (and this in Protestant Boston), and in eighty-six per cent of cases their homes were close to vice spots and in areas infested by gangs.

In spite of the generally unfavourable outlook, continued follow-up over two further periods of five years yielded progressively more encouraging results. After fifteen years the proportion of non-offenders was two and a half times larger, and the proportion of serious offenders smaller by a half, than after the first five years.

* See also pp. 71, 110, 161, 253.
† But see p. 74 for explanations.

Persistent adult offenders are not always juvenile delinquents grown up. A substantial proportion of recidivists start their criminal careers late in life. Of all offenders convicted for the first time for an indictable offence, two fifths are twenty-one years or over. Furthermore, Home Office research on the criminal records of persistent adult offenders, defined as those liable to preventive detention, showed that the majority – fifty-five per cent – had no history of being convicted as a juvenile, and thirty-one per cent were convicted for the first time after reaching twenty-one. The latter figure was the more convincing, since records of convictions as juveniles were not always complete [112].

Research into the personal characteristics of persistent offenders of mature years shows that they are largely recruited from the ranks of the mentally abnormal, being solitary, ineffectual, zestless, and recognizably neurotic personalities [276]. Some of these mental misfits are sadly and consistently wayward from a tender age, but others only take to crime when they reach years of maturity without being ready to meet the demands of adulthood. In either case, the typical adult recidivist has little in common with the typical young offender, whose potentialities are sound even though his energies are temporarily misdirected.

Summing up the situation

Criminal statistics are often quoted in support of the dismal view that crime is increasing all over the world, and that young people are responsible for this. Actually, the picture is more complicated. No one really knows how much of the increase in numbers is due to more diligent reporting and recording. Certainly, most convicted persons are young males, but that is nothing new. The fact that the peak age for convictions is as low as fourteen years and that the incidence gets less and less with increasing age means that for most offenders liability to convictions is a passing phase of youth. The boy who is first convicted at fourteen or earlier is especially likely to be re-convicted shortly, but the boy who goes on to become a persistent recidivist all his life is exceptional in the extreme, and in all probability differently constituted and motivated from the ordinary juvenile delinquent.

The criminal statistics are recording primarily offences of

dishonesty; everything else is in comparison rather unusual. A great deal of the crimes recorded consist of comparatively petty and unimportant incidents. Indeed, it has been a criticism of the way the statistics are presented in England that they allow all the more important matters to be submerged in the sea of petty larcenies.

Most of the offences of juveniles lack the gravity and substance, or the scheming and planning, which the public associates with crime. Even when one examines the crimes of boys from approved schools, many of whom are confirmed recidivists, it appears that their range is mostly limited to minor thefts and traffic offences, and that serious violence, sexual assaults and professionally organized crimes are most uncommon. A somewhat older age group, the late teens and early twenties, includes some of the most dangerously violent offenders in existence, but fortunately they are very rare, and have little in common with the general run of young thieves or sporadic hooligans. The over-all impression left behind from a cursory examination of the statistical trends is that though the numbers are enormous they mostly stand for minor offences. Like an attack of measles, a first conviction in a schoolboy, though it can be serious, does not usually portend a blighted future.

2 The True Extent of Youthful Crime

However valuable a 'virtue' may be as the name of a class of acts, it is not apparent that it has any widespread concrete existence.

Hugh Hartshorne, *Character in Human Relations* (1932). New York, Scribner.

The crime wave

Today's youth worse than ever?

Ever since statistics began to be kept they have been held to prove the increasing lawlessness of youth. The press and television, echoed all too often in official pronouncements by authorities who should know better, find news value in reports of a wave of crime and hooliganism concentrated among teenagers. Talk of the present 'wave' has been going on for at least twenty years, and yet in the perspective of history the present situation is mild. One is certainly much safer from molestation in the city streets today than a century back, and the recollections of older people tell of rowdyism and drunken violence in the poorer neighbourhoods of English industrial towns to an extent quite unfamiliar in today's tame subtopia.

Every age bemoans the follies of the younger generation. The following words appear in a report on the English scene published in 1818.

The lamentable depravity which, for the last few years, has shown itself so conspicuously amongst the young of both sexes, in the Metropolis and its environs, occasioned the formation of a Society for investigating the causes of the increase of Juvenile Delinquency.

A little further on the increase in juvenile delinquency is described as unprecedented in extent and 'still rapidly and progressively increasing' [221]. Thirty years later, another report, written in response to a prize offer of £100 for the best essay on the topic of the fearful and growing prevalence of Juvenile Depravity and Crime, quoted statistics for England and Wales.

The number of juvenile offenders has gradually and progressively increased. . . . Juveniles, aged 15 and under 20, form not quite one tenth of the population, but they are guilty of nearly one fourth of its crime. . . . The period which shows the blackest, whether we look at the proportionate amount of crime, or its progressive increase, is comprised between 15 and 20 years of age [290].

In point of fact, some real changes in social behaviour, especially delinquent behaviour, are extraordinarily hard to prove. Even according to official statistics, though fashions in crime may change, people are not necessarily in all respects more lawless today than they were in the last century. In 1895, about half a million convictions for all kinds of offences were recorded. In 1962, provided one excludes minor traffic offences (i.e. those dealt with summarily), there were still half a million convictions for all other offences, although in the meantime the size of the population had increased some fifty per cent. In 1895, there were considerably more convictions for drunkenness than there are today. Throughout the last half of the nineteenth century the proportion of the population incarcerated in English prisons was considerably higher than it is now; notwithstanding the fact that since the last war the numbers in prison have doubled.

Are the statistics realistic?

The total of convictions rises inexorably year by year, but this could mean no more than that each year a little more of a virtually limitless reservoir of crimes is tapped off and enshrined in official statistics. The larger and more active the police force concerned with detecting and recording, the more offences come to light. Between the years 1931 and 1932, for instance, a dramatic increase of 222 per cent in the total figure of indictable offences in the London area was brought about by the simple expedient of abolishing the book listing items 'suspected stolen' and entering these instead as 'thefts known to the police' [220]. One of the biggest increases in the juvenile crime statistics followed the passing of the Children and Young Persons Act, 1933, which encouraged people to bring to juvenile courts many children who would previously have been dealt with by unofficial warnings and parental discipline. When the level of unrecorded offences (what criminologists like to call 'the dark figure') greatly exceeds the numbers of known offences, slight changes of policy on the part of the police will produce remarkable fluctuations in the crime statistics. Ben Whitaker [278] in his book on the police quoted the example of male importuning in Manchester, for which there was less than one prosecution per year in the period 1955 to

1958. Then a new chief constable arrived, and prosecutions for this offence over the next four years steadily rose from thirty in 1959 to 216 in 1961.

In the year 1958, just before the introduction in England of severer penalties for soliciting under the Street Offences Act, convictions of girls of seventeen to twenty for offences connected with prostitution rose sharply and actually exceeded for the first time the incidence of convictions of girls for theft. Since then, the frequency of convictions of females for sexual offences has fallen to less than a tenth the incidence of convictions for larceny. Nobody believes that there has really been such an enormous fluctuation in the numbers of practising prostitutes. When the new act was under discussion, and the topic of prostitution was given great publicity, the police were doubtless unusually active in trying to clear the streets, hence the unusual frequency of convictions. Subsequently, the development of the call-girl system and other devices have moved the prostitutes off the pavements, without necessarily abolishing their trade.

Changes in the methods of classifying and recording crimes could make the official statistics more realistic as a measure of crime trends. What is needed is some kind of index of crime, analogous to the cost-of-living index, which could take account of the gravity of the offences committed as well as the total numbers recorded. Separate indexes would probably be needed for major categories, such as personal violence, large-scale thieving, vandalism and sexual offences, since these different forms of behaviour do not necessarily increase or decrease in unison.

A courageous attempt to produce a more realistic index of juvenile crime has been made by two American criminologists, Thorsten Sellin and Marvin Wolfgang [237]. A single criminal exploit, such as a 'job' of house-breaking, was defined as an 'incident'. They based their measures on the number of 'incidents' reported to the police, disregarding the number of different charges to which a single incident may have led, or the number of persons involved. Scores were allocated for each element of damage done in an incident (e.g. injury requiring hospital examination, plus theft of more than $250). The scores were derived by sampling the opinions of relevant groups in the community (e.g. police officers, juvenile-court judges) on the relative seriousness of a range of items of damage. Thus the ultimate criteria of seriousness were subjective opinions, which cannot be expected to remain consistent and unchanging. Even so, the Sellin–Wolfgang scale is probably a better measure of social damage than the total of indictable crimes recorded, the statistic upon which most public discussion is at present based. It has in fact been applied by an English psychiatrist P. D. Scott [234], to demonstrate differences in after-conduct of various groups of boys discharged from an approved school, differences which would not have become so readily apparent by the usual process of counting the numbers of re-convictions.

The use of crime indexes might go a long way towards settling the age-old question to what extent the amount of damage done by delinquent youngsters is really increasing. But the difficulty of compiling accurate and comprehensive records must not be under-estimated. If the value of the goods stolen were to be officially recorded against all convictions for larceny, it would not be sufficient to take the uncontested testimony of victims, especially where insurance claims were pending.

The deterioration in morals

The 'disintegration' of the family

The opinion has got about that community standards in England have deteriorated, that relaxation of the moral, religious and disciplinary precepts of former generations has led to weakening of family ties, to insurbordination and selfishness on the part of the younger generation, and that individual effort, self-reliance and sense of duty have been undermined by undue dependence on a state system to provide financial security. Statistics of divorce, illegitimacy, alcoholism, abortion, venereal disease, suicide and crime are often cited as indexes of this rapid degeneration. The motives behind such comments deserve some scrutiny, for in many instances the statistics do not in fact warrant so gloomy an interpretation [75].

In 1951, 38,382 petitions for divorce were filed in England and Wales. This figure was a considerable increase over previous years, and was undoubtedly the consequence of the financial help provided for the first time by the Legal Aid and Advice Act, 1949. By 1955 the number of petitions had stabilized, and was then 28,314. In 1962 it was 33,818. This increase of divorce petitions has to be viewed against a background of increasing population, increasing popularity of marriage (fewer single people), and increasing duration of marriage (marrying younger and living longer). Viewed in proper perspective, it is by no means certain that the average family is less stable and cohesive than formerly, or that the prevalence of working mothers and busy fathers leads to inadequacies in the care and supervision of children. Social change has on the whole operated in favour of a greater home-centredness among the working masses. Shorter working hours, better housing and an enormous increase in household goods mean greater home comforts than ever before, and more leisure to enjoy them. Break-down of the once rigid attitudes to the respective roles of mothers and fathers means that husbands take a more active interest in home and children, and many a public house has lost custom to the home-based television set and to the fascination of do-it-yourself home maintenance [293]. The modern army of health visitors, N.S.P.C.C. officers, school inquiry officers, care committees, marriage counsellors, child guidance centres, and not least the juvenile courts, who have the power to remove children from inadequate parents and place them in the care of the local authority, combine to protect the young against the gross cruelties, exploitations and neglect which were once so frequently the fate of those born into the large families of the urban poor. The low incidence of nutritional disease, the faster rates of growth and development of the modern child and the enormous diminution in infant mortality indicate a great improvement in the health and happiness of the younger generation which one would expect to increase rather than decrease the chances of a young person attaining mature social and moral standards.

Public and private immorality

J. B. Mays [174] has argued that evidence for a deterioration in moral standards is provided by such things as the increase in thefts from railways, hotels and public institutions; the evasion of regulations, which became so prominent in connexion with rationing and black market transactions in the last war; the spectacle of official denials by government spokesmen rapidly being exposed as lies; and the newspaper accounts of business and political scandals. It may be so, but one has to allow the possibility that an apparent increase of moral lapses may be simply the result of a blaze of attention and publicity, or that a real increase in petty thefts may be the result of exposing the same moderately dishonest public to more and more unguarded property.

A. Grimble [107], a venereologist from Guy's Hospital, London, has pointed out that increases in illegitimacy or in sexually transmitted infections do not necessarily support the common assumption that thoughtless youths have become suddenly more promiscuous. A revulsion against shot-gun weddings could produce more illegitimate births. Morally neutral causes, such as changes in the sensitivity of infecting organisms to antibiotics, are too easily forgotten. Guy's Hospital statistics showed that the proportion of males with venereal infections who were under twenty years old actually decreased between 1932 and 1962. Over the country as a whole, however, recent statistics show the increase most marked in the fifteen to nineteen age group. The percentage increase among girls of this age has been five times that among the boys [192].

The supposed sexual laxity and promiscuity of the average teenager, which has been given so much attention by the press and been used as a pointer to the deterioration of moral standards generally, received no confirmation whatever from a careful survey of the sexual behaviour of young people under twenty years carried out in England under the auspices of the National Council for Health Education. In fact, about two thirds of boys aged nineteen and three quarters of the girls of that age were found to be without experience of sexual intercourse. Only a small minority could be called promiscuous. Of all those in the sample of under-twenties who had had any experience of sexual intercourse, not more than a quarter of boys and less than five per cent of girls had had more than ten different sexual partners in their life, and only three per cent of the sexually experienced boys had been with prostitutes [228].

There is no factual reason to assume that changes in public sexual morality have any relevance to the incidence of dishonesty in young people. However, as a supposed worsening in the one respect is sometimes used to explain a supposed worsening in the other, it is worth pointing out that in neither case does the evidence establish any such alarming degree of deterioration as one might gather from the contentions of moral jeremiads.

The extent of unrecorded delinquency

Everyone admits to some delinquency

A good deal of evidence points to the conclusion that delinquent behaviour has always been more or less universal, and that most of the young offenders who come before the courts differ from the rest of the population only in the accidental misfortune that they have been caught and prosecuted and their activities subjected to public scrutiny. If so, belief in an unprecedented wave of criminality among modern youth becomes all the more difficult to sustain.

J. B. Mays [173], in a study of juvenile behaviour in a slum district in Liverpool, suggested that the average lad from a bad neighbourhood participates in delinquent acts because others do so and he dreads to be thought different.* Of eighty youths interviewed, very few gave trustworthy testimony to law-abiding habits. Thirty-four had already been, or were soon after, convicted, but a further twenty-two admitted committing offences for which they never appeared before the courts. They appeared to live the same kind of lives as the boys who were caught, and their offences were similar, namely shop-lifting, larceny from lorries and warehouses, and occasional breaking-in with intent to thieve. Like those who were caught, the majority tended to grow out of their delinquent habits as they passed the age of fourteen. When recalling their juvenile escapades, both the caught and the uncaught offenders described stealing as a natural part of life from which they got some kind of thrill. Most of their exploits were committed in groups, and the sporting and self-proving character of their activities was revealed by the frequency

* See also p. 37.

with which the plunder consisted of articles of no particular interest to them, which they afterwards threw away. On reading descriptions of this kind of delinquent-prone community, one begins to wonder if the minority who are too timid to share the joys of law-breaking are more likely than the delinquents to be maladjusted individuals.

Similar impressions have been gained in surveys in different parts of the world. Kerstin Elmhorn [58] questioned school-children in Stockholm, and found that over a half of all boys admitted having committed at some time one or more of a list of specified offences, such as vehicle theft or damage, breaking and entering, or robbery. In contrast, only 3.5 per cent of the boys were actually known to the police as offenders. Nils Christie [35] questioned samples of young men in various parts of Norway, giving each a crime score according to the frequency and serious-ness of their self-confessed infractions. Less than ten per cent were crime-free with a score of zero, and the crime scores of those from upper-class homes were as great as those from lower-class homes.

Similar impressions have been gained in surveys elsewhere. In the Cambridge–Somerville Youth Study in Massachusetts, in which a group of potentially delinquent boys came under close scrutiny by social workers, the number of boys who were known to have committed offences without being reported to the courts exceeded the number brought to court. In fact, the number of violations of a not too serious kind committed by the uncaught offenders was not much less than the number committed by the official delinquents, but they committed serious offences less often [195].

Wallerstein and Wyle [273] submitted a questionnaire to a cross-section of the New York population asking about law-breaking, and of 1,698 persons who replied, ninety-one per cent admitted that they had committed one or more offences after the age of sixteen for which they might have received penal sen-tences. Of the men who replied, eighty-nine per cent admitted to larceny, seventeen per cent to burglary and eleven per cent to robbery. Results in some ways even more startling were obtained by Porterfield [210], who questioned students attending college in Texas about their juvenile misconduct. They all admitted having committed offences, and furthermore they admitted a frequency of offences which greatly exceeded the frequency with which a sample of official juvenile delinquents had been charged with the same range of offences. Sex offences were especially prevalent, 24.5 per cent of the male students admitting to indecent exposure and 5.5 per cent to attempted rape. Yet hardly any of the students had ever been before the courts for any offence except traffic violations.

Those repeatedly convicted are usually the worst offenders

Short and Nye [244] administered an anonymous questionnaire to 3,000 adolescents attending American high schools, and to a group of official delinquents attending a penal training school. On the whole, larger percentages of the training-school inmates than of high-school boys admitted having committed each of the forms of misconduct specified. Thus ninety-two per cent of the official delinquents admitted having stolen small items worth less than two dollars, compared with sixty-one per cent of the high-school boys. Many more of the official delinquents admitted really serious offences. Thus sixty-eight per cent admitted robbery by force, compared with only six per cent of the high-school boys. On the other hand, as in Porterfield's study, a large number of sexual offences were admitted by the ordinary population. Approximately the same proportion of both groups, eleven per cent, admitted to homosexual relations other than masturbation. Over half the high-school boys admitted to malicious damage to property. On a scale of delinquent behaviour constructed from their responses, there was a definite overlap, the worst fourteen per cent of high-school boys producing scores indicative of worse behaviour than the best fourteen per cent of the penal-school inmates.

In some more recent American research in which 180 youths aged fifteen to seventeen inclusive were interviewed confidentially about their offences, Erickson [62] found that a group of fifty boys who had never been before a court admitted a tremendous number of offences, ninety-nine per cent of which had never been detected or at least never acted upon. Nearly all of the officially 'non-delinquent' had been involved in relatively minor

offences, such as gambling and petty theft, and forty-six per cent
of them had committed more serious offences such as breaking
and entering, automobile theft, forgery and narcotic violations.
In both the frequency of offences and the proportion of boys
who engaged in them the officially 'non-delinquent' closely
resembled the group of thirty boys who had been convicted only
once. A group of one hundred recidivist offenders (fifty on probation and fifty in an institution), however, admitted to something like a ten times higher frequency of violation of the law
than the officially non-delinquent, and in the range of more
serious offences the difference was even more extreme. It was not
that a higher proportion of their offences were detected and
punished, but rather that they committed them so very persistently that penal action was inevitable.

These findings must be treated with caution, since one cannot
place too much reliance on the accuracy and consistency of self-
reporting of delinquency.* Nevertheless, they strongly suggest
that the conventional division between delinquent and non-
delinquent is misleading when applied to adolescent boys, for
delinquent behaviour is a matter of degree, and many of those
who come to court, especially first offenders, are no different in
their behaviour from the majority of the so-called non-delinquents. In a statistical sense, a certain amount of delinquent
misconduct is a normal feature of youth. It is the minority who
keep getting brought back to court whose behaviour is significantly more criminal than their neighbours', and who may be
suspected of being in some way different or abnormal.

Honesty non-existent?

Tests for dishonesty

The investigations so far mentioned were all dependent upon
self-reporting, although of course each investigation included
some check on the truthfulness of responses. For example Short
and Nye included some buffer items to which the correct answer
was already known to be 'yes' for the great majority of persons
who answer truthfully. If a particular subject answered 'no' to

* See p. 60.

several of these items, this indicated that he was probably a pious fraud. Then again, if a particular group of subjects, all members of one school class for example, produce scores very different from the rest of the population, one suspects some deception. Nevertheless, any systematic tendency on the part of all young people to exaggerate or to minimize their delinquencies, which might be either a deliberate or an unconscious tendency, would be difficult to detect and allow for by these methods of indirect inquiry. Actual observation of behaviour in delinquency-inducing situations presents a more immediately convincing, and in many ways a more informative, method of studying the delinquent potential of normal people. The method makes great demands on the skill and ingenuity of the investigator, who has to contrive suitable situations and means of observing subjects without letting them know what is happening. The most important series of experiments of this kind were conducted many years ago by Hartshorne and May [115], who applied classroom tests to 8,000 American youngsters attending state and private schools and ranging in age from nine to eighteen years inclusive.

The observations of Hartshorne and May covered the forms of dishonesty which underlie the bulk of indictable crime, namely stealing, lying and cheating. They used a great variety of test situations, but one or two examples must suffice. In the magic square test the subjects were given a box containing a collection of coins of different denominations. The ostensible task was to fit coins into the circular slots which were of appropriately different sizes, so as to make the rows and columns all add up to the same figure. This gave the children the opportunity to pocket some surplus coins. The puzzle boxes were later returned to a pile with no obvious means of seeing which had been used by a particular child. The number of excess coins retained by each subject provided the measure of stealing in that situation. Cheating was measured by allowing the subjects to report their supposed scores in various tests, under circumstances in which the investigator had secret means of knowing what were the subjects' true results. Sometimes prizes were offered for particular levels of achievement. The dynamometer test of strength of grip made use of the fact that a sharp fatigue effect causes a loss of force after a few quick repetitions of the squeeze. The subjects were therefore given several practice trials under supervision, during which the experimenter observed unobtrusively the maximum figure reached on the dynamometer dial. They were then required to try hard on their own and record their highest score, while the experimenter placed himself so that the dial was outside his view. Those who reported substantially higher scores than in the practice trials were cheats.

Situation counts for more than character

The conclusions to be drawn from this research were important, unexpected, and most revealing as to the origins of dishonesty. The popular assumptions that young people can be divided into groups of honest and dishonest types, that honest types will remain so in all situations, that honesty will increase with age, or that honesty is correlated with acceptance of moral principles on a verbal level were shown to be almost completely mistaken. The most striking conclusion that emerged was that dishonest behaviour was much more closely linked to the situation in which the juvenile found himself than to any characteristic of the child as an individual. Thus, the percentage of cheaters ranged from five to ninety-five or more according to which school or which classroom was under consideration. Whereas a fair degree of constancy was found in an individual's cheating habits in some very specific situation, say mis-reporting of scores on an arithmetic test, or stealing money during a party game, it was not necessarily the same people who behaved dishonestly in these different situations. Few youngsters were honest in all of the situations investigated, and few cheated under all circumstances, the majority were moderately dishonest, that is prepared to be dishonest in some situations but not in others. There was no such thing as a fundamental trait of honesty manifest in all situations.

Since no trait of general honesty could be identified, there was no invariable rule about girls or older children or upper-class children being relatively more honest. There was a slight over-all tendency for older children to cheat more than younger ones, but the frequency of stealing by older and younger children was about the same in the situations tested. The influence of the group in which the child was placed, and in particular the relations between the class members and their teacher, was greater than the difference between individuals. Impersonal and authoritarian teachers provoked the most cheating.

It seemed a little surprising, in view of the reputation enjoyed by girls for better decorum, greater social conformity and less delinquency, that no consistent differences occurred in the amount of dishonesty by boys and girls. Indeed, in word tests which the children were allowed to complete at home, after receiving instructions not to use a dictionary or to seek advice, girls cheated much more than boys. The investigators thought that the probable explanation lay in the stronger motivation of girls to do well at school, hence their willingness to take the trouble to look up the answers, whereas the boys, on account of their relative unconcern about formal scholastic requirements, could not be bothered with the effort involved in cheating in this type of test. Such comparisons suggest that outward respectability, which girls adhere to more than boys, may in some circumstances go together with an increased tendency towards secret delinquencies, stimulated by the need to keep up appearances. In those tests of lying which were based upon the tendency to answer personal questions with an implausible number of claims to virtuous behaviour, girls scored more highly than boys.

The investigators also looked into the question to what extent honest, law-abiding behaviour reflects the youngster's degree of understanding of the moral precepts and codes of adult society. They applied tests to various samples of schoolchildren who had been subjected to special moral instruction, but found no improvement in honesty. In one school, which had optional membership of an organization for encouraging truthfulness and other virtues, boys who joined were more dishonest than those who did not, and the longer they remained in the honesty-promoting scheme the more dishonest they became in practice. Possibly the system failed because it rewarded those prepared to make hypocritical protestations of virtue and discouraged those who cared most for the genuine article. Increasing age, which one assumes corresponds with an advance in social and moral understanding, was not accompanied by generally improved honesty. Clearly, neither familiarity with moral principles nor willingness to profess adherence to them, were effective in promoting honest behaviour.

Is there a specially wicked minority?

The conclusion that most people's dishonest behaviour is largely specific to the situation in hand must not be taken to mean that general trends towards honesty or dishonesty do not occur in some unusual individuals. In fact, Hartshorne and May's own later analyses of integration of behaviour [116] showed that some individuals could be identified who were both unusually honest and unusually consistent in their reactions, and these individuals were also above the average in at least three respects in which delinquents are said to be below average, namely emotional stability, persistence, and resistance to suggestion. Conversely, although the trait of dishonesty was less readily discernible, since consistency was so conspicuously lacking in tests of lying and cheating, in so far as it was possible to identify a minority of children who displayed dishonest behaviour in unusually high frequency in a variety of situations, this group showed just those characteristics that have been repeatedly quoted in connexion with juvenile delinquents seen in remand homes and institutions. These included scholastic backwardness, emotional instability (as indicated by a psychological test), suggestibility, keeping company with other dishonest youngsters, membership of the lower classes (i.e. children of labourers, or others earning small wages) and unfortunate home circumstances (e.g. family discord, poor discipline, neglectful parents, or parents giving a bad example in themselves). Youngsters with an undue share of these handicaps were particularly prone to dishonesty. These findings suggest that the minority of habitually dishonest youngsters have much in common with the habitual delinquents who comprise the bulk of inmates of penal institutions. On the other hand, the majority of dishonest acts, and presumably also the majority of delinquent acts, are the work of more or less normal individuals who break the rules now and then when opportunity arises or occasion demands.

The delinquency problem in perspective

A cool scrutiny of the statistical and historical evidence suggests that the youthful crime situation today is neither unique nor so serious as commonly supposed. Systematic inquiries have demonstrated time and again that nearly all youths commit occasional delinquencies, especially acts of dishonesty and social defiance. There is no reason to suppose this is a new development; but it does mean that the statistics of officially known offences can never do more than scratch the surface. But the deeper and more determined the official scratching, the larger the incidence of convictions will become, and the more alarming the situation will appear.

Undue despondency about the criminal statistics feeds anxiety about the stability of our society, and supports alarmist notions about the wholesale deterioration of family life and the spread of sexual promiscuity and social irresponsibility. In these fields, also, it is not at all clear how far the official statistics of divorce, venereal disease or illegitimacy actually justify such pessimistic interpretations. The results of some serious research surveys run counter to popular views.

While the exact state of the delinquency situation is anyone's guess, experts are mostly agreed on two points. First, the ever-increasing number of convictions and the increasing proportion of the population with a criminal record suggest that some genuine increase has occurred at least in certain kinds of delinquent activity; although the true extent of the increase is open to dispute, since for various reasons the official statistics may exaggerate the trend. Second, convictions are increasing faster among teenagers, roughly the fifteen to twenty age range, than among other age groups, especially in respect of crimes of drunkenness, use of prohibited drugs, vandalism and assaults. These trends, which are common to nearly every European country, as well as to North America, are unlikely to be due solely to statistical artifacts and decreased tolerance of youthful exuberance.

There are obvious practical reasons for authorities expressing disapproval whenever an offender is caught red-handed. However, since the behaviour of most first offenders is no different from that of their friends who don't happen to have been caught, it is important to discipline them without treating them as if they were specially wicked or peculiar. Society's greatest efforts should be directed towards identifying and changing the ways of that small but disruptive minority of recidivists. Their offences tend to be more persistent and serious than ordinary youthful misconduct, and their attitudes and characters are often blatantly deviant.

3 The Social Background of Offenders

Crime belongs exclusively to the lower orders. I don't blame them in the smallest degree. I should fancy that crime is to them what art is to us, simply a method of procuring extraordinary sensations.

The opinion of 'Lord Henry' in *The Picture of Dorian Gray*, by Oscar Wilde (1891).

Il était indulgent pour les femmes et les pauvres sur qui pèse le poids de la société humaine. Il disait: – Les fautes des femmes, des enfants, des serviteurs, des faibles, des indigents et des ignorants sont la faute des maris, des pères, des maîtres, des forts, des riches et des savants.

The attitude of the good bishop in *Les Misérables*, by Victor Hugo (1862). Chapter 1.

Every true man's apparel fits your thief.

The hangman's comment in *Measure for Measure*, by Shakespeare. IV. 2.

Criminals as creatures of circumstance

The response to opportunity and temptation

The sociologist seeks explanations of behaviour in terms of the situation in which a person is placed. The psychologist is more interested in the variations of personality which make individuals respond differently. In real life, the complex interaction between person and situation hardly permits a separation of the two elements, but in trying to analyse the causes of delinquency it is a useful simplification to think of these aspects one by one, and to consider first the environmental and social determinants.

The close dependence of delinquency upon contingent circumstances, which may sometimes over-ride all considerations of individuality, is a fact too easily lost sight of in discussions centred upon the psychology of the offender. In the last chapter, investigations were quoted to illustrate how widespread, almost universal, is delinquent behaviour, and how a youngster's honesty in various test situations depends more upon opportunity, incentives and traditions than upon individual character. Nevertheless, it is sometimes argued that conscience matures later on in life, and that except for a small minority of deviants, mature adults no longer succumb to temptation. Furthermore, some crimes, like murder, produce such a degree of moral revulsion in the average person that it seems they could be perpetrated only by seriously disturbed individuals. Unfortunately, neither of these propositions carries much conviction in the face of historical and social observations on the proliferation of crime wherever opportunity and temptation combine.

In relatively trivial matters, the high frequency of delinquent acts by ordinary, respectable adults can be to some extent measured in such occurrences as the disappearance of 'souvenirs' from restaurants and public places, the steady drain of small items of consumer goods from factories where work-people take things away, or the substantial losses of stock experienced by shops and supermarkets, or the noise of drinking drivers revving

up their cars outside pubs at closing time. A great many people
are deterred from worse behaviour only by the risk of detection.
Stephen Hurwitz [138], the Danish criminologist, noted the
effect of the deportation of the Danish police by the Germans
from September 1944 to the end of the wartime occupation in
May 1945. During this period, in spite of the establishment of
private security organizations, law enforcement was much impaired, with the result that the numbers of thefts and robberies
notified to insurance companies multiplied remarkably, although,
so far as was known, sex crimes and murders did not significantly
increase. Presumably it would need a more drastic and prolonged
change of circumstances to release serious violence among the
civilized Danes.

More serious effects have been frequently reported following
revolutions and great disasters. During the French revolution in
1789, when effective police protection was removed, Paris became
a centre of attraction for marauding ruffians, who terrorized the
citizens, relieving them of money and possessions on the
slenderest pretext of collecting for the national effort. Worse
still, hordes of casual labourers and vagabonds whose criminal
propensities were normally held in check blossomed into fanatic
murderers and pillagers [147]. Pinatel [206], the French criminologist, quotes a number of examples of this kind, including the
pillage of goods which quickly followed the destruction of central
Hiroshima by atomic bombing. More recently, in November
1965, a black-out from a failure in the electricity supply affected
the whole north-east of the United States. Within minutes,
youths in Harlem were smashing shop windows and looting,
while at a prison near Boston the failure was immediately
followed by a mass riot.*

Political and racial conflicts furnish the most blatant examples
of serious crimes incited by external conditions, but sometimes
less dramatic influences produce a similar result. In England in
the nineteenth century, the system of burial clubs, which insured
against funeral expenses in the event of a death in the family,
became all too popular among the poorer classes. Many infants
met untimely deaths, either from neglect or from actual violence,
at the hands of parents interested in securing the insurance

* *Guardian,* 10 November 1965.

money [119]. At that time dangerous opiates could be procured without restriction, and it was customary to use these to quiet fretful infants, so child murders by these means carried little risk of exposure, especially as the natural mortality of infants was high and inquests on infant deaths were exceptional. The death rate of girls, who were of little potential use to parents, was considerably higher than that of boys. The situation became so notorious that a Select Committee on *Friendly Societies* (1854), after hearing evidence that 'child murder for the sake of burial money prevailed to a fearful extent',* recommended that no burial money should be paid out in the absence of a medical certificate as to cause of death, and that a limit should be set to the total sum payable for a child's death.

Special circumstances and terrible reactions

Sharp contrasts in the types of conduct found acceptable in different cultures show how much depends upon the accident of a man's place of birth and upbringing. The Moslem's duty to kill a sister who has allowed herself to become pregnant, or the old custom of the Hindu widow allowing herself to be burned to death on her husband's funeral pyre, would be condemned as serious crimes of violence on Western standards. Love-making practices accepted in one country are found revolting or even criminal in another.

Even within the confines of a single more or less unified culture, namely that of the contemporary Western world, the worst crimes of all, those which many people would regard as beyond the scope of any normal person, do in fact take place with awe-inspiring frequency in special circumstances. The sanctioned killing of enemies in wartime is too commonplace a reversal of behaviour to strike the imagination, but the tortures and mass exterminations of Jews in Nazi concentration camps, to which activity many socially conforming and respectable persons contributed, still act as a chilling reminder of our latent propensities. The belated trials of some of these concentration-camp killers, arrested after twenty years of useful and respected family life in their communities, proves the social normality of many such

* Minutes of Evidence, 1045.

criminals. Likewise, Nils Christie's investigation of concentration-camp guards in Norway suggested that their inhuman attitudes to their charges were a product of the special situation, and not the reflection of a generalized lack of feeling. Similarly, there is no reason to suppose that the supporters of cruel apartheid policies in South Africa, however 'criminal' they may appear to democratic observers, are in any way abnormal or defective in social conscience in other respects.

The idea of a natural reservoir of anti-social energy forms the theme of William Golding's imaginative novel *Lord of the Flies*. It describes how a band of respectably reared British schoolboys, stranded on an island, quickly regress from democratic orderliness to rampant barbarity and tyranny. In reality, children's reactions to extreme neglect prove how dependent is law-abiding behaviour upon consistent social training and control. A great proportion of crime a hundred years ago was the work of bands of homeless waifs who roamed the streets of industrial Europe and America. Sutherland and Cressey [258] refer to 'Arab street boys' of New York, forlorn offspring of drunken or vanished parents, who banded together to save themselves and to prey upon the community that had thrown them out. In the more highly developed countries today, the floating population of homeless children from which these gangs were recruited no longer exists. It takes war or national disaster to create a comparable situation. In the aftermath of the atomic destruction of Hiroshima, vividly described by Robert Jungk [144], orphaned and abandoned children ran wild in gangs, learned to live by their wits amidst the general chaos, and were ultimately persuaded back into civilized community only with difficulty.

Experimental demonstrations of the release of criminal behaviour in normal subjects are understandably difficult to set up. Stanley Milgram [179] of the Harvard Department of Social Relations came close to succeeding in some tests of obedience. Unsuspecting volunteers were told by an authoritative experimenter to administer to a fellow volunteer (actually an accomplice of the experimenter) electric shocks of increasing severity every time he made a mistake in a learning task. The supposed shock apparatus bore horrific labels ranging up to 'danger, severe shock'. In some of these experiments the subjects could hear from the adjacent room, where the victim sat in an 'electrified' chair, cries of protests (actually tape-recorded). In other experiments there was no audible voice but at 300 volts the victim pounded on the wall, and then fell ominously silent. In the stiffest test of all, subject and victim were together, and the subject had to force the victim's hand on to the electric plate when the voltage reached a level at which, apparently, the victim could not bear to maintain the contact voluntarily. The proportion of subjects who obeyed the experimenter completely, working up to maximum shocks, varied from thirty per cent to sixty-six per cent, according to the conditions imposed. The setting must have seemed frighteningly realistic, judging by the sweating and trembling and anxious comments of the volunteers, but they still continued to give painful and possibly dangerous punishment to an unwilling and protesting stranger. The experimenter's conclusion, that a relatively mild form of authoritative persuasion suffices to overcome the scruples of many normal adults, has implications at once frightening and humbling.

Low social class

How many delinquents come from low-class homes?

Granted that we are all potential delinquents, what are the factors liable to bring it out? Two of the most important, namely age and sex, have been described in the first chapter, when it was explained that the great majority of thieving and violence is the handiwork of boys and young men. Other important factors are low status in the social-class system, educational deficiency, poverty, inadequate or broken home backgrounds, residence in a bad neighbourhood, and belonging to a large family.

Although the links between these factors and delinquent behaviour must be known to all, it is perhaps worthwhile, before discussing the theories put forward to explain them, to give some examples to illustrate how close are the associations revealed by some research surveys. The matter is complicated, of course, because the factors are not independent of each other. Thus, among families of low occupational status, many reside in slums, do not limit the number of children they produce, and suffer from poverty and lack of education. In other words, adverse factors tend to occur in clusters and to interact to make a very potent crime-producing situation.

In England, social-class membership can be gauged in a rough and ready manner from one's occupation (or father's occupation in the case of young people), which may be placed into one of five groups according to the Registrar General's classification. The lowest, Class V, comprises unskilled manual workers and casual labourers. The solid middle-class occupations, like doctors, teachers and businessmen, belong to Classes I and II. Classes III and IV comprise the bulk of workers, the distinction being between skilled and semi-skilled respectively. This system of ranking goes more by the prestige of one's job than the level of earnings, although, of course, the two are highly correlated.

All investigators are agreed that persons from the lowest social class are over-represented, and persons from the middle classes under-represented, in samples of delinquents brought to justice, but the true extent of the class bias is not yet clear. Little and Ntsekhe [157] found that among 381 boys in a London remand home in 1957, twenty per cent came from Class V, approximately double the proportion in which this class occurs in the London population. Only 7.5 per cent came from Class I or II, less than half the proportion of these classes in the London population. In other words, the lower-working-class boy had at least four times as great a chance of being found delinquent as the middle-class boy. A similar, but slightly more extreme, trend was recorded by Gibbens [83], from a sample of London youths who were serving sentences of borstal training in 1953 and 1955. Of fathers with classifiable occupations, twenty-six per cent fell into Class V. In an earlier study A. Gordon Rose found that forty per cent of borstal youths who were released during the last war had fathers in unskilled occupations [223].

Differences considerably more extreme have been reported in other studies. Terence Morris [188], in a well-known survey in Croydon, found none at all from Classes I and II in a small sample of seventy-nine juvenile delinquents, and a great excess from Class V. In a study of juveniles before London courts in 1952 Mannheim and others [167] found about half came from Class V. Possibly the class bias of young offenders has become less extreme in recent years. Certainly the increasing number of young people brought before the courts means that whatever their relative proportions there must be substantial numbers from all classes. Even on Little's figures, which are already out of date, it appears that the majority of delinquents originate in the average working-class home which makes up the bulk of the population.

Grading people according to the nature of their job gives no more than a rough indication of the whole complex of attributes included in social class. Educational background, family contacts, social aspirations, leisure pursuits, choice of companions, type of upbringing, and the whole style of living and outlook on life are involved in the notion of social class. Any or all of these different things may have an influence upon potential delinquency. Resentment and self-consciousness on the part of those of inferior status is an aspect of social class very much emphasized in contemporary theories of delinquency. One of the ways in which this may operate in the development of juvenile delinquents was shown in a recent study in Flint, Michigan [100]. A sample of recidivist delinquent boys and a control sample of non-delinquents of similar age, race, intelligence and social class (rated on father's employment) were interviewed and questioned about attitudes to their parents. Among the delinquent group, those with fathers in lower-status occupations had less respect for their parents. Fewer of the low-status boys said they would talk to their parents about personal problems, or do things in the company of either parent, and relatively few of them felt that their father's decisions counted for more at home than their mother's, or that they wanted to become the kind of person their father was. This tendency for low-class fathers to be less attractive to and less influential with their sons was also present among non-delinquents, but to a lesser extent. The investigators concluded that parents of low status are at a disadvantage in trying to exert control over their sons, and that this factor aggravates the tendency for their sons to react to social frustrations in a rebellious and delinquent fashion.

The educational retardation of delinquents

Another feature of low social status, namely poor educational attainment, is one of the most prominent and characteristic features of juvenile delinquents. In most cases this does not arise from lack of intelligence, but it may be due to lack of opportunity. Although state education for all has reduced the grosser differences between social classes, the fact remains that dirty and uncouth children from poor-class homes are unpopular with teachers, don't get much encouragement from their parents to do well in school, and often play truant. On the other hand, individual as well as social troubles must also play some part, since the child misfit, whether he be a noisy rebel or an over-anxious conformist, does not concentrate so well or learn so rapidly as his better adjusted colleagues.

Whatever the explanation, the facts are sufficiently striking. Eilenberg [56], in a study of a sample of boys in a London remand home for juvenile delinquents in the year 1955, found that thirty-nine per cent were up to or above the population average on intelligence tests, but only ten per cent were up to or above the average in scholastic attainment. Only twenty per cent were substantially below average in intelligence (i.q. less than 85), but sixty-four per cent were retarded educationally by three years or more. A similar but rather less extreme trend was recorded by Gibbens [82] in his study of youths in borstals. Only fifteen per cent were substantially below average on an intelligence test (i.e. Grade E, the lower tenth percentile and below on Raven's Matrices Test) but twenty-five to thirty per cent were in the corresponding range of retardation on verbal and spelling tests.

In Ferguson's survey [69] of Glasgow boys (in which he took an unselected sample of 1,349 boys leaving school in January 1947 at the earliest permissible age) poor scholastic performance was very closely associated with likelihood of being convicted, both while still at school and subsequently. Thus, among the ten per cent of school leavers who had the lowest scholastic assessments, the chance of being convicted before the age of eighteen was over five times what it was among the top ten per cent.

Low socio-economic status is not the sole reason for the educational retardation of delinquent groups. When delinquents and non-delinquents were first matched for social class and then compared, as was done in the Flint Youth Study [101], delinquents still appeared worse in scholastic performance. The Flint study also showed that the delinquents' awareness of their poor scholastic showing was accompanied by a depressingly low level of expectations and declared aspirations in regard to their own future employment careers. Thus it would appear that many delinquents show in more extreme form the patterns of discouragement and social alienation which are, in lesser degree, shared by the whole of the lower social classes.

Is the class bias spurious?

Some authorities have challenged the assumption that delinquent behaviour is more prevalent among lower-class youngsters, and explain their over-representation at the courts by the greater liability of the lower classes to be apprehended and brought to justice for misdemeanours which would be otherwise dealt with if committed by middle-class persons. Doubtless private schools are more likely than state schools to discipline their pupils caught stealing without calling in the police, and middle-class parents are more likely to protect their children by making good loss or damage so as to forestall complaints and prosecutions. Perhaps, also, the badly dressed, badly spoken urchin found by the police in equivocal circumstances stands a poor chance of avoiding official arrest. Support for this point of view comes from researches on undetected delinquency. Short and Nye's questionnaire [244], referred to in a previous chapter,* showed that, according to their own self-reporting, American high-school adolescents of differing socio-economic class behaved equally badly. R.L.Akers [5], in a later study of a thousand high-school students in Ohio, confirmed that no significant relationship existed between the incidence of confessed delinquency and socio-economic status as graded by the North-Hatt prestige-ranking scale applied to the father's occupation. E.W.Vaz [265]

* See p. 41.

came to similar conclusions from questioning 1,639 high-school boys in Canada.

The conclusions of these American questionnaire investigations must be treated with some reserve, since innumerable studies of the characteristics of impoverished and socially alienated sectors of the community suggest that these classes have a high incidence of persistent delinquents. While the work of Hartshorne and May, and many others, has demonstrated that occasional delinquency, mostly unrecorded and not very serious, is the rule among normal youngsters of every class, it is possible that real differences between classes occur in respect of boys who commit serious and repeated transgressions. The proportion of boys who have ever committed crimes is of less significance than the quality of the delinquency in different classes. Another complication in interpreting questionnaire findings is the greater verbal fluency, and readier adaptability to interviews and tests, displayed by middle-class children, which may have the effect that they report a larger proportion of their transgressions, and so put themselves in an unfavourable light in comparison with lower-class children who may be less ready to confide. Even though the class bias of apprehended delinquents may be largely a product of selective arrests, this does not invalidate the observation that captive delinquents, who, after all, are the people the penal system must cater for, are preponderantly lower-class.

This argument about the association between delinquency and social class illustrates a difficulty that constantly crops up when research workers try to demonstrate the peculiarities of samples of delinquents. One can range offenders along a scale of increasing seriousness, beginning with those whose activities are known only from confidential questionnaires, to those known only to teachers and parents, to those known to the police, to those brought to court, and finally to those sent to penal establishments. With each succeeding step along this scale, the selection processes tend to pick out the more deviant and troublesome individuals. The ones at the end of the penal line, who are most often sampled by research workers, are by and large extreme cases whose characteristics are likely to be exaggerated compared with those at the beginning.

Financial hardship

Absolute poverty

In considering the role of poverty in producing crime, the state of affairs today hardly compares with the situation in Western Europe in former times, or with the present situation in some undeveloped countries, where a large part of crime consists of thefts of the very necessities of life. In Victorian England sheer want was such an obvious cause of theft that it seemed plausible to expect that relief of poverty would bring about a dramatic reduction in delinquency. The *Second Report of the House of Commons Committee on the State of the Police in the Metropolis*, published in 1817, referred to 'this alarming increase of Juvenile Delinquency' which it was inclined to attribute to 'the existence of poverty and distress, unknown perhaps at any former period to the same extent. But your Committee hope, that with the gradual removal of these causes, their lamentable effect will cease'. The same Report also stated:

The condition of these poor children is of all others the most deplorable; numbers are brought up to thieve as a trade, are driven into the streets every morning, and dare not return home without plunder; others are orphans, or completely abandoned by their parents, who subsist by begging or pilfering, and at night sleep under the sheds, in the streets and in the market places; when in prison no one visits them ... [136].

Other careful observers shared the sentiments of this Committee. The *Fourth Report of the Committee of the Society for the Improvement of Prison Discipline and for the Reformation of Juvenile Offenders*, 1818 [221], referred to a cause of juvenile crime

which every humane mind must contemplate with deep regret and compassion; the strong temptation to dishonesty, which has too frequently of late years prevailed, from a want of the necessaries to support life. ... It not infrequently happens, that boys, committed to gaols for petty offences, are discharged upon the wide world, without any alternative, but plunder or starvation.

In England, in spite of numerous legal and social reforms designed to prevent the exploitation of workers and to protect their children, such was the plight of the urban poor during most of the nineteenth century that a high level of delinquency from want seemed almost inevitable. Worsley [291] described the 'jaded operative, his wife and children returning together from the factory to an unwholesome hovel, in which the very air is pestilential' to find 'his only solace in the delirium consequent upon dram-drinking'. He went on to criticize employers for exposing their child workers to 'a fermenting mass of sin and vice' in the factories, and to trace 'the causes of juvenile depravity' to 'intemperance, as a most prolific source, which ministers to, or originates almost every vice . . .'. Clearly, therefore, Worsley, who saw poverty at its worst, did not regard material want as the only cause of juvenile crime, but emphasized the association of poverty and other factors, such as parental example, and methods of child training and scholastic instruction.

Poverty, in the sense of lack of basic necessities, has undoubtedly been an important concomitant of juvenile delinquency up till quite recently, especially in economically depressed areas. Bagot [12], in a study of juvenile delinquency in Liverpool before the war, found a surprising concentration of serious want among the families of his sample. On the Rowntree Human Needs standard, thirty per cent of Merseyside families were then below the poverty line, compared with 85.7 per cent of the families of delinquents. Taking a more extreme definition of poverty, adapted from previous surveys of Merseyside, more than half of the families of delinquents were seriously poor compared with only sixteen per cent among the Merseyside population. Cyril Burt [26], in a survey in 1923, found that over a half of the juvenile delinquents in London, compared with less than a third of the general London population, came from poor homes. There was a high correlation (.67) between delinquency rate and percentage of poor homes in the various London boroughs.

Relative poverty and temporary unemployment

The general impression today seems to be that the English welfare state has abolished all but limited pockets of physical want, and that what remains is associated with particular groups in the community, such as aged social isolates, problem families incapable of managing on limited incomes, and fatherless families. Such special groups cannot account for the great bulk of young offenders. Indeed, interest in the question of family income in relation to delinquency has fallen to such a low ebb that not much hard data on the topic is available.

Nevertheless, though serious poverty no longer explains the majority of crimes, the influence of financial pressure is still perfectly apparent, even if nowadays the hire-purchase commitments on a motor cycle or a television set may have replaced lack of food as the typical precipitant. Comparisons of fluctuations of economic indices, such as unemployment rates or production figures, with changes in crime rates have revealed distinct correlations. Although there are many exceptions (especially if one considers small areas where local conditions may outweigh national economic changes), the general rule seems to be that crimes against property increase more than usual whenever national prosperity decreases, and this appears to hold true even though the depression may still leave the population comparatively wealthy. Glaser and Rice [93], in an extensive survey over a twenty-five-year period in the United States, found substantial positive correlations between unemployment rates and the rates of convictions of adults for crimes against property. On the other hand, the crime rates of juveniles showed either no such relationship, or else a slight paradoxical trend in the opposite direction, that is less crime during periods of economic depression. It is readily understandable that juveniles should be less directly affected by unemployment than their wage-earning fathers, and furthermore, if it is true that most juvenile offences today arise from youthful exuberance and desire for thrills, it is conceivable that unaccustomed hardship might have a sedative effect.

The effect of financial pressure upon individuals is shown in the work records of offenders, among whom temporary unemployment, and hence temporary shortage of the cash needed to maintain an accustomed style of life, increases the likelihood of criminal behaviour. In a survey of 4,000 borstal youths, Norwood East [54] found that only about thirteen per cent of their working lives was spent in a state of unemployment, which was not appreciably above the average at that period for the general population of young males. At the actual times when their last offences were committed, however, the incidence of unemployment was very high, from forty-five to fifty per cent. The clear inference was that these young men were much more prone to commit offences during periods of unemployment than at other times.

Today it is relative deprivation rather than absolute poverty that provides the stimulus towards crime. Rapid advance by the community as a whole, and the assumption that reasonable material standards should be within everyone's reach may lead to sharper awareness of contrasts between different sectors of the community, and correspondingly greater discontent.

The continued operation of economic pressures tends to be somewhat obscured by the steady increase in crime rates which has accompanied increasing affluence in industrial countries. Many authorities interpret this as cause and effect, since the enormous increase in volume of material goods, and the corresponding increase in the number of property transactions, both legitimate and illegitimate, must have added greatly to the opportunity for and the temptation to criminal activities.* However, a long-term trend towards increasing social wealth, accompanied by a gradual increase in crimes, does not preclude the existence of temporary economic recessions during which offences precipitated by hardship become apparent in unusually steep increases in crime rates. The lower classes are always the hardest hit by temporary increases in unemployment. Moreover, it is the offspring of the lowest classes who experience most acutely the dreary homes, lack of educational stimulus, and other handicaps which cut them off from the benefits of the affluent society. But of course many other matters besides level of earnings enter into these social-class differences.

Bad neighbourhood

In most countries, townspeople contribute more than countrymen to the total crime rate per head of population. England is no exception, although the contrasts are less striking than they once

---

* This interpretation fails to explain why crimes of violence and of sex should also have apparently increased with affluence, but that is another question.

were, probably because of the widespread infiltration of urban development and urban attitudes into rural areas. Thus the county police forces, which cover a more rural population than the various city police forces, record only about two fifths of the total of indictable crimes, although they actually serve about a half of the total population. (This generalization does not, of course, apply to every individual category of crime: certain sex offences, for instance, are substantially commoner in rural areas.)

Within the urban regions, slum districts and densely populated industrial areas contribute most to crime. Clifford Shaw *et al.* [238], in a classic survey of juvenile delinquency rates in various zones within the City of Chicago, was one of the first to document the magnitude of the variations, and to identify the characteristics of the high delinquency neighbourhoods. Dividing the city into concentric zones, it was found that the innermost circle had a delinquency rate more than five times that of the most peripheral zone, with the intermediate zones showing a steady increase as one approached the centre. This curiously regular distribution was no doubt due to the way the city had developed, with the more prosperous families moving out to newer homes on the outskirts, leaving the centrally situated homes dilapidated, cheaply rented, overcrowded, and largely populated by recent immigrants with nowhere better to go.

In England, slum districts inhabited by poverty-stricken families or poor-class coloured immigrants are less sharply delineated than in some American towns, but to some degree a similar situation prevails. Grunhut [108] found that areas with a high rate of juvenile delinquency usually have a high rate of adult crime as well. In spite of social changes, delinquent areas maintained some consistency. He showed that well-known juvenile trouble spots, such as Bootle and Birkenhead, had disproportionately high delinquency rates both before and after the war. Some recent work by Rodney Maliphant on the distribution of offenders in London has shown the persistence of high delinquency rates in the same areas that Cyril Burt had identified as the trouble spots of a previous generation. Areas of high juvenile delinquency rate tend to coincide with areas of overcrowding, poor housing, low rents and few owner-occupiers, and to be accompanied by high rates of illegitimacy, infant mortality, tuberculosis, alcoholism and suicide. Grunhut calculated the delinquency rates for juveniles in different areas of England in the years 1948 to 1950. Oxford City, for example, had double the rate of the predominantly rural Oxford County, and the predominantly working-class industrial town of Swansea had almost double again that of Oxford City. The mean rate for selected industrial areas was 10.8 per thousand, compared with a mean rate of 4.4 for rural areas.

Within the towns themselves, the areas where the majority of juvenile delinquents live can be mapped with some precision. In the desirable residential neighbourhoods, patronized by middle-class professional and clerical workers, the delinquents appear sparse; in the older, poorer and more densely populated regions occupied largely by unskilled labourers, delinquents appear in large numbers. Some local-authority development schemes, where former slum-dwellers are re-housed in modern blocks of flats, appear on maps as black islands in a white sea of sparse delinquency [140]. As T.P.Morris [187] pointed out in a well-known survey of delinquent areas in Croydon, the locations of black spots do not always coincide with the most physically dilapidated areas; some newer housing estates have higher delinquency rates than older and more densely populated central areas.

In some recent research into the court appearances of juveniles in east London, M. Power* has shown that, depending upon which secondary school they attended, anything from three up to twenty per cent of the population of boys aged twelve to fourteen are found guilty in any one year. Furthermore, whereas over the whole survey area about one boy in four was likely to be found guilty at some time before reaching seventeen years of age, in some notable black spots, which were quite narrowly localized, every other boy was likely to achieve a juvenile court record.

These comments apply to areas of residence and are not necessarily true of areas in which the crimes actually take place. Areas of well-stocked shops or warehouses, large transport termini, the dockland region, places of amusement and centres of city night life, are likely to have a high incidence of crimes committed, although the delinquents responsible may have been

* (1966) Proceedings of the Royal Society of Medicine, 58, 704-5.

drawn there from living quarters some distance away. On the whole, however, petty crime in one's own neighbourhood, like breaking open next-door's gas meter, is more typical of juveniles than ambitious excursions to residential areas to burgle the houses of the rich.

Race and colour

Racial affiliations have furnished a traditional hunting ground for American criminologists, who regularly discover enormous over-representations of Negroes, Italians, and Puerto-Ricans among their delinquents. Argument then arises on how far this may be due to some intrinsic quality of racial groups or cultures, or how far it simply reflects the under-privileged position of these minorities in the American socio-economic system or the experience of emigration and unsettling changes of habit to which the foreign-born and their offspring have been subjected.

In England, statistical data about race and delinquency are hard to come by, although everyone knows from experience that Jewish families are under-represented and Irish families over-represented among the clients of the juvenile courts. One would have thought that this experience might lead to a proliferation of research; but whether from distaste or discretion, English investigators have mostly fought shy of such topics. None of the three most modern English text-books of criminology [139; 166; 268] quote any investigations into the ethnic affiliations of English delinquents. Some of the findings of American research in this connexion have a special importance, not just because they probably apply to most other countries, to a greater or lesser extent, but because the general conclusions of such research have formed the basis for a good deal of sociological theory about crime causation.

In the United States, the reported crime rates are often ten times as high among Negroes as among whites. In order to find out if the high crime rate of Negroes was associated with their relative poverty, Earl R. Moses [193] carried out a classic sociological survey of contiguous areas in Baltimore inhabited by whites and Negroes respectively. The white and black areas were well matched in regard to age and sex distribution and density of population, size of households, type of housing, and the high proportions of the inhabitants belonging to the lower occupational and educational strata. In other words, on a number of objective social criteria the areas and their people were similar, apart from the matter of race. Nevertheless, the crime rates in the Negro areas were some six times as high as among the corresponding white areas, and crimes of serious violence were particularly common in the Negro areas.

Similar situations arise in connexion with other racial groups. In a study of crimes committed by Arabs in Metropolitan France, C.A.Hirsch [122] estimated that, of the total males in the Seine department in the age range eighteen to fifty years, only ten per cent were North Africans, whereas 15.6 per cent of offences were committed by North Africans. However, the situation varied with the type of crime. Relatively few North Africans committed frauds, false pretences, or offences against morality, whereas many were guilty of violence. Violence in personal relations, especially in avenging insults and marital infidelity, seems to be tolerated in places like Moslem Africa, Puerto Rica, and at one time in Sicily and Southern Italy, rather as motoring offenders are tolerated by the British and American public.

Explaining the statistics

Evidence suggests that the differences between crime rates of different races arise more from their cultural and social background than from any biological peculiarity. Some of the persons officially classed as American Negroes, and sharing the same behaviour patterns, are actually near-white in colour, and biologically closer to European than African stock. Races which are notably law-abiding in a primitive rural setting become rapidly delinquent when they migrate to industrial urban areas, either in their own country or abroad. Immigrant minorities, whatever their race, or whatever part of the world they settle in, are generally vulnerable to delinquency so long as they remain under-privileged minorities. They are also apt to bring with them habits at variance with those of the host country. Sutherland and Cressey [257], in their well-known text-book, quote the U.S. Prisons Report for 1933 showing that among inmates committed for serious violence, men born in Italy were over-represented by eight times their number in the general population. Men born in America but with one or both parents born in Italy were not over-represented, which suggests that fortunately such habits are not necessarily passed on to the next generation.

Although, as Moses [193] showed, the high crime rates of Negroes in America cannot be attributed solely to their immediate economic distress, many other forms of hardship, arising from the American caste system, weigh more heavily upon the Negroes. Segregation in poorer areas of the towns, enforced by custom if not by law, restrictions on range of employment, inferiority in the face of officialdom (revealed in such matters as the smaller proportion of accused Negroes allowed bail, and the heavier penalties awarded if a white person is involved as victim) must all aggravate the Negro's aggressiveness. Negro crime rates vary enormously according to the conditions of the area in which they live. The differences in crime rates between Negroes and whites in the same region are less than the differences between persons of the same race living in contrasting areas like Georgia and New England. L. Savitz [226], in a study of migration of Negroes into a high-delinquency area in Philadelphia, found that local-born Negroes had a higher juvenile delinquency rate than the children of Negro families coming in from less turbulent neighbourhoods. However, the longer the immigrant Negro children had lived in the area, the greater was their delinquency rate, thus confirming the effect of living in a bad neighbourhood.

Broken homes

How close is the connexion with delinquency?

The special liability of children from broken homes to become juvenile delinquents has been the starting point for a great many psychological theories about the effects of loss of parents, or separation from parents, upon character development.* However, the closeness of the association between delinquency and broken homes is sometimes overestimated. The incidence varies

* See p. 157.

according to the area and generation from which the sample of delinquents is taken, and whether they are recidivists, and whether they are in institutions.

In a survey based upon a sample of 500 youths discharged from English borstals during the years 1941 to 1944, A. Gordon Rose [223] found that at the time of being committed half of the boys were from homes permanently broken by parental death, desertion, separation or divorce. In the later survey by Gibbens [84] just over a third of borstal boys from the London area had experienced such a break before reaching the age of fifteen. In an unselected sample of 100 boys committed to approved schools and sent to Aycliffe for classification, J. Gittins [92] found that in half the cases either one or both parents were dead, or else they were separated, deserted or divorced, the latter categories being much the more numerous. In only one third of cases did the boys come from apparently normally constituted parental homes. In a sample of 300 boys in detention centres in 1961, Charlotte Banks [15] found that forty-four per cent were from broken homes.

Although these figures seem quite striking, they are difficult to interpret for two reasons. First, in the absence of control groups of non-delinquents of the same age and social class, one does not know the incidence of family breaks among non-delinquents. Second, among the inmates of institutions, an over-representation of boys from broken homes may occur as a consequence of the policy of the courts, who are more likely to commit a boy if he has no stable home.

This last objection could not apply to the results of the survey of 700 young soldiers in a disciplinary unit for delinquents by Trenaman [263]. In this case there was no question of preferential selection of those without homes, but nevertheless a history of broken homes occurred with approaching double frequency in the delinquents compared with the ordinary soldiers, and was cited by the investigator as a major causal factor. In another well-known survey by Carr-Saunders *et al.* [28], covering nearly 2,000 English schoolboy offenders, comparisons were made with an equal number of non-delinquents from the same schools. The proportion of delinquent cases in which one or other natural parent was missing was approaching double that of the control group: twenty-eight per cent and sixteen per cent respectively. The difference in incidence was mostly accounted for by the larger number of instances of parental divorce or separation in the delinquent group.

American research has in general confirmed the genuineness of the statistical association with broken homes, while demonstrating how the magnitude of the association may vary according to circumstances. In the Cambridge–Somerville sample studied by William and Joan McCord [164], only a fifth of the delinquents came from broken homes, but still this was significantly more than among non-delinquents of the same neighbourhood and social class. T.P.Monahan [184] made a survey of the family composition of first offenders under eighteen years of age appearing before the juvenile courts in Philadelphia during the years 1949 to 1954. For comparison, similar statistics relating to the same age group in the total population were obtained from a census taken in 1950. The Census revealed that seven per cent of white children and thirty-three per cent of non-white children were from broken homes, that is not living in census-classified husband-wife families. The comparative incidence of broken homes among the first offenders was twenty-two per cent for white boys and forty-nine per cent for Negro boys, forty-two per cent for white girls and sixty-eight per cent for Negro girls.

While this result demonstrated that in both sexes and both races the delinquents more often came from broken homes, the contrast between delinquents and non-delinquents in this respect was greater for girls than for boys, and greater for whites than for Negroes. The high incidence of broken homes in the Negro population as a whole to some extent masked the effect. This survey also investigated the incidence of broken homes among those committed to institutions, and showed, as many have suspected, that the delinquents sent to institutions included a greater proportion from broken homes than delinquents dealt with in other ways.

Separation has worse effects than bereavement

Homes can be 'broken' in various ways. Most surveys which have taken this into account suggest that breaks caused by parental

desertion or separation are more closely associated with delinquency than breaks due to parental deaths. In his borstal survey,
Gibbens [84] commented that the proportion of youths who had
lost a parent by death before they were fifteen was no greater than
in a sample of young men from the R.A.F. It was broken homes
from other causes, such as illegitimacy or desertion, which distinguished the delinquents. A similar observation was made by
Ferguson [70] from his follow-up study of boys leaving school
in Glasgow. He found that boys who had lost a parent by death
were no more liable to court convictions than other boys. On the
other hand, among the six per cent of the schoolboys who had
lost a parent from other causes before reaching fifteen years of
age, a disproportionately large number were subsequently
convicted. Charlotte Banks [15], who also divides the broken
homes of her delinquent boys in detention centres into those due
to deaths and those due to separations, compared her incidence
figures with those of a recent National Survey by J. W. B.
Douglas and others.* Whereas homes broken by deaths were
three times as frequent as in the normal fifteen-year-old population, homes broken by divorce or separation were five times as
frequent. The fact that bereavements seem less significant than
breaks occasioned by separation or divorce suggests that discord
between parents may be more closely associated with delinquency
than actual loss of a parent. The offspring of a stable marriage
can withstand the shock of a parent's death, especially if adequate
arrangements for continuity of care are made.

Two large-scale studies of earlier generations yielded somewhat different results. In their large American survey, Sheldon
and Eleanor Glueck [95] found that sixty per cent of delinquents,
twice as many as among the matched controls, had lost a parent
during the first ten years of life, and that all types of family
breach, including those produced by parental illness and death,
were more frequent in the histories of delinquents. Cyril Burt
[26], in his classic study of London delinquents, found that
maternal (but not paternal) death was commoner among delinquents than non-delinquents, although, as usual, the high
incidence of parental separations and desertions among the
delinquents provided the more striking contrast. Illness and

* See p. 160.

death of parents were certainly commoner and possibly more damaging under the social conditions prevalent in previous generations.

Another more recent American survey [251], of 1,000 first offenders coming before a juvenile court in New Jersey, found that thirty-one per cent came from broken homes. The investigators tried to see if those from broken homes tended to commit the more serious offences. They also inquired whether the kind of break – divorce or death – made a difference, and whether such matters as the number of years a home had been broken, or the presence of a step-parent, or the sex of the parent having custody of the child had any bearing upon the seriousness of the offences committed. Contrary to what might have been expected from previous work, the differences were mostly insignificant, and the author concluded that the broken home was not of very great importance in determining the severity of a boy's misbehaviour.

Without going to extremes of scepticism, it is plain that the broken home, like all the other factors discussed in this chapter, cannot be more than a contributory cause of delinquency. Even in bad neighbourhoods, delinquents from intact homes outnumber delinquents from broken homes.

Too big a family

Another point on which investigators all agree is that families with a large number of children contribute a disproportionately large number of juvenile delinquents. T. Ferguson [71] demonstrated this most convincingly with his sample of 1,349 Glasgow boys. Of those from families of not more than four children, eight per cent were convicted by eighteen years of age. Of those from families of more than four children, sixteen per cent were convicted. A similar finding was reported by Trenaman [262] from his sample of 700 young delinquent soldiers. Compared with a control sample of ordinary servicemen, the average size of the delinquents' sibling family was nearly twice as large, 6.3 compared with 3.6.

Of course, as has already been pointed out, size of family is strongly linked with other social factors, notably poverty and overcrowding. Ferguson's survey showed that boys from homes overcrowded to the extent of four or more persons per room had an expectation of being convicted three times as great as the boys from homes with less than two per room. When there are many children at home, an unskilled worker's earnings may be but little above the subsistence level allowed to such a family if they go on National Assistance. If the mother of a very large family happens to be a not particularly efficient manager, the children are likely to be deprived both physically and emotionally, meals become erratic, attention spasmodic, and the absence of clean clothes or dinner money may lead to staying away from school.

Size of family is also linked with social-class membership and religious and racial affiliations. Lower-class families and Roman Catholic families more often have a large number of children than middle-class or Protestant families. Trenaman noted that twenty per cent of his delinquent soldiers were Roman Catholics, twice the proportion to be found at a normal army intake. F.H. McClintock [162], in his survey of crimes of violence in London, found that over a quarter of convicted offenders were either immigrants from the Irish Republic or coloured persons from the Commonwealth, obviously an enormous over-representation compared with the numbers of such persons in the London population. This link between size of family and other things shows once again how consideration of any one of these social background factors leads to all the rest. From the familar conglomeration of social handicaps (labouring class, poverty, overcrowding, immigrant, Irish, Roman Catholic, bad neighbourhood, poor schooling, broken home and large family) it seems futile to single out any one as the prime factor in the development of juvenile delinquency.

Combinations of adversity

The characteristics of unrespectable, delinquent-prone families

In view of the clustering together of adverse social factors, and the impossibility of understanding the operation of one factor in isolation from the rest, a more realistic approach would be to start with the individual delinquent families and investigate the whole constellation of circumstances which differentiate them from the law-abiding members of the community. This was actually attempted some years ago by a research team from Nottingham University in one of the few really detailed studies of a high delinquency area so far undertaken in England [249]. They noted that in the working-class district of 'Radby', a mining town in the Midlands, five selected areas, which contained in total a third of the adult population, contributed sixty-three per cent of the adult offenders and seventy per cent of the juvenile delinquents. They also noted that these same areas had particularly high rates of infant mortality, divorce, tuberculosis notifications, and other indexes of social malaise.

Examining the situation more closely, they found that in some areas delinquency was concentrated in certain 'black' streets, and that neighbouring 'white' streets, inhabited by respectable working-class families, housed very few delinquents. They interviewed families and graded households on a five-point scale according to the degree of social competence and attitudes displayed. In the worst grade (I) they placed the real problem families, chronic social misfits who made no pretence of keeping up with accepted standards of honesty, hygiene or household management. Into the highest grade (V) they put the socially aspiring families, people who wanted to better themselves and openly condemned the fecklessness and immorality of their 'black' neighbours. The bulk of ordinary working-class families, who believed in 'live and let live', trying to preserve reasonable standards themselves while remaining on friendly terms with their neighbours, went into the middle grade (III). While some streets had an extraordinary conglomeration of families in the worst grades, and were readily identifiable as 'black', other streets had poor-grade households dotted about among rows of more respectable families. The variability from one house to the next in the same street was often greater than the difference between the average of one street and another, or one district and another. Something in the 'under the roof' culture of individual families was often more important than the effect of the place they were living.

The Nottingham workers tried to pinpoint the differences

between 'black' and 'white' families. In the former, juvenile delinquency was very much more frequent (fifteen instances among seventy-two families in Grades I and II, none at all among fifty-nine families in Grades IV and V), so was the number whose children had a bad educational record (twenty-two out of seventy-two compared with none out of fifty-nine), and the number of broken marriages (eight out of seventy-two compared with none out of fifty-nine in which the woman of the house was living with a man not her husband) and the number living in big families (forty-four out of seventy-two compared with twelve out of fifty-nine in households containing five or more persons). The 'black' families lived in an atmosphere of squalor; possessions were untidy and uncared for, and individual ownership was not prized. In the 'white' families people took a pride in their own things, and house and garden were carefully tended. In the 'black' families leisure was largely taken up with gambling, whereas among the 'whites' this was only a minor interest. In the 'black' homes irregular sexual unions were frequent and openly discussed, whereas the 'white' families, at least in public, adhered to the conventional code of sexual morality. Minor acts of physical aggression – mothers clouting children, boys hitting their sisters – occurred much more often among the 'blacks'; whereas 'white' mothers made deliberate efforts to refrain from hitting their children in temper. Since both sets of families belonged to the working class, differences between the 'blacks' and 'whites' in regard to occupational status and amount earned were relatively slight.

Some of the most conspicuous differences lay in the field of child care. In the 'black' homes, parents quarrelled openly and violently, whereas the 'whites' tried to conceal their disputes from their children. In the 'black' homes, only the mother showed concern for the children, whereas in 'white' homes responsibility was more often shared between both parents. In 'black' families, children were given pocket money casually to spend as they felt like; the 'white' parents usually made their children put away savings, and made an effort to train their children in thrift and the use of leisure. For instance they encouraged Sunday schools and youth clubs, whereas 'black' parents did nothing to persuade their children to attend organizations, and their children were apt to find such places over-disciplined or too 'stuck up'.

The poorest group of all

Another way of investigating the relation between adverse social factors and likelihood of juvenile delinquency is to identify the most unfortunate or vulnerable group within the community, and see to what extent delinquent habits prevail among them. Something of this kind was done in a study of juvenile delinquency in an English seaport by Harriet Wilson [287]. She selected a group of unfortunate children from families referred to welfare agencies on account of various indications of neglect, such as shortage of clothing, inadequate meals, being sent to school in a dirty condition, or being kept away from school. The family had to show a certain minimum number of these un-favourable features in order to be included in the survey. This method of selection produced a group conspicuous for the presence of a large number of factors known to be correlated with delinquency. Thus, the average size of family was very large (7.4 children per family) and there were many cases in which a fluctuating family income repeatedly fell below subsistence level. Partly owing to the housing policy of the local authority, many of these families, who often owed money and were regarded as unsatisfactory tenants, were accommodated in old council property in close proximity to other unsatisfactory tenants in a squalid neighbourhood that was notorious for stealing and violent quarrels. Over a third of the fathers had bad work records, which were usually associated with mental or physical disabilities, and only a small minority of the children attended school regularly.

A large majority of boys from this type of background became juvenile delinquents. Thus, eighty-five per cent of the boys aged seventeen had had one or more convictions. The delinquency rate for boys in the sample was some eight times that of the average for the total population of boys in the city. When compared with a control group of boys from the same bad neighbourhoods, the boys in the sample had a cumulative delinquency rate which, at every age level, was more than double. This finding suggests that, given a sufficient combination of adverse social factors, most boys will become juvenile delinquents. From a theoretical standpoint, and as an exercise in teasing out possible causes of delinquency, this result is most important, but of course one has to remember that the majority of boys who become delinquent do so without having been through anything like such extreme adversity.

Social pressures not the final answer

The level of crime in a community appears to be largely determined by external pressures. In Victorian times, the prevalence of poverty and poisonous medicines led to a high rate of child murder. Wars and social disasters release phenomena of looting, violence and racial murders, which are normally held in check by police and government authorities. It is hardly surprising, therefore, that social pressures such as unemployment, lack of education, disrupted homes, over-sized poor families, and run-down neighbourhoods are all found to be correlated with delinquency rates. At one time or another, every one of these factors has been heralded as a prime cause of crime. But this is out of fashion. Professor Radzinowicz wrote recently:

I am strongly convinced that the unilateral approach, the attempt to explain all crime in terms of a single theory, should be abandoned altogether with such expressions as crime causation. The most we can now do is to throw light on factors or circumstances associated with various kinds of crime [216].

Multi-factorial explanations remain possible. Although no single type of hardship has a monopoly in relation to delinquency, it could be that delinquents experience an accumulation of adverse pressures which build up to the point where restraints are overcome and crimes occur. This way of looking at the matter fits in rather nicely with the results of surveys, like those of Sprott and Wilson, which reveal the thick web of misfortunes in which the highly delinquent problem families, or the rougher slum elements among the working class, seem to be enmeshed. Lack of education, poor health, broken homes, low earning capacity, slum housing, inadequate child-rearing techniques, and general social ineptitude are merely the constituent elements of a powerful compound social handicap, which looks like the most important causal nexus in delinquency.

Unfortunately, things are not really so simple. Statistically speaking, though each factor of social-background adversity correlates positively with delinquency, none of the correlations is spectacularly large. Narrowing one's sights to the minority with a serious accumulation of adversities produces a very large correlation indeed, but in the process one has eliminated most of the population, and most of the delinquents as well. In other words, notwithstanding the great importance of these readily identifiable forms of social handicap, other factors must be operating. How else to explain the increasing numbers of apprehended delinquents who come from socially secure homes, or the fact that middle-class youngsters confess to as many unreported delinquencies as their working-class peers? Perhaps the secret will be found in more subtle social factors, or in different stresses operating in different social classes; or perhaps, after all, the psychological make-up of the individual youngster holds the answer.

4 Some Social Theories

Contrary to current ideas, the criminal no longer seems a totally unsociable being, a sort of parasitic element, a strange and unassimilable body, introduced in the midst of society. On the contrary, he plays a definite role in social life.

E. Durkheim, *The Rules of Sociological Method* (1895). Translated by J. Mueller, Glencoe, Ill., Free Press (eighth edition 1950).

If you steal what you want from the other, you are in control; you are not at the mercy of what is given.

R. D. Laing, *The Divided Self* (1960). Tavistock Publications; Penguin Books (1965). p. 62 (Penguin).

Schools of crime

Crime as a style of life

Modern sociologists follow Durkheim in interpreting the bulk of criminal behaviour as a normal response to a bad environment. Instead of singling out individual scapegoats for punishment or psychiatry, they advocate social reform as the best means of tackling the true causes of crime. In many departments of human activity, such as personal hygiene, eating habits, dress and language, conformity with social custom comes about for the most part without reference to criminal law by a gradual and largely unconscious absorption of conventions universally accepted in a particular community. Persons deviating too far from such conventions, even if not actually locked away as madmen, would soon find themselves rejected by family and by employers, and left without means of gaining food and shelter. Against criminal habits the taboo is less strong, and among certain groups and in certain circumstances law-breaking is recognized, even tolerated, as a possible style of life. Furthermore, the choice between criminality and conformity is not an 'all-or-none' decision. Selective disobedience to the law is rife. Many drivers who exceed speed limits, or get into their cars after drinking parties, many tourists who pass through customs with undeclared goods, many retailers who disregard the permitted hours for sales, and many businessmen who fake expenses, or devise misleading advertisements, or take advantage of office facilities for private purposes, would never class themselves as criminals, although they soundly condemn the more overt dishonesty of the housebreaker. On the other hand, the common crimes against property incur less disapproval among rough working-class groups than they do among those of respectable middle-class standards. Much of the contemporary sociological theories of crime concern the ways in which particular groups within the community succeed in evading or rejecting some of the moral restraints accepted by the predominantly middle-class law-makers. Understandably, most of these theories have originated in the United States, where the flaunting of political and business corruption, the more or less open pursuit of profitable 'rackets', and the conflict of ideals between different segments of a complex and fluid society, present to the young a particularly wide range of good and bad choices.

In view of the multiplicity of social factors concerned, no single causative principle can ever hope to provide a satisfactory insight into crime. Unfortunately some theorists have a partiality for over-simplified versions of events which they build up into supposedly universal explanatory principles. If, instead, the theories about to be mentioned are regarded as descriptions of different aspects of the problem, their real worth can be better appreciated.

Differential association

Broadly speaking, most sociological theories start with the assumption that the criminal way of life is something that has to be learned from experience. Whether a youngster becomes a crook or a respected and honest citizen depends upon the environment in which he has grown up. This is the idea behind the theory of 'differential association' first put forward by Edwin Sutherland in the 1939 edition of his *Principles of Criminology*. It has been castigated by one psychologist as the most sterile theory of crime ever devised, and lauded by numerous sociologists as the starting point of the modern approach. Basically, it consists of the simple principle of bad example. Young people develop into criminals by learning wrongful ways from bad companions, and by seeing powerful and successful adults breaking the law. Thus, the youngster from a bad school and bad neighbourhood comes into contact more often than not with older persons of confirmed anti-social attitudes, from whom he learns to reject law-abiding principles and acquires skill in rule-breaking and evasion. Everyone is to some extent exposed to conflicting possibilities, temptations and restraints, but where the young person perceives or experiences more in favour of crime than against it, he will become delinquent. On this theory, the budding criminal strives for money, status and happiness just like everyone else, but the attitudes with which he has come into contact, especially in his strongest personal relationships, have been such as to teach him unlawful rather than lawful ways of attaining his ends.

Sutherland himself recognized the existence of criminogenic factors other than association; for example the role of opportunity in the making of the embezzler, or the influence of poverty in making theft seem appropriate, so it is clear that the theory cannot provide a complete explanation. It explains the transmission of the criminal outlook, but says little about how antisocial attitudes originate. Furthermore, the assumption that all criminality is learned from others has been challenged by those who believe that, although social restraint has to be learned, aggressive and predatory behaviour comes all too naturally from the cradle. To make the theory workable, Sutherland had to accept that the age of the potential criminal, and the perceived importance and status of the persons whose example is being taken influences the learning that takes place; otherwise one might predict that prison officers, police and criminologists would become criminals by association.

. Sutherland's views were much influenced by two sets of phenomena; career criminals and adolescent gangs. In the criminal records of burglars, for instance, it was sometimes possible to discern a progression 'from a sport to a business', from petty crimes committed on the spur of the moment to highly organized and skilfully executed professional operations carried out with the minimum of risk for the maximum reward. Such offenders learn their techniques from older and more experienced criminals, and gradually earn for themselves an accepted place in the society of professional crooks, whose self-justifying philosophy they adopt along with the tricks of their trade.

Gangs as training for the criminal career

Affiliation to neighbourhood gangs of adolescent delinquents has always been a particular feature of juvenile offenders in America. In his classic study of juvenile gangs in Chicago, F.M. Thrasher [260] saw gangs as a training ground for crime. First encouraged to join gang companions in truancy, then

drawn into dare-devil adventures and the experience of getting a
kick out of disobeying rules, a boy is led step by step into actual
crimes. The gang provides a reservoir of technical knowledge
'how to procure junk, open merchandise cars, rob bread boxes,
snatch purses, fleece a storekeeper, empty slot machines . . .'
Along with demoralizing personal and sexual habits, it instils
'attitudes of irresponsibility, independence, and indifference to
law' along with 'an attitude of fatalism, a willingness to take a
chance – a philosophy of life which fits him well for a career of
crime'. As they grow older, youths thoroughly schooled in
criminal ways in their juvenile gangs gravitate readily to the
hierarchy of professionals ranging from 'silk hat' bosses with
impressive business and political interests, to the 'numerous
bums, toughs, ex-convicts, and floaters who frequent underworld
areas . . .'.

Later students of the Chicago scene such as F. Tannenbaum
[259] and W. F. Whyte [279] saw delinquent gangs as the
inevitable outcome of the failure of the community to provide
reasonable and constructive outlets for spirited and frustrated
youth. Such gangs always flourished in the worst slums, where
street-corner society provided a refuge from miserable and overcrowded homes, and an opportunity for self-expression, leadership, excitement and *esprit de corps*, otherwise denied to the
uneducated and impoverished segments of the community.
Whyte, in his description of the Norton Street gang, was quite
clear that in spite of its lawlessness the group performed a constructive social function through the mutual support and
solidarity of its members in the face of the misfortunes of
economic depression and unemployment.

Nevertheless, it is towards a criminal mode of adult living that
American adolescent delinquent gangs set their sights. Block and
Niederhoffer [20], who studied gangs in East Side New York,
described how the adolescent Corner Boys emulated and tried
to join up with the older Pirates, whose delinquent coups were
more sagaciously planned and more successful. In turn, the
older groups formed a training ground and a source of recruitment for the really professional adult racketeers and criminals.
Such organized gangs thrive best in communities, like the
Cornerville society described by Whyte, in which the rackets

extend from top to bottom, and form a large part of the life of the district, with prominent members of the respectable business and political world participating at the higher levels. Under these conditions, the frustrated youngster from the slums who finds legitimate avenues blocked has the ready alternative of a career structure in crime, beginning on the street corner, and ending up a big-time operator.

From such observations Sutherland and later theorists of this same tradition derived the conclusion that young offenders are on the whole normal members of a sick society. They differ from respected citizens only because they have had the misfortune to be reared among a class of society in which the delinquent style of life is more accessible and more easily learned than conformity to middle-class ethics.

Social protest theories

Anomie

Whereas Sutherland emphasized the normality of delinquent behaviour, other sociologists have explained it as a sympton of frustration which is liable to become pronounced among groups undergoing special stress. Durkheim coined the word 'anomie' for a form of social malaise in which the regulating and controlling pressures of accepted social custom are reduced, so that people find themselves without guidance or constraint, so that unrest and delinquency multiply. This is an opposite state of affairs to that of a tradition-bound culture where everyone knows his place, and where, though they may suffer poverty, discrimination, or even slavery, people accept their lot without protest. Industrial progress tends to destroy the stability of tradition. As social mobility increases, as goods appear in unfamiliar abundance and new career prospects open up, the individual no longer has any fixed limits of expectation with which to curb his appetites and ambitions. The greater the possibilities, the higher the sights are set and the more fluid the social situation, the greater the danger of dissatisfaction and disillusionment. Durkheim pointed out that too much freedom could have repercussions in private life no less than in business and public affairs, so that men without wives were more prone to suicide and mental illness. Modern freedoms have exposed the younger generation to greater opportunities both good and bad. An abundance of leisure, greater scope for getting about and meeting other young people, faster growth and earlier physical maturity, the extraordinary proliferation of products for youthful consumption (pop records, scooters, transistors, teenage fashions), and a growing tradition of free thinking and independence of the ideas of the older generation have brought increased opportunity for self-expression, but at the same time have also increased the temptations and chances to commit illegitimate acts.

The notion of social anomie and its dangers has been taken further by modern sociologists, notably R.K.Merton [176]. He redefined anomie as a form of cultural chaos due to an imbalance between the approved goals of society and the legitimate means of attaining them. He noted the tremendous emphasis in America on 'getting ahead', making money, and acquiring the trappings (mostly consumer goods) which symbolize status and success in contemporary society. While these goals are accepted by people in all walks of life, access to the socially approved means of attaining them varies. According to one's starting position in the social hierarchy, the social system can act as either a barrier or an open door. Young people with poor backgrounds and education are handicapped in the race towards success symbols, although they are under the same pressure to make good. Hence comes the temptation to take illegitimate short cuts. Merton and Durkheim agree about the danger of unleashing unrealistic aspirations, but Merton goes on to explain why this should happen especially among the lower classes. In effect, his theory suggests that by organizing itself so as to arouse and then to frustrate lower-class aspirations, society gets the criminals it deserves.

Merton described several types of response to anomie, of which perhaps the most serious is 'retreatism' or contracting out. This refers to persons who repudiate the whole frame of reference of conventional society, rejecting both the goals and the means. Beatniks, vagrants, drug addicts, and other self-determining outcasts fall into the category. The 'innovators' as Merton called them, the ones who twist the rules of the game so as to have a better chance of winning, are less personally maladjusted, but are labelled criminals. They mostly belong to classes of society where the chances of self-improvement in a conventional job cannot compare with the rewards of a criminal career. Another outlet Merton called 'ritualism', an over-valuation of the rules at the expense of the goal. Such people make a great show of 'playing the game', but the prize has faded into some unattainable distance. These are the assiduous bureaucratic form-fillers and report-compilers, the regular attenders who always make the right gestures and obedient noises, but their activity has become an end in itself, divorced from any realistic purpose.

Delinquent sub-culture

Merton's theories have inspired other writers to examine in more detail the reactions of those groups within society which deviate from or positively reject the morality of the majority. Such groups have come to be known as 'sub-cultures'. One of the most obvious examples of a criminal sub-culture is that of the delinquent gang. Albert Cohen [41] studied the social outlook and origins of members of delinquent gangs of juveniles, and produced some penetrating observations which he and others have elaborated into a general theory of delinquency causation. He observed that American juvenile delinquent gangs are recruited from working-class boys frustrated by lack of status. The emphasis among middle-class parents on self-discipline, planned ambition, and constructive use of leisure by their children paves the way to educational and social advancement; whereas the freer and more spontaneous, but less ambitious, attitudes of the working class leave their children less capable of benefiting from conventional opportunities for advancement. Lower-class boys find themselves at a disadvantage because success in business and education is largely reserved for those with middle-class ideas, values, skills and contacts. Being sensitive to their inferior status, and finding the effort to adopt middle-class standards too great, some of these boys react by repudiating middle-class values altogether, and holding up to ridicule conventional respectability and morality. The sub-culture thus formed stands in relation to dominant culture rather like a witches' coven in relation to orthodox Christianity; so that what was most condemned is now most admired. The boy who has made no headway among his more respectable peers now gains status by acts of aggression, theft and vandalism. By demonstrating his defiance and contempt for the authorities who have rejected him, he relieves his own feelings, and also wins the admiration of others. Wherever this reaction is commonplace, the affected individuals are likely to come together to form a group solution to their status discontent, each member of the group obtaining support and encouragement from others similarly placed and similarly motivated.

Cohen pointed out that his interpretation satisfactorily explained some otherwise puzzling aspects of juvenile delinquent behaviour. A lot of delinquent activity cannot be accounted for in terms of simple material gain, since very often great risks are taken and effort expended to steal articles which are so little valued by the thief that they are soon discarded or given away. Boys who like thieving often also like bullying better-behaved children who are not members of their gang, as well as playing truant, defying teachers and destroying property. The common motive behind all these forms of anti-social behaviour is malicious delight in annoying the representatives of respectability. A resentment against being pushed around and exploited by authorities also accounts for two prominent features of the gang ethos, hostility towards any form of outside control, and 'short-run hedonism'. Gang members are very resistant to efforts by teachers or social agencies to regulate their lives or supervise their leisure activities. They prefer to hang about idly, without set purpose but out for fun, until some impulse of the moment takes them off to a football game or a delinquent exploit. Gang members especially resent attempts by parents to control them, and in Cohen's view gang loyalties may contribute as much to the break-down of family life as family conflicts contribute to gang recruitment.

Advocates of the delinquent sub-culture theory argue that the reactions described are essentially normal and inevitable responses to a given set of social circumstances. Cohen himself, however, was willing to admit individual differences in type of reaction. Some boys, like Merton's 'retreatists', instead of transferring their allegiance to a sub-culture, simply gave up trying and lapsed into apathy. Despite the common core of motivation in the sub-culture, different individuals might come to join it for somewhat different reasons.

After Cohen, various writers have put forward variations on the delinquent sub-culture theme, but without much change in the basic concept. W. B. Miller [181] suggested that working-class sub-culture in America is such as to generate gang delinquency of itself, without any need for a reaction against middle-class ideas. The focal concerns of lower-class youth, toughness and masculinity, cleverness in making easy money and not being duped, excitement in chance and risk-taking, and the wish to be independent and not bossed about, encourage attitudes that are already half-way delinquent. The ideal of the super-manly fighting tough guy, intolerant of personal affronts, contemptuous of sentimentality, regarding women as objects of conquest and 'queers' as targets for abuse, has much in common with the traditional gangster hero. Skill in outwitting others in street-corner gambling and in exchanging insulting repartee brings increased status. Weekly 'binges', with the prospect of sexual adventures, brawls, and unrestrained excitement relieve an otherwise dreary and unrewarding routine. Resentment of coercion, exemplified by walking out on jobs, breaking away from homes and wives, or running away from penal institutions, may represent a compensation for dependency cravings, obliquely revealed by the compulsive way absconders seek out further 'trouble' and bring about inevitable re-commitment to institutional care.

The increasing rejection of deviants

Leslie Wilkins [282] has produced a theoretical model which seeks to explain further the social dynamics of delinquent sub-culture formation. He began by pointing out how much tolerance of deviant or undesirable behaviour varies according to the way a community is organized. In general, personal experience of individual variations leads to greater tolerance. In a village, where everybody knows the local idiot, and the local drunk, they are less likely to be shut away in institutions. In a tightly organized urban community, where ordinary persons are shielded from direct dealings with deviants by professional social and medical workers, personal experience and information about deviants will be rather small. Hence, any deviation that actually obtrudes will appear subjectively more unusual and extreme, and the reaction to it will also be more extreme and intolerant.

Referring back to the theories of the delinquent sub-culture, Wilkins noted that decrease in tolerance of deviation can lead to a vicious circle (or negative feed-back system, to use the modern idiom). The greater the pressure towards conformity, the greater the strain on the socially handicapped, and the more likely they are to react negatavistically and to seek solace in the delinquent sub-culture. Participation in the delinquent sub-culture in turn produces a sharp retaliation by authority, the effect of which is to aggravate still further the deviant's status frustration, and provoke still more hostility. And so round and round again.

In summary, the model proposed runs roughly as follows. Inadequate information leads to a wider range of acts being defined as intolerable. This means that larger numbers of individuals are cut off from social acceptance, and these people, perceiving themselves as outcasts, begin to develop their own deviant values. This leads to still further rejection, and to still greater emphasis on conformity by the community in general.

Coherent and incoherent forms of protest

D. J. Boruda [21] has put his finger on a curious feature of the modern theories of the delinquent sub-culture. Whereas Thrasher and the older exponents of gang dynamics admitted the exhilaration and satisfaction experienced by boys skipping school and being chased by coppers, the later theorists, such as Albert Cohen, depict boys driven by grim psychic necessity into rebellion. It seems that 'modern analysts have stopped assuming that "evil" can be fun and see gang delinquency as arising only when boys are driven away from "good"'. In this respect these modern social theorists have come closer to psychological theories, which regard delinquency, or at least persistent or compulsive delinquency, as a sign of personal maladjustment.

A survey of aggressive gangs in New York by Lewis Yablonsky [292] suggests that the modern gang is less well organized and socially purposeful than those of previous generations described by Whyte and Thrasher. The modern gangs indulge in brutality for no logical purpose except to boost a sinking morale. Youths embittered by personal inadequacies and social failures fulfil their fantasies of power and success by terrorizing others. Unlike the old gangs, which at least provided some elements of friendship, camaraderie and leadership, these groups lacked stability of membership, or any spirit of cohesion, acting in a mob-like fashion to relieve themselves in spontaneous bursts of irrational violence. In other words, these gangs had sunk to the level of loose collections of handicapped or inadequate individuals, and could hardly be looked upon as useful or coherent forms of protest against social injustice.

Cloward and Ohlin [40] have put forward an ingenious theory to explain the contrasts between the miserably frustrated delinquent sub-cultures, typified by Yablonsky's gangs, and the well-socialized delinquents marching up the ladder of a comfortable criminal career, as described by the earlier writers. They point out that a successful protest reaction against middle-class values depends upon the availability of opposing values and alternative courses of action. Illegitimate means as well as legitimate means vary in accessibility. Only those neighbourhoods in which a criminal community flourishes offer the youngster easy opportunity for learning the criminal role. In the heyday of the Chicago gangs, when at least the higher echelons of the criminal organizations were well integrated into normal business society, criminality offered a natural and rewarding career. In the more socially alienated type of slum, populated exclusively with the failures and outcasts from society, delinquency remains unsophisticated and impulsive, and professionally organized crime has no chance to develop, since the requisite links with the dominant culture do not exist. In the bad old days, lawless districts were relatively stable and cohesive, and people stayed there all their lives. In modern times, with greater social mobility, and massive housing projects, transience and instability are the chief features of slum life. The juvenile gangs in these areas have no opportunity for getting ahead by crime, so they can only work out their grudge against society in futile violence. In Merton's terms they are really retreatists from life, failures in both the criminal and the legitimate worlds. Hence the popularity of other retreatist reactions, notably drug-taking, which has become so prevalent among young people in America's urban slums.

When gangs dwindle away

In keeping with the assumption that delinquent sub-cultures are not so well developed in England, one finds that organized gangs of young delinquents do not flourish to anything like the same extent as in the United States. Dr Peter Scott [232], a psychiatrist at the London Remand Home for boys, made a special study of the habits of juvenile offenders in this regard. In the first place, he emphasized that the street-corner and coffee-bar groups, among whom so many adolescent youths spend their leisure hours, are not really much concerned with delinquency, and although their members may become offenders, they do so on their own initiative, and not as part of the group. Many juveniles committed offences on their own, but even when they offended in company their most frequent companions were their own brothers or regular friends. Such associations, not being ordinarily committed to delinquent activities, could not be called gangs. Indeed, delinquent gangs with a definite membership and a recognized leader were rather unusual, and apprehended juvenile offenders who had committed crimes as part of organized gang activities were quite exceptional. On the other hand, temporary associations between some three or four boys who committed their offences together were not uncommon, but these were often composed of personality-handicapped boys, whose emotional immaturity unfitted them for normal companionship.

When social conditions approximated more to those in America, as for instance in the slums of Liverpool a generation ago, juvenile gangs were more in evidence. When conditions change in such a way that the normal, average youngster no longer craves the support of an aggressive body of youths committed to social warfare, then the gangs dwindle away or change their character. One Liverpool student described vividly the transformation of adolescent gangs in Liverpool with the advent of the craze for beat music [74]. Boys who had previously spent their time fighting, or breaking into cigarette machines, got interested in forming themselves into musical groups, collecting equipment, practising, and attending dances. Belligerent and criminal gang leaders lost their sway, since the majority of the boys now had both the money and the aptitude for indulging this new interest. Adults might doubt the good taste of the product, but at least the activity was not inherently destructive, and in the form of Beatle exports was eventually to prove a national financial asset. Unfortunately, the poorer and less competent boys couldn't keep up with the new development. This hard core of misfits and criminals remained behind in the depleted gangs. It is always the weaker brethren, those least effective in social skills and manners, those most disliked by authorities, those most confused by faulty upbringing, who cling to the remnants of the protest group long after others have progressed to marriage or other interests.

Observations like these run counter to expectations based upon purely social factors, and draw attention to the importance of individual deficiencies and quirks of character in the development of persistent habits of delinquency. In the past, sociologists have tried to explain everything in terms of external pressures; but clearly individuals react differently, and one is not likely to get further towards understanding delinquency without some scrutiny of the offender as a person.

Second thoughts on the delinquent sub-culture

Delinquents not fully committed?

D. Matza [172] has called attention to the lack of factual support for the existence of the attitudes commonly imputed to delinquents. He points out that the sociological stereotype of a juvenile delinquent as a person committed to an oppositional culture does not ring true for most delinquents actually met and spoken to. For instance, when questioned in the abstract about offences like car theft or fighting with a weapon very few express approval or admiration for such violations. Their indignation if falsely accused of more offences than they have actually committed suggests that they share to some extent in the common feeling for justice and condemnation of wrongdoing. Likewise, they are insulted rather than flattered to have their mothers called immoral or their fathers described as rogues and criminals. If they really were fully conditioned to an oppositional system, they would hardly drop out of crime and 'go over to the enemy' in such large numbers on reaching the age of discretion. Except perhaps for some spies, the apprehended criminal does not usually feel a martyr to his cause (like members of persecuted political or religious minorities); instead he either admits to remorse or puts forward mitigating excuses like 'You have to defend yourself, don't you?' or 'What do you expect when there's nothing else to do?'

In Matza's view juveniles are less alienated from the wider society and not so uncompromising in their anti-social attitudes as the sociological theorists would have us believe. He thinks it implausible to credit children with the ability to initiate and promulgate an oppositional culture. After all, children still come under the influence of parents, and most parents strive to keep them law-abiding. Even in the most delinquent neighbourhoods one hardly ever finds parental Fagins setting out to teach their children the thieving arts. Most of the time delinquents behave just like everyone else, only now and then they have lapses from the accepted norm. Matza believes they evade rather than oppose the dominant morality, and they do this by selecting and extending trends that already exist in the wider culture. For instance, they may extend the accepted justifications for violence from protection against attack to protection against insult. They may extend a common disregard for the property rights of monolithic organizations to the idea that big stores are 'fair game'. Furthermore, the non-criminal American community is far from homogeneous, and in certain sectors of society attitudes flourish which have a strong affinity to those of the delinquent sub-culture. The cult of cowboy masculinity in the mass media, the 'freedoms' of Bohemia, and the fatalistic philosophy that puts down all individual badness to social causes, reflect and lend support to the cruder versions prevalent among delinquents.

Matza's criticisms do not really contradict the idea of a delinquent sub-culture, but they warn against exaggerating the power and consistency of the anti-morality and anti-establishment attitudes. Most observations on sub-cultures have been made in towns in the United States where social discrimination on racial and economic lines is in particularly blatant conflict with the American ideal. Under these conditions, protest reactions are intense and in some degree realistic. In England, with its more muted versions of social conflict, the delinquents' allegiances are likely to be more mixed and vacillating.

The stresses of an educational meritocracy

American literature on sub-cultures stresses the stark contrasts between rich and poor, or white and Negro. T. R. Fyvel [80], in a colourful description of some features of modern working-class youth in England and in some other European countries, has drawn attention to other kinds of class conflict which can equally well give rise to a class of aggressively disillusioned, socially alienated, and delinquent-prone youth. Fyvel points to the peculiarities of the English educational system as one of the worst sources of trouble. As the Crowther Report of 1960 pointed out, enormous numbers of fifteen-year-olds are released on to the labour market with insufficient training or preparation for anything but dead-end jobs. These hordes had been virtually condemned to second-class citizenship ever since the age of eleven when they were excluded from grammar school promotion and relegated to what were then called secondary modern schools. Finding themselves in boring jobs, but with more leisure and ready cash than their better-class peers, who were busily occupied in higher education or apprenticeships, these working-class youths, lacking the self-discipline necessary to organize their time constructively, remained bored and aimless. Having been turned off the middle-class ladder to success, and resenting their status as social failures, they tried to compensate by self-display, by extravagant spending on pop-music and exotic clothes. First the Teddy-boy outfits, then the Italian styles, then the long-haired, leather-jacketed Rockers spread across England in successive waves. The attractiveness of the new fashions to rebellious youth is doubtless much increased by the displeased reactions of teachers and authorities generally. Of course, fashions tend to spread in time throughout the population, and some are taken up by students at grammar schools as well as pop-art entertainers, but the delinquent groups are always way out at the current

D

extreme, as evidenced by the extraordinary wardrobes collected from boys entering remand homes.

Clothes are a harmless form of protest, but of course England's delinquents share, at least to some extent, many of the inverted ideals described by Cohen, especially the resentment of organization, the belief in living for the pleasure of the moment, and the importance of not letting a chance 'to get away with something' go by. One English writer of what might be called the social protest school, Alan Sillitoe, in his well-known short story (also filmed) *The Loneliness of the Long Distance Runner*, depicted his delinquent hero as being so deeply imbued with the idea that he was being pushed around and bamboozled by middle-class authorities that he deliberately let himself be overtaken in a race that he had worked hard to win rather than give the impression of cooperating. This hero's disillusionment with conventional morality is completely understandable, especially when he fumes against toleration of the atom bomb, or the combination of puritanical restrictiveness with the exploitation of sex and snobbery in commercial advertisements. Among sub-cultural delinquents in real life, the frustration and disillusionment are felt and acted upon in a confused way without any such attempt at intellectualization.

The class conflicts assumed to be responsible for delinquent sub-cultures may take different forms according to the nature of the dominant culture from which they derive. Fyvel contrasted the state of affairs in Moscow and London. Both cities have experienced growing social protest groups of delinquent-prone youngsters, but the precipitating stresses have been slightly different. In London inadequate guidance and training allows lower-class youngsters to drift into difficulties. In Russia, where the educational system is much more tightly organized and adolescents of all classes are directed and disciplined to a high degree, it is those who do not make the grade, and find themselves threatened with banishment to uninteresting menial jobs in far-distant places, who are liable to take to hooliganism, drunkenness, and social subversion. Thus American-style clothes and music may serve to symbolize rejection of an over-regimented meritocracy by those frustrated youngsters who suffer its restrictions without achieving the rewards that are supposedly open to all.

Choosing between the theories

An outstanding weakness of the social theories of delinquency is absence of factual evidence in support of any one in preference to the rest. The few hard facts that have been established, such as the social-class and neighbourhood distribution of offences, are for the most part consistent with all the theories. The different viewpoints represent more or less plausible intuitive interpretations, based upon general experience of offenders and their outlook. Criminological research findings on the attitudes and family backgrounds of offenders do have relevance, but researches planned specifically to test a particular theory are almost completely lacking.

The criminologist Nigel Walker [269] looks forward to the day when sociologists will select groups of people on the basis of the various social causes of delinquency to which they have been exposed or not as the case may be, and then compare their actual delinquency rates so as to get some measure of the practical importance of the causes in question. That day seems still far-off, and in the meantime one can do no more than appraise the merits of the theories in very general terms with reference to their compatibility with the results of delinquency surveys and with one's own experience.

All the social theories have one feature in common: they make no assumption about the supposed peculiarities of delinquency. They interpret delinquent behaviour as a natural response, sometimes even a constructive response, to the situation in which the youngsters find themselves. Since social circumstances vary so much from one country to another, it is only reasonable that sociological interpretations should vary also.

Whenever an urban society is so organized as to produce a ghetto situation, with an identifiable segment of the population condemned by educational and social disadvantages to slum life and third-class citizenship, then one finds delinquency highly concentrated in poorer neighbourhoods and closely associated with social deprivation and social protest. Where a well-established wealthy community attracts an influx of poor migrants, especially if the migrants are of a different race, religion and culture, class conflicts are exaggerated, and alienated groups of

socially handicapped and discontented youths come into prominence. In such situations, of which prime examples are to be
found in some large American cities, the formation of self-
assertive and rebellious 'sub-cultures' is both eminently understandable and rather patently obvious. An important point made
by the more recent sociological observers is that sub-cultures
may be, according to circumstances, relatively purposeful and
successful, as in the heyday of the Chicago gangs, or relatively
ineffective, frustrated and irrationally violent, as in the Yablonsky
type of gang.

It is open to question how far the delinquent sub-culture
theories apply to contemporary English society. Slum clearance,
and social welfare generally, have greatly reduced both the ghetto
situation and the sad inferiorities of dress and physical wellbeing
that at one time distinguished youngsters of the lower classes. On
the other hand, as Fyvel points out, an educational meritocracy
has developed that tends to relegate the less fortunately endowed
to an inferior status that is all the more humiliating because it
cannot so easily be attributed to wicked injustice. An interesting
implication of this view is that, after all, it may be personal inadequacies that are responsible for some individuals falling
behind in a competitive society and joining the ranks of the
socially inept and delinquent-prone.

Statistics suggest that delinquent habits are no longer limited
to the socially under-privileged, but are permeating upwards
through the class barriers. The Oxford sociologist B. R. Wilson
[286] has suggested that the contemporary emphasis on 'success',
based upon intellectual and material superiority, and widely
diffused via the mass-media, has the effect of inducing a sense of
frustration among the younger generation which is by no means
limited to the very poor. A further source of stress is the imper-
sonality of modern social organization and control, well exemplified by the anonymity of ownership of industrial concerns, which
does little to foster the old-fashioned virtues of individual
loyalty. Furthermore, while current ideas of child-rearing favour
a permissive, indulgent and affectionate attitude to children,
adolescents find themselves thrust abruptly into an impersonal
and demanding world. The modern youth culture, with its
rebellious, anti-establishment overtones, provides adolescents

with an alternative and self-comforting system of values and status. The pop-singer idols capture the imagination of the under-achievers, because they symbolize the fantasy of a meteoric rise to the top without visible effort or conventional virtue. While not overtly delinquent, the modern youth culture, in Wilson's opinion, by its emphasis on protest, excitement, kicks and short cuts to success, erodes moral restraints, and lowers resistance to delinquent temptations.

All this sounds very plausible; but as with so much of present-day theorizing, speculative interpretation has far out-distanced the facts of research.

5 The 'Bad' Seed?

Whence and what art thou, execrable shape?
Milton, *Paradise Lost*. Book II.

Everyone is as God made him, and often a great deal worse.
Miguel de Cervantes, *Don Quixote*. Part 2, Chapter 4.

The born criminal

The dubious concept of one criminal type

Even in neighbourhoods or social classes where the risks of delinquency are at their highest, not everyone takes to crime. Unless one believes the selection occurs by pure chance, it seems reasonable to look for the qualities which render certain individuals relatively vulnerable. Research on these lines has proved fascinating but very complex. At first, attention was directed more or less exclusively to individual weaknesses or pathology, to factors like ill health, mental subnormality or neurosis, but of course a delinquent response to a bad environment can be associated with more positive qualities, such as adventurousness, vigour, and self-assertion. Clinical studies of small groups of untypical offenders, for instance those whose anti-social outbursts are the result of epilepsy or of neurotic tensions, have led to dubious claims as to the relevance of such abnormalities to the generality of delinquency. Delinquent behaviour has a multiplicity of origins, and however closely tied it may be in a given case to an identifiable abnormality, it does not follow that the next case will show the same abnormality, or indeed any abnormality at all. Furthermore, the concept of delinquent susceptibility is itself an obvious over-simplification, for even when only thieving is under consideration it is likely that susceptibility to being caught once or twice at an early age is a different matter from susceptibility to becoming a recidivist. Likewise, susceptibility to delinquency probably means very different things in a person from a delinquent-ridden slum and in someone from a respectable middle-class environment. The dangers of generalizing too readily are very great.

Apart from the intrinsic complexities of the topic, research in this field also has to contend with strong emotional resistance to any findings which suggest that delinquent-prone individuals have identifiable psychological peculiarities. Sociologists are sceptical of the importance of individual differences in the face of massive social forces. Authoritarians don't want to know about anything that seems to provide excuses for bad behaviour. Lawyers don't like anything that detracts from the basic principles of self-control and personal responsibility upon which all justice rests. Yet it was in the relatively conservative atmosphere of the last century, and long before modern psychological ideas had taken root, that the most extremist of theories concerning the individual peculiarities of criminals gained widespread acceptance.

Nineteenth-century theorists believed that criminal habits signified some inborn moral deficiency. Some went so far as to suggest that criminals represented a reversion to an earlier stage of man's evolution, children with the mental endowment of primitive savages unluckily born into a civilized age. Others looked upon the criminal as a degenerate type, sharing with the mentally subnormal an incapacity to attain normal social standards because of some innate brain defect. This way of thinking lay behind the preoccupation with criminal anthropology, which in those days meant studying the bodily measurements, skull shapes and facial characteristics of criminals.

Alleged biological inferiority in criminals

As long ago as 1869, Dr G. Wilson read a paper to the British Association seeking to prove the moral imbecility of habitual criminals by showing that their skulls were smaller than average. The ultimate expression of this school of thought is to be found in the work of the Italian forensic psychiatrist, Dr Cesare Lombroso, whose investigatory zeal was stimulated through being called upon to carry out a post-mortem on the body of a famous brigand, during the course of which he came across a curious hollow on the man's skull which reminded him of similar features on the skulls of lower animals. Lombroso, in his famous treatise *L'Uomo delinquente*,* claimed that many criminals had physical anomalies bearing a striking resemblance to the physical features of primitive savages, apes, and in some cases to animals even lower in the evolutionary scale, such as the fierce carnivora. Thus, like apes, many criminals had an arm span

* Turin, 1895.

exceeding their height, a flat nose and sugar-loaf form of skull, and palms marked with few creases. Their lower face and jaw were often unduly developed and protuberant, in striking contrast to their narrow forehead and low skull vault. Tests revealed that their sensory powers were blunted, they could not interpret light touches on the skin as readily as the average, and a sharper stimulation was needed to produce any feeling of pain. Lombroso believed that the typical attitudes of criminals, their lack of moral sense, their immunity from remorse, their cynical attitudes, their impulsiveness and inability to restrain their passions, their violence and cruelty, were likewise attributes of a primitive constitution [73].

Today, such views seem quaint, and modern research has produced no support for Lombroso's ideas about the physical stigmata of criminality. Nevertheless, at the time, the work of the criminal anthropologists undoubtedly gave a boost to the popular notion that moral turpitude, feeble-mindedness, and coarse or deformed physique represent different aspects of degeneracy, and therefore tend to occur together in the same individuals. Belief in the existence of a congenital weakness of moral sense, analogous to or coincident with a congenital mental defect, led to the inclusion in the English Mental Deficiency Acts of 1913 and 1927 of a legal category of 'moral defectives' who were defined as persons 'in whose case there exists mental defectiveness coupled with strongly vicious and criminal propensities, and who require care, supervision and control for the protection of others'.

In point of fact, although modern evidence does not support the idea that either physical or mental defects are necessarily linked with immorality, it is true that the severer forms of mental subnormality are often accompanied by physical anomalies. In these cases, not only has there been gross interference with the growth of the brain and nervous system, but many other structures show signs of stunting or deformity. A brief walk round any hospital for the mentally subnormal should suffice to convince anyone of the prevalence among such patients of the stigmata that Lombroso associated with criminality. Indeed, one of the factors responsible for his results could well have been the number of mental defectives in the prison population in nineteenth-century Italy. In modern times, these people are sifted out and cared for in hospitals instead of being allowed to sink into destitution and crime.

Refutation of Lombrosian ideas

The most determined critic of criminal anthropology was an English prison medical officer, Charles Goring [104], who published a survey of 3,000 prisoners, comparing them with a control group from the normal population, from which he concluded that a physical type specific to criminals did not exist, although he agreed that, as a group, criminals were physically and intellectually below the average. Even this conclusion must not be taken too seriously, since Goring compared his criminals with quite different groups, particularly undergraduates, whose racial backgrounds, level of nutrition during growth, exercise habits and social advantages presented a marked contrast to those of the average prisoner.

A brief recrudescence of Lombrosian ideas was produced by Hooton [135], who compared American prisoners with samples from among the general population. He found that white, native-born American male criminals compared with white American civilians were on average smaller (lighter and shorter, with smaller heads) with a higher incidence of misshapen ears (one of the Lombrosian stigmata), snubbed noses and narrow jaws. Dividing the criminals according to the nature of their offences showed that the differences between civilians and prisoners were practically the same regardless of the type of crime. Hooton concluded that 'the primary cause of crime is biological inferiority – and that is exactly what I mean'.

As in so many researches in this subject, the fatal flaw in Hooton's work probably lay in the manner in which he selected the 'control group' with which to compare his prisoners. In the case of his native-born whites, half of the controls consisted of a group of firemen in Nashville, Tennessee, and the remainder were drawn rather haphazardly in Boston from men found on bathing beaches or attending hospitals or from soldiers at drill halls, and were measured by a different observer. There was no guarantee that these volunteers were truly representative of Americans in general. Furthermore, since physique is known to be linked with social class of origin and with choice of occupation, it is not established whether the alleged physical differences between prisoners and civilians had any connexion with the causes of their criminality, or were merely secondary consequences of the fact that the criminals belonged to a different range of social and occupational classes from that of the controls.

The dim-witted delinquent

Results of intelligence tests

One of the most constant of an individual's psychological qualities is intelligence. Barring accidents like brain injuries or disease, a child who ranks high among his contemporaries on the results of intelligence tests will usually continue to do so throughout life. Although the tests measure something surprisingly constant, the nature of intelligence eludes precise definition. Some psychologists dismiss the problem by saying that intelligence is whatever the tests measure – rather like the criminologists who say that a crime is whatever the courts declare a crime. Perhaps the nearest one can get to it is to say that intelligence tests measure general intellectual capacity for grasp and insight into new and puzzling situations and problems. The individual who lacks this capacity to a serious degree is recognizably dull and stupid in everyday life, and only those who achieve above average scores on intelligence tests are able to become successful students or pass examinations for professional careers.

At one time leading psychologists believed dullness of intellect to be the commonest characteristic of the criminal. In the early decades of this century, Goddard applied tests to various groups of American prisoners and declared anything from a quarter to nine tenths feeble-minded. More recently, Mary Woodward [289], in a comprehensive review of the results of intelligence tests applied to offenders, suggested that the average intelligence quotient of delinquent groups, both in England and America, was not more than eight points below that of the normal population.

Since samples of criminals, especially those taken from institutions, regularly include an over-representation of socially deprived and educationally backward persons, they will always be found to perform far below average on questions involving scholastic skills, upon which the older tests of 'intelligence' relied. In the more modern types of test, which involve non-verbal puzzles, like fitting shapes and patterns together, the un-educated are no longer at such a disadvantage, and when these tests are administered to samples of remand-home boys, borstal youths, or older prisoners, the intelligence scores obtained are not so very different from those of the normal population, except that there are relatively few really bright individuals, and an excess in the dull to average range [56].

Even this undramatic difference might melt away if, instead of comparing the delinquent groups with the average for the whole population, one compared them with a control group of non-delinquents of similar social background. This is not so easy to do in practice, because the commonly used criterion of socio-economic status, namely father's occupation, in the case of delinquent families may not provide a reliable guide to educational opportunity. In their analysis of the Cambridge–Somerville Youth Study, W. and J. McCord [164] were fortunate in having available a large sample of young working-class males who had been selected at the early age of eight years, for the most part because they were judged potential delinquency risks. Actually, forty-one per cent were convicted at least once during the ensuing seventeen years, and of those who were convicted there was indeed an over-representation (forty-two per cent) of individuals of rather dull intelligence, with quotients not more than 90. However, the unconvicted group had just as high a proportion (forty-four per cent) of individuals with the same range of intelligence scores. The excess of dullards in both groups was accounted for by the fact that the whole sample came from broken-down delinquent neighbourhoods, where the intelligence range of the population is generally depressed. The follow-up study showed very neatly that under these circumstances individual dullness bore no significant relationship to likelihood of a criminal conviction.

Previous work has not always yielded the same result. Cyril Burt [26], in his great study of London juvenile delinquents more than forty years ago, compared his delinquent group with non-delinquent children of the same age and social class, living usually in the same streets and attending the same schools. He found that both intellectual dullness and actual mental subnormality were three or more times as common among the delinquents. The improvements which have since taken place in the social and educational services may have prevented many dull children from lapsing into delinquency, and probably accounts for the fact that modern delinquents are not conspicuously duller than their social peers.

Types of intelligence and types of crime

A modified version of the theory that delinquents are intellectually inferior suggests that their main characteristic consists less in generalized dullness than in a selective lack of verbal skills compared with their relatively better performance on practical, manual tasks [211]. This suggestion seems plausible, because it fits in with the popular impression of the delinquent as a person who expresses himself more readily in action than in thought. However, it is singularly difficult to establish this as a characteristic peculiar to delinquents, since it has often been held to be typical of lower-working-class males in general, because of their traditional contempt for book-learning, abstract vocabulary, and middle-class subtleties of speech. Furthermore, as a recent review of research on the point has shown [196], actual findings have frequently failed to conform to the theoretical prediction. In fact, some recent research on English schoolchildren by P.E.Vernon [266], in which performance on a wide range of tests was related to the presence of environmental adversity, showed that children from homes of a low cultural level, where educational and linguistic stimulus was lacking, were as badly handicapped in practical-spatial tasks as in verbal comprehension or scholastic achievement.

It is sometimes suggested that criminals of above-average intelligence do not appear as often as they might in the criminal statistics because they use their intelligence to develop skills to evade being caught. By the nature of the case one can't know about those who have never been caught at all, but likelihood of re-conviction among those who already have a record bears no significant relationship to intelligence. The prison psychologist B. Marcus [170] reported on the re-convictions of 800 men followed up for three years or more after discharge from Wakefield Prison. On average, according to their test scores in prison, the ten per cent who were re-convicted during this period were no less intelligent than those who stayed out of trouble. A similar result in the case of juveniles was obtained by J. W. Anderson [9], who compared first offenders and recidivists in a sample of boys in the London Remand Home and found no significant difference in intelligence scores.

There is a demonstrable relationship, however, as Marcus and others have shown, between the average intelligence scores of those who commit different types of crime. As groups, sexual offenders and those guilty of personal violence are on average less intelligent than thieves, and of course considerably less intelligent then embezzlers. This might well be the consequence of the lowest social class, whose intelligence as a group is below average, being relatively uninhibited in sexual and aggressive behaviour, and so contributing large numbers of these types of offender.

Sub-cultural and pathological subnormality

When it comes to the minority who are sufficiently deviant to be classed as mentally subnormal, a more definite relationship with criminality emerges, although even then it is not so close as has often been supposed, and may be due in large part to the methods of selecting persons for legal ascertainment. The English Mental Health Act, 1959, defines subnormality as 'a state of arrested or incomplete development of mind ... which includes subnormality of intelligence and is of a nature and degree which requires or is susceptible to medical treatment or other special care of training of the patient'. Such a patient, if under twenty-one years of age, may be compulsorily committed to a mental hospital on the appropriate medical recommendations.

In practice, persons whose scores on tests place them in the bottom five per cent of the population on measurable intelligence are liable to be admitted to institutions [30], but in fact this happens to not more than one in a hundred among the dullest five per cent. In spite of their intellectual disadvantage, the great majority fit into the community in simple, undemanding jobs. However, those whose dullness is combined with a wayward temperament, or those whose training has been neglected on account of bad family backgrounds, find themselves in social difficulties, and are liable to be referred for examination and officially ascertained as subnormal. The selection process accounts for the fact that, among children below the age of puberty attending state schools for the educationally subnormal, boys invariably predominate. At this age, teachers find boys more often troublesome than girls, so boys are preferentially selected for disposal in special schools. Stein and Susser [250] demonstrated a great preponderance of lower-class, badly educated, and socially unaspiring families among those whose children were ascertained subnormal. In institutions, there is always a relatively large number of admissions of subnormals after adolescence, at an age when the guiding influences of school and parents begin to wane, and young persons are expected to assume some individual responsibility.

This way of looking at the problem emphasizes the cultural determinants of subnormality. Intellectually, subnormals fall on the dull side of the average, but most of them are within the natural range of variation, they have no obvious physical defects, and they generally come to notice on account of social as much as intellectual incompetence. The families least able to contend with difficulties, those in which the parents are themselves dim-witted, ineffectual or neglecting, and who often produce large numbers of children, are the ones least able to cope with the training of children of low intelligence. Hence the duller off-spring from such families are very liable to be ascertained subnormal, thus perpetuating from one generation to the next a complex of social problems that is likely to include both subnormality and delinquency.

There seems no doubt that the increasing complexity of urban civilization makes heavy demands upon the duller members, who find learning to read, write and calculate, learning to handle machines, use a telephone, drive a car, or master a trade, or learning the complicated array of attitudes and habits required by society comes less easily to them than to their brighter neighbours. Most instances of moderate subnormality result from a combination of below-average intellectual endowment and deprived upbringing, which has the effect of stunting mental growth and discouraging social learning. It was once popularly believed that intelligence, as measured by tests, was essentially a fixed, unalterable attribute, determined exclusively by hereditary endowment. Modern research suggests that not more than three quarters of the variation in intelligence between individuals is due to innate factors, and this leaves a lot of scope for environmental influences. Uninterested and neglectful parents, who are often dull themselves, give their offspring insufficient stimulation. They don't bother to talk to them or explain things, they don't give that loving encouragement which is an essential part of training, and as a result their children never learn to take things in properly. Extreme examples are on record of unwanted children, usually illegitimate, shut away in solitude in an attic. Such children, if they pass the critical age when social contacts and language are normally learnt, may remain permanently imbecilic. In less extreme cases, transfer to a good foster home, provided it takes place while mental growth is still possible, results in a considerable increase in test scores. Clarke and Clarke [38] studied the changes in intelligence quotient among subnormals which took place over a period of eighteen months following committal to an institution. The prospects of improvement with training were better with those from the worst homes, presumably because in their case environmental factors predominated. The subnormal children who came from very adverse backgrounds made an average increase of ten points of I.Q., compared with an increase of only four points in those from less bad homes. A follow-up investigation six years after first committal showed continuing improvement.*

Severe subnormality, legally defined as 'of such a nature or degree that the patient is incapable of living an independent life or of guarding himself against serious exploitation . . .', constitutes a different and more strictly medical problem. Most such persons give scores on intelligence tests worse than 99.8 per cent of the population, which means, in the case of adults, that they

---

* The difference between the changes in the two groups was the important finding. The statistical phenomenon of regression to the mean might explain some degree of apparent improvement on re-testing.

have a 'mental age' of less than six years. Most of them have demonstrable physical abnormalities, paralyses or deformities. In other words they are pathological cases in which, as for instance in the common 'Mongol' type, some developmental flaw (in this instance associated with an identifiable chromosomal abnormality) has prevented the normal development of the brain and nervous system. Many such unfortunates require skilled nursing care just to keep them alive. They contribute very little to crime statistics, partly because they are comparatively rare outside of institutions, and partly because their incapacities, both mental and physical, are too severe to allow much scope for criminal activities. They differ from the 'cultural' type of moderately subnormals in that they are as likely to appear in better-class homes as in the poorer homes [202], and they have not usually been deprived of affection or training.

Since there is such a clear association between social adversity and moderate subnormality officially ascertained, it is not surprising to find, in clinical surveys of mentally subnormal individuals, that those who have come from the worst environments are often the most unstable in behaviour. Dr Michael Craft [44] made an interesting comparison between a series of subnormals transferred to the special hospital at Rampton on account of their violent or obstreperous behaviour, and a control group of patients of similar grade of defect who remained in the ordinary hospital. The former group had a much higher incidence of unsatisfactory backgrounds as judged by interventions by the National Society for the Prevention of Cruelty to Children, the absence of one or both parents, or indications of severe poverty.

Subnormal offenders

East, in a survey of 4,000 youths examined at Wormwood Scrubs Prison as to their fitness for detention in borstals, found 3.5 per cent potentially certifiable as mentally subnormal [53]. In his smaller sample of 200 youths actually committed to borstals, T. C. N. Gibbens [82] found three per cent of unstable dullards whom he described as 'borderline defectives'. Although this is several times what one would expect of a normal young male population, subnormals obviously do not account for more than a small minority of the population of young criminals. However, it is of interest to isolate the subnormal group and consider their special characteristics.

Like any other under-privileged minority, mentally subnormal people, especially if they have been forcibly detained in institutions, may develop attitudes of resentment and revolt. They may also feel at a loss to make their mark among their peers, so when opportunity presents itself to participate in delinquent activities they are easily led into stupid exploits in the hope of winning acceptance. Sexually, they have normal physical and mental urges but often without the ability to make social contacts with the opposite sex and achieve their goal in a conventional manner. G. de M. Rudolf [225], in a survey of the incidence of crime among subnormals released from English hospitals, demonstrated that patients discharged or released on licence have a considerably higher incidence of criminal convictions than the population average. He noted that all kinds of offences of all degrees of seriousness were committed by subnormals, but that sexual crimes were particularly common. Liability to minor crimes seems to be rather widespread among subnormals. Nigel Walker [270] pointed out that of the 305 male offenders of seventeen years of age or more who were committed to hospitals by English courts on account of mental subnormality during the year 1961, as many as thirty-two per cent were guilty of sexual offences. (Of all males of seventeen or more convicted of indictable offences that year, only five per cent were convicted of sexual offences.) Crimes of serious personal violence, on the other hand, are not particularly characteristic of subnormals in general, and murder is rarely committed by them.

In subnormals, as in other types of mentally abnormal person, background and personality count for more than the degree of handicap in determining criminal habits. The general run of subnormals are not particularly criminal, but those with an intellectual handicap combined with temperamental aggressiveness or psychopathic disposition can be quite a menace.

Rudolf did not follow up his cases long enough to see if they gradually got adjusted to life outside the institution. The few long-term surveys that have been done tend to show that the ultimate prospects of mentally handicapped people are not so bad as one might expect, that very few commit serious crimes, and only a small minority become persistent offenders. Thus D.C. Charles [32], in a survey of 127 cases ascertained mentally retarded during their schooldays, and traced some twenty years later, found no very serious crimes had been committed, although sixty per cent of the men had been convicted on one or more occasions. Petty crimes, especially traffic violations and drunkenness, accounted for the great majority of convictions. At the other extreme a twenty-year follow-up of cases from two Danish island colonies for subnormals, which receive unruly or criminal patients, revealed a much more depressing picture [280]. Of fifty-eight men, eight had died, one while trying to escape from the mental institution, three by committing suicide. Two of the suicides occurred in prison, one by a man who had committed 400 burglaries, the other by a man who had committed murder. Of the fifty surviving at follow-up, about a half were 'managing decently' in the community. However, it was also about a half who had received one or more sentences for criminal offences, some of them of quite serious nature. Repeated thefts were the most frequent of their offences, but crimes of fraud, sex and violence were not uncommon.

The contrast between the ordinary harmless subnormals and the psychopathic types accounts for the fact that whereas serious crimes of violence are untypical of the general run of subnormals, nevertheless, among the minority of serious criminals, for instance those who commit murder, rape, and sexual assault with violence, a surprisingly high proportion are drawn from the ranks of the more unstable and aggressive subnormals. It seems that the conjunction of impulsiveness with lack of imaginative appreciation of the consequences or gravity of their acts makes a few subnormals a real danger.

The classification of subnormals into the more severe cases who are organically damaged, and the less severe cases, who are culturally deprived dullards, useful as it is in identifying general trends, cannot be applied in a hard and fast way to every individual case, since some people display varying mixtures of both kinds of handicap. The combination of social adversity and organic defect can sometimes produce quite monstrous and dangerous deformities of character.

Physical defects

Minor physical handicap

According to some theorists, people take to crime because they find difficulty in competing according to the rules. Hence, any kind of physical handicap or disease which interferes with social adjustment might be expected to predispose to delinquency. In practice, it has not been convincingly demonstrated that criminals as a group, and especially young criminals, are any less healthy than their non-delinquent peers. Earlier surveys often found a high incidence of physical disease and malnutrition among delinquents. In the 1920s, Cyril Burt [26] found that defective physical conditions were roughly one and a quarter times as frequent among delinquents as among non-delinquents. Nearly seventy per cent of his delinquents were suffering from some degree of bodily weakness or ill-health, and fifty per cent were in urgent need of medical treatment. With improved social conditions this no longer holds true. In a comparison of the medical records of delinquent boys in a London remand home in the years 1930 and 1955, Eilenberg [56] found that over this period serious physical disease and serious malnutrition had virtually disappeared as a feature of young delinquents. In fact the delinquent boys were slightly heavier than the average for London schoolboys. However, he did note a significantly higher incidence of minor physical ailments in the remand-home boys, including skin complaints, visual defects, ear discharges and deafness, and skeletal deformities. Some of these were treatable conditions that had been neglected.

The slightly raised incidence of physical anomalies among delinquents may be merely a feature of the social class from which they come. Larger studies, using control groups taken from the same social class, have not shown any consistent trend. Thus E. and S. Glueck [95] found that most of the defects which cause embarrassment, such as squints and genital peculiarities, were, if anything, commoner among the non-delinquents. W. and J. McCord [164], in their analysis of the Cambridge–Somerville youth project, found no correlation between general physical ill health and delinquency proneness. Ferguson [69], in his Glasgow survey, showed that boys from schools for the physically handicapped were no more frequently delinquent than those from ordinary schools – although those who were tended to be unusually persistent. A reaction of social withdrawal and shyness may possibly be more typical of the physically handicapped than one of rebellion and delinquency, although the rebellious reaction may be an important characteristic of certain handicapped individuals.

D.H. Stott [252] attempted to show that the more maladjusted among delinquents are more likely to have physical defects. Applying a maladjustment questionnaire addressed to school-teachers, he found that among a sample of 400 boys on probation in Glasgow, those rated 'maladjusted' had a much higher incidence of physical ailments. In order to see if this association was simply the consequence of both the socially maladjusted and the physically inadequate coming from the same poor backgrounds, he separated out a group from satisfactory homes and found that the relationship still held good even in the absence of obvious environmental adversity.

As usual, when one comes to consider special groups of offenders the incidence of abnormalities increases. Borstal youths are on the whole more serious and persistent delinquents, and come from worse backgrounds, than the average boy in a remand home, so it is not surprising to find that they have a larger proportion with physical defects. T.C.N. Gibbens [82] found that among his borstal sample double the expected proportion had been rejected on physical grounds when called up for military service.

Whatever one believes about the importance or otherwise of the presence of physical defects in fostering delinquent tendencies, clearly nothing but good can come from trying to correct them when their presence is detected. This was done, for instance, by Ogden [198], who arranged surgical treatment for borstal inmates with minor deformities, and showed that their reconviction rates appeared to decrease. He believed the procedure worked by liberating these youngsters from chronic embarrassments and irritations, and so rendering them more susceptible to training. In a more recent Canadian project [153], 450 young male prisoners who had disfigurements improved in behaviour after plastic surgery.

Brain damage and bad behaviour

A somewhat more subtle version of the physical-defect theory
has gained acceptance in recent years, based upon evidence that
relatively slight degrees of brain damage, sustained perhaps
during development in the womb or in the process of birth,
although insufficient to cause paralysis or other physical symptoms, may nevertheless result in emotional instability and possibly
delinquency. One of the best pieces of evidence for this view has
been produced in a Scottish survey by C.M.Drillien [50], who
followed up a sample of prematurely born infants, and, at the
age of seven years, had their teachers rate their behaviour on a
questionnaire designed to elicit signs of maladjustment (Stott's
Bristol Maladjustment Guide). Children who were maturely
born (i.e. over $5\frac{1}{2}$ lb. at birth), and without complications in
pregnancy or delivery, produced the fewest indications of
maladjustment. A history of premature birth, of complications of
delivery or pregnancy, or of family stress, each added a considerable increment to the maladjustment score. Such findings
lend support to the theory that a series of minor neurological
impairments can produce a cumulative deterioration of behaviour, and that individuals so affected are rendered particularly
vulnerable to adverse environmental influences.

Unfortunately, much of the evidence bearing upon this theory
is somewhat complex and equivocal. Clinical experience of
persons with epilepsy, head injuries, brain infections, or other
conditions liable to damage the brain shows that some of these
patients, especially if they are young and of unformed character
at the onset of the illness, afterwards become extraordinarily
irritable, aggressive and sometimes delinquent. However, the
outcome is very unpredictable, and large-scale surveys of the
after-careers of patients who have had encephalitis or epilepsy
have failed to confirm any conspicuous general trends towards
delinquency. For example, C.H.Alström [7], in a careful follow-
up study of 345 adult male epileptics over a ten-year period,
found crimes of violence recorded in seventeen per cent of the
sample compared with eleven per cent in a control group. There
were no instances of homicide, and nearly all the crimes were
minor, usually related to alcoholic abuses.

D.A.Pond [209] has pointed out that the over-activity and aggressiveness of epileptic and brain-damaged children brought to psychiatric clinics are very similar to the symptoms of children brought on account of purely emotional disturbance. Furthermore, the organically impaired children with behaviour problems usually came from broken or disturbed backgrounds such as are also associated with bad behaviour in organically sound children. He quoted in support a Swedish study by Dencker and Löfving, in which a large series of twins, one of each pair having sustained a serious head injury, were followed up years later. Often the uninjured twin showed similar symptoms, although in a milder degree. The work strongly suggested that the psychological disturbances following brain injury had more to do with the previous personality and background of the patient than the extent or nature of the injury. A fair statement of the position would seem to be that even minor degrees of neurological disease, injury, or congenital abnormality are liable to exaggerate the effects of an adverse environment or of underlying defects of personality; but that in the absence of these additional factors even very serious injuries may not produce any permanent deterioration in behaviour.

From a research standpoint, the difficulty of sorting out the effects of organic and environmental handicaps is greatly increased by their tendency to occur together in the deprived section of the community. Thus J.W.B.Douglas [47], in a national survey of all children born over a given span of time, found a very significant correlation between bad behaviour, as evaluated by primary-school teachers, and a history of premature birth. However, among the children of better-class mothers, the association between prematurity and bad behaviour no longer held true. He concluded that the connexion was not a matter of cause and effect, but was largely due to the high incidence of premature births among the unsatisfactory mothers who reared badly behaved children.

It seems clear that physical defect, either in general or more specifically neurological form, does not account for the bulk of delinquent behaviour, although it may be a contributory factor in many cases, and an important factor in a few.

Brain waves in delinquents

The electro-encephalograph, which records in wave tracings the
electrical activity of the brain, might be expected to provide
further evidence as to the neurological abnormalities of certain
delinquents. Applied to persons of epileptic tendency, the instru-
ment can be used to show that fits are associated with paroxysms
of fast waves of high amplitude, indicative of numerous brain
cells discharging in unison. When this abnormal rhythm spreads
too far, generalized convulsions and loss of consciousness occur.
Rather similar paroxysmal disturbances, but limited to areas of
the brain where they do not cause convulsions, have been found
in tracings obtained from individuals of abnormally aggressive
temperament. This has led to the theory that explosive outbursts
of rage may sometimes represent the 'equivalent' of an epileptic
fit, a theory reminiscent of the traditional notion of a 'brain-
storm'.

Apart from these paroxysms, a commoner indication of cerebral instability is the presence of waves slower than those which
are usually found in the records of normal, wakeful adults. It is
possible to classify people as 'normal' or 'abnormal' on their
E.E.G. records according to generally agreed criteria, such as the
system evolved by F. A. Gibbs, which depends upon counting
the frequency of various types of deviant waves. Anything up to
one fifth of the population may be classified as 'abnormal' on
these grounds. When the same tests are applied to E.E.G. records
taken from mental patients, a much greater incidence of abnormality has been found. Unselected groups of criminals, however,
have shown no such trend [89], but of criminals classified as
'unstable and aggressive' or 'psychopathic' something like a
half have been found to have 'abnormal' brain rhythms [57].
In one of the most famous investigations of this kind Hill and
Pond [121] examined the records of a series of 105 English
murderers, and found that of those who had committed clearly
motivated crimes only ten per cent had abnormal E.E.G. records,
but nearly all of the irrational murderers showed abnormalities.

In a more recent research by Loomis [159], who examined the
E.E.G. tracings of 100 young delinquents (modal age fifteen to
sixteen years) in an American reform school for boys, the propor-

tion with specifiable abnormalities was no greater than that found in unselected school populations of similar age. On the other hand, among a group of fifty delinquents from the same reform school who had been specially selected for psychiatric examination on account of peculiarities noticed by the staff, the proportion with E.E.G. abnormalities was almost double the ordinary figure. Impulsive violence was only one among many symptoms displayed by the youths with abnormal E.E.G. recordings.

In so far as these abnormal tracings may be thought to signify the presence of a constitutional neurological defect, they provide another piece of evidence for innate delinquent propensities in some individuals. However, the findings refer only to specially selected groups of violent and peculiar offenders. E.E.G. abnormalities also occur in individuals of 'psychopathic' temperament who do not happen to have committed crimes. Individuals with abnormalities of the E.E.G. must not be regarded as doomed, for a great many improve or 'mature' with time. Judged on adult standards, the E.E.G. tracings of most normal children would be classed as abnormal. Among adults, the proportion found to be 'abnormal' decreases steadily with age. Curiously enough, Gibbens and others [86], in a follow-up study of a series of psychopathic recidivists, found that those with E.E.G. abnormalities on first examination did rather better than those with normal records. This confirms the impressions of other workers [55], who find that psychopaths with normal E.E.G. records are relatively more aloof and set in their ways, and more obviously strongly conditioned by a very bad social background; whereas those with abnormalities have slightly better backgrounds, more frequent histories of brain injury or disease, more signs of conflict within themselves about their behaviour, and a greater potentiality for change. Thus, the connexion in certain people between unstable and anti-social behaviour and E.E.G. abnormalities is beyond doubt, but the details of these relationships, and their meaning in regard to cause and effect, have yet to be worked out. Modern anti-convulsant drugs, which have a stabilizing effect upon brain rhythms, without actually putting the patient to sleep or causing too much drowsiness, have proved most effective in controlling epileptic attacks. The same drugs have been given to aggressive psychopaths in the hope of controlling their emotional outbursts, but on the whole without any great success, except in those cases associated with definite clinical epilepsy.

Insanity

Mental diseases, like manic-depressive psychosis and schizophrenia, which are probably due to some underlying but as yet not precisely identified organic defect are hardly worth mentioning in connexion with young offenders, since their incidence is so small. Melancholia is a disease of middle age, and schizophrenia does not usually manifest itself before early adult life. Occasionally young schizophrenics under the influence of delusions of persecution or preoccupied with bizarre sexual impulses commit family murders or other atrocious acts of violence, but fortunately such events are rare. Among young delinquents examined in remand homes, schizophrenia is rarely diagnosed, and probably no more often than might occur in routine examinations of a normal population during an army call-up.

The criminal physique

Sheldon's body types

In recent years techniques known as somatotyping have been developed whereby individuals may be classified according to their characteristic physique by measuring the relative size of the muscular, bony and fatty components of the body. The pioneer in this field was a psychiatrist, E. Kretchmer, who was interested in the observation that susceptibility to one mental disease or another was apparently associated with body build. He divided people into asthenic (the thin, lanky type), athletic (the muscular type), pyknic (squat, barrel type), and dysplastic (mixed) types, and found that the asthenics were prone to introverted temperament and schizophrenic illness, while the pyknics were more prone to mood fluctuations and manic-depressive psychosis. W. H. Sheldon [240] developed a method of rating numerically these various bodily elements by measuring the contours on photographs taken in the nude. He later introduced his system into the criminological arena by claiming that the physical types were related not only to temperament, but also to delinquent tendency.

On Sheldon's system each person receives three numerical ratings according to the strength of three primary bodily components called endomorphy, mesomorphy and ectomorphy. Although many people score equally on more than one rating, others show a predominance of a particular component. Endomorphs have large body cavities and viscera (barrel chests and pot bellies) with soft, rounded surface contours. Mesomorphs are solidly built and heavy, with a lot of muscle. Ectomorphs are light-weight skinny types with slender bodies. The names of the three body types were taken from the three layers of the developing embryo, which form respectively the viscera and body linings; the muscle, bone and connective tissue; and the nervous system and surface skin. The body types were thought to result from differential development of one or other of these fundamental tissue components. Whether the measurements used in Sheldon's system really do have these biological implications is doubtful. The Sheldon types correspond roughly, but not exactly, to Kretchmer's system, the endomorphs having much in common with the pyknics, the mesomorphs with the athletics and the ectomorphs with the asthenics.

Sheldon applied his typing system, using photographs, to 200 male students at a university and to another 200 youths resident in a Boston institution for difficult and delinquent boys. He found that whereas among the college males there were as many ectomorphs as mesomorphs, among the institutional youths there was a heavy preponderance of mesomorphs and few ectomorphs. The preponderance of sturdy mesomorphs was most noticeable among the healthiest of the institution youths, those who were simply delinquents without having any accompanying psychiatric or medical disabilities. Sheldon identified this type of physique with the boisterous, affable, out-going, yet fundamentally aggressive and undisciplined, temperament (Dionysian) that predisposes to a predatory rather than a subservient or docile attitude to life. He saw the delinquents as individually unsuccessful predators, whereas some political bosses and irresponsible jingoists in the community at large were examples of the same type who had won themselves social status. Sheldon thought selective breeding was a cause of the delinquency problem and eugenic measures a possible long-term remedy. He argued that 'our best stock tends to be outbred by stock that is inferior to it in every respect' [241]. The parents of the delinquents were producing many more offspring than the parents of college students. They were 'expending a greater proportion of their energies on uninhibited or irresponsible sexuality'. The predatory types were reproducing themselves at an alarming rate, thus causing a population explosion that could only end in a death struggle for survival.

Fortunately, an acceptance of some of Sheldon's research findings does not force one to share his alarming speculations about the deterioration of the race. Indeed it is arguable that the beefy, vigorous mesomorph is biologically an admirable type who is apt to become delinquent only under adverse conditions. The same type of youth in a different social class might be a successful rugger captain or rowing blue.

The physical and temperamental differences outlined by Sheldon are detectable from quite an early age, which is in keeping with the idea that these are largely inborn qualities. R. W. Parnell [200] found in a sample of Oxford schoolchildren of eleven a high positive correlation between ectomorphic physique and traits of meticulousness and susceptibility to anxiety and guilt feelings, which were assessed by psychological testing and psychiatric interviews. In contrast, 'muscularity' (Parnell's version of mesomorphy) correlated with traits of aggressiveness and restless or explosive behaviour.

Physical types among delinquents

The largest and most famous application of Sheldon's system to delinquents was made by S. and E. Glueck [97], who compared 500 delinquent youths attending two correctional schools in Massachusetts with 500 youths, who were believed to be non-delinquent, from state schools in Boston, who were matched with the delinquents for age, intelligence level, racial origin and residence in poor urban areas. The results confirmed Sheldon's claims. There were twice as many mesomorphs among the delinquents (60.1 per cent compared with 30.7 per cent) but less than half as many ectomorphs (14.4 per cent compared with 39.6 per cent). The matching procedure ensured that these findings were not due to differences in race or social class between the delinquents and non-delinquents. Assessments of the boys, made by means of psychiatric interviews and psychological tests, showed that, among both delinquents and controls, those of mesomorphic physique tended to be relatively more powerful and energetic, more apt to work off their tensions or frustrations in action, and less inhibited by feelings of inadequacy, submissiveness to authority or by sensitivity to conflict situations. It is easy to see how these traits might predispose to aggressiveness and delinquent behaviour, although of course only a minority of mesomorphs actually become delinquent.

In contrast, the ectomorph was characterized by greater liability to feelings of inadequacy and to emotional conflict, a more sensitive and imaginative turn of mind, and less out-going energy. These traits acted as a curb on aggressive impulses, so that frustrated ectomorphs tended to bottle up their emotions, and to react to difficulties by blaming their own inadequacies or by generating nervous symptoms, rather than by resorting to rebellion and delinquency.

Although the degree of vulnerability to delinquency varied, the Gluecks found that the adverse factors associated with the onset of delinquency (such as poor homes, bad relationships with parents, lack of self-control, undue suggestibility, and delinquency in other members of the family) were much the same in all types of physique. But the association between disharmony in the home and delinquency was closer in the case of ectomorphs than mesomorphs, presumably because ectomorphs are more sensitive to environmental conditioning, whereas mesomorphs, being more robust and self-assertive, become slap-happy delinquents without necessarily having a very disturbed background, or, in other cases, resist becoming delinquents in spite of bad home influences. Some of the most intractable delinquents, however, were mesomorphs with the aggressive drive typical of their physique, but unhappily coupled with emotional instability, mental conflicts and feelings of inadequacy such as more often occur in ectomorphs.

Sheldon's system of typing human physique has been subjected to considerable criticism in recent years. The shapes of photographic silhouettes may not give the best indication of physique. More recently other workers have used quite different procedures, for example taking X-rays of limbs and counting the ratio of muscle to bone at a particular level across the calf or upper arm. Another way of estimating muscular development uses strength of grip, as measured by squeezing a dynamometer bulb. Sheldon hoped to eliminate the complicating factor of the amount of fat present, which of course varies with age and feeding habits, but in this he probably did not completely succeed. Furthermore, it remains an open question at what stage of growth the bodily configuration becomes stable and permanent. Some authorities consider that the whole idea of dividing people into types is misconceived, and that better correlations between physique and behaviour might be had by using an array of simpler variables such as height, weight and shoulder width. Sheldon's types, although thought by their originators to arise from genetic differences, may well be connected with other factors. The muscular, hyper-masculine mesomorphic youth, for example, may well owe the splendours of his physique largely to his endocrines which are certainly prompted by nutritional and environmental circumstances as well as by the genes.

These and many other technical difficulties serve to emphasize the complexity of the relationships between physique and temperament, but they in no way invalidate the fundamental principle, pioneered by Sheldon, that the individual physical constitution has an obvious bearing upon human behaviour, and in particular upon delinquent behaviour. The measures relevant in this context, such as height, weight and muscularity, are variants of the normal, and in this respect quite unlike the Lombrosian stigmata, which were thought to indicate degeneration or pathology. Nevertheless, they are measures which, to a large extent, appear to be predetermined by inborn or hereditary factors. Although it is highly unfashionable to suggest that delinquent propensities may have some hereditary basis, research evidence compels one to consider carefully some of the links that have been discovered between delinquent behaviour and certain physical and psychological traits presumed to be inherited.

Inherited criminality

Familial incidence of criminality

The individual qualities so far discussed as possibly related to criminal propensities have in common the factor of being supposedly determined to a large extent by heredity. Hence it seems relevant to mention at this point some attempts to obtain direct evidence for the inheritance of criminal tendency.

The first problem is whether in fact criminality does run in families from one generation to the next. If it does not, then the question of heredity hardly arises. If it does, then one has to try to sort out how far this can be accounted for by environmental factors, such as contamination through contact with criminal relatives, or adverse influences acting upon the whole family.

In countries like England, where for many years a central register of all convicted persons has been kept by the police at the Criminal Records Office, one might expect to have a lot of information available on the distribution of criminals between families from one generation to the next. It would be most interesting to know, for instance, whether the children of criminals, if they take to crime, have any tendency to commit the same kinds of offences as their parents. Does violence breed violence, or sex offences breed further sexual offences? Unfortunately, this type of investigation has been almost totally neglected.

Some studies of samples of young offenders have noted the presence or absence of criminality in their parents. Although these often rely on local police or probation reports rather than on a systematic name search, they are sufficient to demonstrate a high incidence of convictions among the parents and siblings of juvenile offenders. Nevertheless, surprisingly large numbers come from apparently law-abiding families, and in the case of those who commence a persistent criminal career only after reaching adult years, the presence of criminal convictions in their parents is the exception rather than the rule [276]. Such observations suggest that extraneous environmental influences are often more powerful than any direct transmission from parents to children, whether by bad example or bad heredity. All the same, as every probation officer or social investigator well knows, many notorious families exist among whom nearly every member is either a known criminal or a social menace in other ways. Where one member is alcoholic, another a prostitute, another a hospitalized mental patient, and the rest petty criminals, some familial weakness is obviously present, although criminality is only one of a number of ways in which it may manifest. The environment has to be suitable for bringing out such tendencies. No one is born a skilled safe breaker.

Seriously defective characters, with marked aggressive tendencies and shallow, callous emotional responses, who are diagnosed by psychiatrists as psychopaths,* may be suspected of having some innate abnormality. Franz Kallmann [145], who investigated the genetics of various human abnormalities, noted that psychopathy may be passed on through generations of disorderly families, but it was doubtful how far hereditary mechanisms were involved. The transmission did not follow the lines of closest blood kinship. The children of psychopaths showed a higher incidence of disorder than the brothers and sisters of psychopaths, which is what one would expect of a condition produced by faulty child-rearing rather than pure inheritance.

Twin studies

A classic method of sorting out the effects of heredity and environment makes use of comparisons between samples of identical and non-identical pairs of twins. Identical twins supposedly come about by the splitting of a single fertilized egg to produce two separate individuals with precisely the same genes. Since they have exactly the same hereditary endowment they are always of the same sex, blood grouping, eye colour and so forth. Any differences between them must be the result of environmental influence (although one has to remember that in this context environment begins in the womb). Non-identical twins come from different eggs, and from the physical standpoint are no more alike than ordinary brothers and sisters, except for being of the same age. Qualities like physique and intelligence, on which identical twin pairs are much more alike than non-

* See p. 150.

identical twins, can generally be assumed to be hereditarily determined. A complication arises, however, if one believes that identical twins actually experience more similar environments than non-identical twins, and that this might account for their more frequent concordance. Some identical twins look so alike and dress so alike that parents and others treat them with greater equality than if they had been non-identical. Thus, identical twins may to some extent generate their own similar environments. This argument cannot apply in the case of twins separated from birth or soon after and reared apart. Studies of twins have shown that in such matters as intelligence and extraversion the degree of concordance between identical twins is as great or almost as great when they are reared apart as when they are brought up together, and very much greater than the concordance between non-identical twins reared together [242].

In the 1930s, a number of large-scale surveys of twins were published, purporting to show that where one member of an identical twin pair was criminal the other usually was as well, but that non-identical twins were much less often concordant. This work has been reviewed by Slater [248]. The earliest, as well as the most startling, result was published in Germany by Lange in 1929, and subsequently translated under the dramatic title *Crime as Destiny*. He found that in ten out of thirteen pairs of identical twins, that is seventy-seven per cent, both members had a criminal record; whereas out of seventeen pairs of non-identical but same-sexed twin pairs only two, that is twelve per cent, both had criminal records.

In two later series of criminal twins, also German, smaller differences were reported. Stumpfl [255] found that of eighteen pairs of identical twins eleven, that is sixty-one per cent, had criminal records in both members, but, of nineteen same-sexed non-identical twin pairs, seven, that is thirty-seven per cent, both had records. H. Kranz found that fifty-five per cent of thirty-two pairs of identical twins were concordant on the possession of a criminal record, but so were fifty-three per cent of forty-three same-sexed non-identical twin pairs. However, both these investigators found a much greater concordance between non-identical twins on temperamental qualities like aggressiveness and social rebellion which underlie serious criminality.

Stumpfl noted that if he counted only the more serious or habitual criminals, the difference in concordance of identical and non-identical twins became much greater. In the case of juvenile twins, concordance on juvenile delinquency is greater than concordance between adult twins on adult criminality. However, the concordance is almost equally great for non-identical as for identical twins, thus confirming the common-sense view that juvenile misbehaviour for the most part reflects environmental influences.

The distinction between identical and non-identical twins may not always have been too certain in these earlier investigations, which used general physical resemblance as a criterion instead of more exact measures like blood groups and fingerprints. A more serious objection, however, concerns the method of selection. Unless one can be sure that all examples of twins in a particular population have been studied, those left out may bias the findings. In the case of criminal twins, for instance, identical brothers, being more noticeable and striking, might be more easily picked out in a search than non-identical twin brothers. For the reason that identical twins reared together may in effect have more similar environments than non-identical twins reared together, the most convincing observations are those made on twins who have been reared apart from an early age. There have been too few such cases in the studies of criminal twins to provide conclusive results. It is unfortunate that interest in the question of the hereditary element in crime has dwindled, and repetitions of earlier work using improved modern techniques have not been tried.

A conclusion

Although inherited attributes may favour a delinquent outcome, environmental circumstances finally bring it about. In observation of infant behaviour, certain primary patterns of reaction (e.g. active–lethargic, intense reactors–mild reactors) appear very early and persist through childhood. But the ultimate effect on social adjustment depends upon how these tendencies are absorbed or exaggerated by training and other social influences [34].

The upshot of all this work amounts to this: a strong case has been made out for the existence of an inherited factor contributing to the behaviour of some serious and persistent criminals. However, owing to technical imperfections in the evidence, resolute sceptics can still argue that the case has not yet been adequately established. Furthermore, in relation to most juvenile delinquency, and to the less serious types of occasional criminals, the influence of heredity seems negligibly small. Even in regard to the persistent criminality of pathological individuals, case histories of identical twins taking different paths demonstrate the importance of life experience in determining whether or not a particular predisposed individual will in fact turn into a criminal. Such case histories show that incidents like a minor brain injury in childhood or an unwise marriage serve to tip the balance and provoke a criminal pattern in the less fortunate member of a twin pair.

6 Some Psychological Theories about the Development of Criminals

(imitating judge)
'In the opinion of this court, this child is depraved on account he ain't had a normal home.'
'Hey, I'm depraved on account I'm deprived.'
'So take him to a head shrinker.'
Leonard Bernstein and Stephen Sondheim, *West Side Story* (1957). London and New York, Chappell & Co.

A behaviouristic view of criminal traits

Psychomotor clumsiness

Psychologists of the behaviourist school believe in studying people's actions, which can be objectively observed and measured rather than their thoughts and feelings, which can only be deduced somewhat indirectly and inaccurately from what they are able to put into words. Behaviourists categorize people according to their measurable reactions to various set situations or stimuli. For instance, given a situation in which a reward is offered for solving a puzzle which is actually insoluble, some individuals, characterized by 'low frustration tolerance', will quickly lose patience and behave aggressively. By classifying people in such terms, some behaviourists believe they can identify personality traits which correspond to innate or constitutional differences in the physiological reactivity of the nervous system. In England, a leading exponent of this approach, Professor H. J. Eysenck [64], claims to have identified a constellation of traits characteristically associated with criminality, a constellation which he believes to be largely determined by heredity. Since the evidence for a connexion with criminality is better in the case of some traits than others, it will be convenient to consider them separately. One of the traits described by Eysenck, namely mesomorphic physique, has already been discussed in the preceding chapter.

Another trait is what might be called psychomotor style. This was discovered as long ago as 1914, when the American psychologist Porteus introduced a paper-and-pencil test of intelligence in which subjects had to trace their way through a series of printed mazes of increasing difficulty, being told to make one continuous pencil line from start to finish, not to lift their pencil until reaching the end, not to turn down any blind alleys, and not to cut or touch any of the lines marking the borders of the maze paths. Porteus found that subjects varied in the way they heeded or disregarded the test instructions. Persons who were swift and careless, and did not bother about cutting corners or touching edges, were particularly prevalent among delinquent types. Porteus developed a method of scoring based upon counting the number of careless errors, and this 'Q' score, as he called it, was used thereafter in many criminological researches. It invariably proved to be on average significantly higher among delinquents than among non-delinquent controls. In a survey of borstal youths from the London area, Dr T. C. N. Gibbens [82] confirmed that, compared with a control group of youths of similar age and social class attending a training establishment, a higher proportion of the delinquents had high 'Q' scores. He also confirmed Glueck's finding that the delinquent youths were more frequently of mesomorphic physique, very much more so than comparative groups of male undergraduates or officer cadets. Unfortunately, whereas virtually all the borstal youths produced maze scores, many of them had doubts about letting themselves be photographed in the nude, but the numbers were sufficient to show that high 'Q' score and mesomorphy tended to go together in the same individuals.

Several explanations of the connexion between 'Q' score and delinquency have been suggested, based upon the different types of error which make up the score. For instance, disobeying the test rules might indicate a defiant attitude typical of delinquents. On the other hand, a slovenly wavy pencil line that touches sides and cuts corners in a clumsy, careless manner might be a sign of poor muscular control. H. S. Anthony [10] tested the accuracy of movements of a sample of R.A.F. recruits, using an apparatus that had been developed for investigating accident proneness in Air Force pilots. She found that those young men who were subsequently convicted of offences differed from the rest in the poorer quality of their psychomotor performance. More recently, H. B. Gibson [90] compared a group of ordinary schoolboys aged about twelve with a group of boys in a remand home for delinquents. He used a refined form of printed maze consisting of a spiral track along which were scattered obstacles, in the form of a letter O in heavy type, round which the boys had to trace their way with a pencil, being told to go 'as quickly as you can'. The test gives two scores, time taken, and number of errors, the latter given by the number of 'collisions' with obstacles or sides. Those with large error/time ratios, that is the quick and careless types, were over-represented among the delinquents. Applying the same test to a large sample of young schoolboys, aged eight to ten, none of whom had yet been found guilty in the juvenile courts, he found a significant difference between a group classed by their teachers as well behaved and another group classed as poorly behaved. The naughty boys, like the delinquents, included a disproportionate number of quick and careless boys. This test probably identifies the type of person who can be easily induced to risk speeds beyond what his manual dexterity permits, and who remains undeterred by his own mistakes. This may be one reason why men convicted of offences against property have a much greater than average likelihood of also being convicted for motoring offences.

If this new development in research is confirmed, a quick-careless response on psychomotor tests at a relatively early age may prove to have some predictive value in identifying groups likely, in later years, to prove particularly prone to delinquency. Since psychomotor performance is closely bound up with the functioning of the nervous system, and probably derives more from constitutional differences than from social training, these results tend to support the unpopular view that an individual's inherent qualities count as much as his environment in determining whether he will become delinquent.

Resistance to conditioning

Another half-physiological, half-psychological attribute which Eysenck believes has a close connexion with potential delinquency is 'conditionability'. Experimental psychologists nowadays lay great emphasis on the factor of conditioning in habit-training and indeed in all aspects of learning. Pavlov started the whole idea with his famous dogs salivating at the sight of food. By ringing a bell just before he showed them the food, he found that the dogs soon responded by salivating automatically at the sound of the bell, even when no food followed. Their response had been linked with an associated or conditioned stimulus learnt by experience. Similar conditioned responses can be demonstrated in humans, for instance by blowing a puff of air at the eye and showing an ace of spades simultaneously. After a number of repetitions, the mere sight of the ace of spades becomes sufficient to elicit an automatic blink response. In humans, responses which are normally involuntary or automatic, such as the reflex contraction of the pupil of the eye when a bright light is shone into the face, are the ones which most easily become conditioned to extraneous stimuli, and, the link once established, the subject has no control over the automatic reaction.

One of the most powerful of our innate, automatic responses is the reaction of fear and avoidance of painful stimuli. According to one theory of learning, the infant acquires the self-restraint which underlies all social conformity by a process of conditioned avoidance. Certain situations and types of behaviour – for instance screaming, punching, urinating on the carpet – are swiftly followed by slaps or other punishments, which in turn cause fear and withdrawal. Thus, frequent repetition of punishment, by means of the conditioning mechanism, gradually establishes an automatic conditioned reaction of anxiety and withdrawal in the face of situations liable to provoke bad behaviour. The process is aided by a characteristic of conditioning, known technically as generalization, whereby avoidance responses readily become linked with a wide range of associated stimuli. Furthermore, in humans, because of the ability to increase associations by the use of language, and in this context to define a wide range of behaviour as bad, conditioned avoidance reactions can be greatly reinforced and extended.

This theory explains rather neatly the development of the conscience, in terms of a built-in, automatic avoidance of bad behaviour, which works independently of the chances of being observed or found out on any particular occasion. Positive items of conditioned behaviour, like the dog preparing for food at the sound of a bell, tend to disappear rather swiftly, if the bell sounds a few times and no food follows, but the extinction of conditioned avoidance behaviour is much slower. The child who has once been conditioned to avoid punching his sister may go on restraining himself indefinitely because the act of avoidance itself eliminates the possibility of experiencing loss of control without punishment.

The ease with which conditioned responses become established, and their persistence, differ from one individual to another. H. J. Eysenck [65] cites some amusing experiments by R. L. Solomon, at Harvard University, in which the investigators taught puppies that a particular dish of food was taboo by swatting them with a newspaper whenever they approached it. Later, with the experimenter absent but observing, the puppies were let into the room again. Some of them overcame the taboo without difficulty. Others dithered about and whined before taking the food. Others fasted so long they had to be rescued from the situation. Differences between individuals in respect of conditionability probably depend upon some innate quality of the nervous system. Long ago Pavlov demonstrated in conditioning situations that there was a varying balance of reactivity (excitation) and resistance (inhibition) demonstrable in the nervous system of dogs. The strength of a conditioned response is prevented from building up and up as stimuli are repeated by the development of an inhibitory or fatigue factor. After a rest pause, however, the inhibitory factor diminishes, so that when the stimulus reappears the response occurs more strongly than ever, even though no learning practice has taken place meantime. People differ in the degree to which they build up this physiological inhibition. A simple method of demonstrating this consists of recording electronically a subject's performance on a tapping test in which he has to keep on tapping a metal stylus on a plate as fast as possible. Every so often the fast sequence is interrupted by involuntary pauses as inhibition builds up. People who condition slowly (or are of extraverted temperament) produce more pauses.

In experiments with humans in which a noise and a puff of air to the eye are given together, the number of repetitions required to establish a blink reaction to the noise alone gives a measure of the speed of conditioning. To test Eysenck's theory, it needs to be shown that persons resistive to social learning are relatively slow on conditioning. Eysenck maintains that experiments with psychopaths, who represent the most extreme examples of badly behaved and socially unconforming characters, show that they are both slow on conditioning and high on tests of Pavlovian inhibition. The same is true of children with brain damage, who also tend to be badly behaved and resistant to social training. Gordon Trasler [261] has compared the main assumptions of

Eysenck's theory with descriptions of criminals and found that
they fit rather well. In the first place, the disturbances of upbringing which are so commonly found among the more serious
and persistent of juvenile delinquents, as well as among adult
psychopaths, are of just such a kind as would be expected to
interfere with smooth social conditioning. Broken and disharmonious parental homes, erratic or inconsistent discipline,
parental absence or neglect, are cases in point. Second, it has
been frequently reported by clinicians that one of the most
noteworthy features of the more unrepentant and unconforming
types of offender is that they are strikingly untroubled by guilt,
and that they have a slap-happy, devil-may-care attitude to life.
This absence of anxiety and guilt is just what one would expect
on the theory that these are individuals in whom, either on
account of constitutional resistance, or through ineffective training, or both, social conditioning has been inadequately established. Because training in honesty and conformity to legal
requirements proceeds in infancy simultaneously with training
in social skills generally, one might expect the individual who
has failed in learning in one sphere to show incompetence in
others. Studies of the personality and mode of life of habitual
criminals strongly suggests that this actually happens, for a great
many of them are described as socially immature and have
enormous difficulty in fitting into any ordinary group, settling
to work, or getting on with their wives. Since conditioned
avoidance depends on situations provoking a certain level of
tension or anxiety, any influence which damps down anxiety may
be expected to reduce the avoidance response. Tension-relieving
drugs, of which alcohol is the best-known example, in fact have
just this effect. It has been shown in laboratory experiments with
animals that alcohol makes their conditioned avoidance responses
much less reliable, and it has been noted often enough that man's
conscience is soluble in alcohol.

Extraversion

Extraversion–introversion is another important personal quality
which is said to correlate with both conditionability and delinquency potential. The terms were first introduced by Carl Jung

[143] in intuitively based clinical descriptions of two contrasting types of temperament, the introvert, who tends to be thoughtful, reflective, cautious, introspective and concerned about his own feelings, and the extravert, who is more out-going, sociable and more concerned with action and practical matters than with feelings and theory. In recent years, with the development of personality questionnaires, it has been confirmed, notably by Eysenck, that certain attitudes, collectively suggesting a sensitive, imaginative, reflective and somewhat inhibited temperament, tend to cluster together in the same individual; while another cluster, suggesting a cheerful, matter-of-fact person who adapts himself readily without much need for thought, occur together in individuals of opposite temperament. These clusters represent the opposite extremes of a continuous variation from pre-dominantly introverted to predominantly extraverted individuals, with the majority falling somewhere in between.

Introversion–extraversion seems to be a very fundamental personality measure. In any given individual it remains sur-prisingly steady over years, and evidence has been adduced that it is to some extent an inherited attribute [67]. Furthermore, it is correlated with a large number of other measures, both psycho-logical and physiological. For example, introversion correlates positively with being of ectomorphic physique, with quick conditioning, with high level of aspiration, with anxiety reactions and marked physiological changes in response to stress, with a high threshold to sedative drugs, and with certain perceptual habits (such as high degree of rigidity in seeing only one aspect of an ambiguous picture, and small figural after-effects). In con-trast, below-average introversion (in other words above-average extraversion) is associated with mesomorphic physique, slow conditioning, low aspiration, low reaction to stress, low sedation threshold, low persistence, etc. [68].

Crucial to the present discussion, criminal types are said to be more predominantly extravert than law-abiding or socially con-forming individuals, who are more often on the introverted side. Evidence for the extraverted characteristics of samples of criminals comes first from clinical experience, especially with young delinquents, among whom the sociable, adventurous, but relatively unreflective type of youth seems particularly common.

Systematic testing with questionnaires, for example in a survey of borstal inmates by Alan Little [155], has not always confirmed this impression, but Eysenck cites a number of confirmatory studies, including some work by F. Warburton in which a group of particularly recalcitrant inmates of Joliet Penitentiary in Chicago were found to be highly extraverted [64].

Neurotic extraverts

Another important dimension upon which individuals vary is in neurotic tendency or emotional instability. Eysenck and others have developed tests for grading people on this trait. Those who are prone, when under stress, to produce neurotic symptoms give high scores on these tests. Although, according to Eysenck, neurotic tendency and introversion are completely independent, the quality of neurotic reactions varies according to one's position on the extraversion–introversion continuum. Thus, the introvert who is also neurotic suffers from excessive anxiety, and sometimes from obsessional and phobic symptoms, and tends to be miserable, over-inhibited and self-punishing. In contrast, neurotic extraverts, whom clinicians identify as hysterics and psychopaths, are misfits who are apparently oblivious of their own peculiarities, and apt to attribute their difficulties to imaginary ailments or adverse circumstances for which they feel no personal responsibility. Tests given to psychopaths, whether they be patients in hospitals or criminals in prison (as for instance the Warburton investigation quoted above), confirm that as a group they tend to be both markedly neurotic and markedly extraverted. On the other hand, unstable introverts, because of their over-inhibited quality, are likely to be over-conforming rather than social rebels or delinquents. In a recent investigation in which the present writer was concerned, using a sample of schoolboys, it emerged that those graded unstable extraverts on psychological tests were significantly more often than the rest graded badly behaved by their teachers. Neurotic tendency, therefore, would seem not to be closely related to delinquent trends except when combined with a marked degree of extraversion.

Some confirmation of these ideas about the character traits of young delinquents was produced in an interesting project carried out by the psychologists Hathaway and Monachesi [117], who administered the questionnaire known as the Minnesota Multiphasic Personality Inventory to 4,000 children in the ninth grade of the state schools in Minneapolis. The youngsters, most of them were fifteen years old at the time of testing, were followed up for two years to see which of them appeared in the official records of the Juvenile Division of the Police Department. Of the boys, twenty-two per cent, and of the girls, eight per cent, were found to have police records. The sample was sub-divided into those who had not committed offences until after the time of testing (who were in the majority) and those who had already committed some offence, but since both these groups differed from the non-delinquent children in rather similar ways, the distinction can be ignored for present purposes. The non-delinquent males gave scores indicative of a greater degree of introversion than the delinquents. The delinquents' scores indicated greater sociability and a higher level of energy and enthusiasm. They showed no particular excess in emotional instability, in fact it was the non-delinquent males who, more frequently, gave scores indicative of depressive trends and femininity of interests. In particular, the neurotic introvert, the self-critical, inhibited type of personality, was more in evidence among the non-delinquents. Despite these trends, the findings were very variable, with numerous inconsistencies. The prediction of delinquency in an individual case is way beyond the scope of present questionnaire methods. In fact, the most significant difference statistically between delinquents and non-delinquents was the high scores given by the former on the validity scales which are meant to detect unreliability of response. An implausible excess of claims to virtue ('faking good') and a suspicious excess of self-denigrating responses ('faking bad') were both features of the delinquent group.

Conclusions still tentative

The cluster of traits identified by Eysenck as criminogenic, namely mesomorphic physique, poor conditionability, psychomotor clumsiness, and emotional instability when combined with extraversion, certainly presents a challenging subject for research, although the evidence on some of these points remains weak. In particular, measures of conditionability applied to humans are relatively new, and results are often inconsistent. The techniques are not very easy, and many extraneous influences, such as motivation, distractions, and physical fitness, may possibly interfere with the responses. It has yet to be established how far conditionability can be regarded as a unitary trait, or to what extent a given individual varies in his speed of conditioning according to the kind of situation in which he is placed. The correlations emerging from this kind of research are usually quite small, which means that the factors dealt with represent only a small part of the total situation. Conditioning theory, at least in the elementary form here described, seems to be a gross over-simplification of the problem. The extraverted, slap-happy personality, with a careless disregard for social rules, represents a well-recognized type among criminals, but not by any means the only type. He is probably most typical of the vigorous, unreflective, practical-minded youngster from the working class who so often passes through a rebellious, delinquent phase on the road to maturity. On the other hand, although persons of anxious or introverted temperament do not ordinarily take to delinquency at all readily, if they are serious social misfits, and if their circumstances are such as to bring crime into their ambit of personal experience, a minority of these people will take to thieving as an escape from the difficulties of a more conventional adjustment. Such maladjusted introverts are most prevalent among older recidivists, especially those commonly described as of inadequate personality. Since these cases are so frequent among the inmates of our prisons, they may account for surveys based on prisoners not always showing the expected excess of extraverts and poor conditioners [276]. Eysenck himself [66], in discussing the varying response of different groups of criminals to the same treatment régime, appears to recognize that an introverted group exists for whom conventional penal discipline may be inappropriate treatment. Finally, some people find the conditioning theory unconvincing because the picture it gives of an automatic assimilation of good and bad reactions leaves out of consideration the human qualities of thought and feeling. In the context of child–parent relationships, where social learning takes place, love and hate still count in the estimation of many traditional psychologists.

Psychoanalytic theories about the origins of the anti-social character

The scope of psychodynamic interpretations

The evidence so far discussed suggests that inborn, constitutional features may predispose certain individuals to criminal behaviour, but many psychologists, particularly those of the psychoanalytic school, believe that more important distinguishing features of the criminal character derive from attributes of personality acquired, or at least emphasized, through early upbringing. For instance, whatever the explanation, it seems that children of cruel, rejecting parents are prone to develop undesirably aggressive traits [63; 158]. This kind of observation might furnish a link with sociological findings if it could be shown that the delinquent propensity of certain groups or cultures was due to their peculiar child-rearing practices. The psychodynamic theories, which interpret human character as the outcome of conflict of feelings, have a strong popular appeal. Everyone can understand theories about aggression born of fear, or hostility due to anticipation of rejection, since, in some degree, we have all felt that way ourselves. For scientific purposes, however, empathy is no substitute for objective verification.

Psychodynamic explanations of delinquent behaviour vary enormously in scope. Some refer to patterns commonly found among the generality of delinquents, others to behaviour unique to a particular person or to a specific type of offence. For example, compulsive stealing of women's underwear from clothes-lines is associated with a particular sexual perversion, which in turn is often associated with a recognizable personality type and pattern of upbringing, but it would be ridiculous to expect to find the same pattern among thieves in general. Stealing by small children from mother's purse may sometimes signify a feeling of deprivation of maternal love and attention, but although 'stealing love' by an emotionally deprived person may provide an unconscious motive, or part motive, for some adult larceny, this would be an implausible explanation in the majority of cases. On the other hand, the identification of a personality type who is impulsive, incapable of strong personal attachments, and unrestrained by guilt feelings might provide an explanation for the behaviour of a large proportion of persistent offenders. It is this theory of a recognizable personality type underlying a wide variety of delinquent behaviour, and supposedly attributable to a substantial proportion of delinquents, which needs to be considered first.

Neurotic conflicts in delinquents

Some of the most detailed and useful theories about the origins and significance of character traits derive from psychoanalytic studies. When the subject was first being developed by Freud, interest centred upon patients with neurotic complaints, such as irrational and excessive anxiety, phobias, obsessional habits and preoccupations, or aches and pains traceable to nervous tension rather than to organic disease. Exploration of the emotional life of such sufferers led to the theory of unconscious mental conflict, of individuals torn between the irreconcilable demands of instinct and the restraining forces of social conscience. Neurotic patients seemed to have developed super-sensitive consciences, especially in matters concerning sexual or aggressive feelings, which they could not experience without a strong sensation of guilt or worry. Many of these neurotics had been brought up by strict and repressive parents. Freud advanced the theory that the human conscience (or super-ego) derives from parental injunctions, which the small child incorporates at a very early age, often in somewhat distorted, primitive and literal forms. The child of repressive parents stands in danger of absorbing particularly rigid taboos, which handicap him permanently in his efforts to make a flexible and realistic adjustment to life's conflicting demands, rendering him a prey to paralysing anxiety or other crippling symptoms. The chief aim of early psychoanalytic treatment was liberation from inhibitions and guilt feelings by bringing the patient to recognize and accept his own nature, and to allow himself ordinary ways of fulfilment.

The bold and uninhibited young delinquent, who is conspicuously untroubled by guilt, remorse or nagging anxiety, presents a very different picture. Some psychoanalysts have tried to reconcile this stubborn fact with the contention that delinquents are neurotic by suggesting that their apparent unconcern masks serious mental conflicts which have been so deeply repressed that no trace of them remains in conscious thinking. Unless the existence of such conflicts can be demonstrated in some way, and this does not seem possible in most cases, the theory remains unconvincing.

The anti-social character

A more recent and more plausible psychoanalytic theory suggests that the typical delinquent deviates from the normal character in a direction opposite to that of the anxiety neurotic. Instead of being, like the neurotic, a prey to acute conflict between instinctual impulses and an uncompromisingly rigid super-ego, the delinquent has a very weak, unformed super-ego, which leaves his instinctive impulses unrestrained and unmodified by social considerations. On this theory, the anti-social character, who strikes observers as a self-centred, overbearing individual who must have his own wants satisfied immediately regardless of consequences to other people, becomes like this very early in life through failure to incorporate the inhibiting influences which, in the neurotic, are taken up and developed to excess. In this respect the anti-social character is correctly described as retarded or immature. Like the young infant, he cannot postpone immediate gratification, but gives free vent to his covetousness and aggression even when, in his own interests, self-restraint would be more advantageous. He cannot tolerate present frustration for the sake of future benefit, and so lacks the patience necessary to scholastic learning. Because he lacks the restraining force of a guilt-inducing conscience, he succumbs to the temptation of the moment, truanting, lying or stealing as occasion arises, and suffering no remorse afterwards. Furthermore, and this seems very fundamental, he seems to lack the capacity for forming those stable, loving attachments to others which, in adults, as well as children, provide the incentive for considerate

and altruistic behaviour. Perhaps for this reason, even as a schoolchild, the anti-social character, despite the kudos associated with daring and rebellion, is not usually popular with his classmates.

Features of early upbringing cited by psychoanalysts as likely to interfere with super-ego formation centre upon the emotional tone of the child's earliest experience of other persons, namely his relationship first with his mother and later, and to a lesser extent, with father and other adults. Where the relationship is close and loving, this favours the process of identification, whereby the infant comes to develop a self-reference ideal based upon his image of the parent. A loving relationship acts as a powerful incentive to conformity, since rebellion or badness risks the withdrawal of love, upon which the child feels utterly dependent. When the maternal relationship is less close, as for instance if the parents are over-burdened, preoccupied, uninterested or neglectful, opportunity to learn and absorb the rules is correspondingly reduced, and the situation is worse still if the parents are inconsistent, sometimes condoning and sometimes punishing a particular act. If mother is positively hostile towards the child, the threat of further rejection loses its force, so the child obeys when under observation, but acquires no internal constraints. In short, unloving, erratic and neglectful parents, by failing to teach their babies to curb their impulses properly, and by failing to inspire a restraining ideal or super-ego, leave an indelible mark upon the character of their offspring, who risk growing up into anti-social adults with a permanent incapacity for love and kindness.

The anti-social character type as described by psychoanalysts is virtually the same as what psychiatrists commonly describe as a psychopath. The label psychopath, however, is usually reserved for particularly bad cases who are very set in their ways, and the term is sometimes used to imply the existence of inborn pathology. The psychoanalytic emphasis on the psychological determinants of the anti-social character seems to carry with it a relatively optimistic view as to the fluidity of the situation and the prospects of change for the better, and to avoid implying that normals and anti-socials are separated by any clear or fixed dividing line. Furthermore, the term psychopathy has come to be used with greater reserve since the English Mental Health Act, 1959, gave doctors the power to detain compulsorily in mental hospital anyone under twenty-one (or a person of any age convicted of an offence for which a prison sentence can be given) who is certified as suffering from 'psychopathic disorder'.

The psychoanalytic and the sociological viewpoints

It is not always easy to see clearly how psychoanalytic ideas differ from sociological theories of delinquency causation, since both seem to describe a similar situation in somewhat different language. The unusually lucid statement of the psychoanalytic theory of anti-social character formation put forward by the late Kate Friedlander [79] allows one to discern some of the points of contrast. Friedlander classed as secondary causes all those environmental factors which affect the child from the age of seven onwards, including the influence of companions, the use of leisure, the type of school and neighbourhood, and the experience of frustration or satisfaction in employment. In her view such factors can be very important in increasing the incidence of delinquency, but they affect only those youngsters who have some degree of pre-existing anti-social character formation. The important, primary causes operate in infancy, largely through the mother's handling of her child. Psychoanalysts do not deny the existence of constitutional differences – indeed Friedlander points out that with some children instincts are particularly difficult to bring under control – but they suggest that the outcome in any individual case can be greatly modified for better or worse by the type of upbringing received.

Apart from drawing attention to the temporal sequence of events, the psychoanalytic distinction between primary and secondary factors does not seem to have much practical value. The factors in infancy which make for anti-social character formation do not necessarily lead to actual delinquency unless the secondary environmental influences are present at a later stage, and, conversely, the secondary influences are relatively ineffective in the absence of the primary factors. The real difference between the psychoanalytic and the sociological viewpoints rests upon the emphasis placed by the analysts upon the very great importance of upbringing in the early years, and upon defective character formation as the essential precursor of chronic delinquency. If the analysts are right about all this, it should be possible to demonstrate objectively that the confirmed delinquent differs from the average youngster on specified traits of character, and that a close relationship exists between the events of early childhood and subsequent delinquent tendencies.

The 'neurotic' criminal

Franz Alexander [6], one of the first psychoanalysts to sub-divide criminal behaviour into distinct psychological groups, labelled one type the 'acting-out neurotic' criminal. Like many psychological terms, this has degenerated with popular usage, so nowadays it sometimes seems a mere synonym for a badly behaved person. Correctly used, it describes a person who as a result of mental conflict behaves badly in a particular sphere, although in other respects displaying a definite conscience. Unlike the psychopath, or the delinquent character described by Friedlander, whose childish unrestraint is a consistent feature, the acting-out neurotic, when closely observed, can be seen to be irrational and inconsistent, at times condemning or disowning his own actions, at other times behaving like an anti-social rebel. A classic example of acting-out neurotic behaviour is seen among certain opulent women shop-lifters, usually of mature age and respectable antecedents, who appear under a compulsion to steal (kleptomania), when they could with much less trouble buy what they need. Apart from their one anti-social gesture, which they cannot explain other than as an irresistible urge, they are generally law-abiding and conventional. In such cases strong but unconscious motives are at work. One such motive, identified by Freud, produces what he called the 'criminal from a sense of guilt'. Like all neurotics, these unfortunates have highly sensitive super-egos, and suffer chronic feelings of guilt, usually related to repressed sexual complexes. Unlike ordinary neurotics, whose tensions burst forth in symptoms, they relieve themselves in actions of a more or less reprehensible kind. This enables them to rationalize their feelings as legitimate remorse, and if their actions provoke punishment, so much the better, because thereby they assuage some of their guilt without needing to look closer into its origins. This explains the curious way in which many neurotic criminals persistently commit their offences under circumstances that invite detection. Unconsciously, they seek punishment, and if they bring down upon themselves the full rigours of the law, this enables them to displace their guilt from their private sin on to the publicly condemned act, and to obtain relief through the public atonement that follows. Although in behaviour they resemble the bold, carefree psychopaths, these guilt-ridden neurotic criminals have as much inner conflict as any ordinary neurotic, and clinical examination soon reveals their malaise.

Everyone with experience of forensic psychiatry can recall incidents and individuals conforming to this 'acting-out neurotic' pattern. Sometimes the psychological process seems quite transparent, and close to the surface of awareness. For example, one young man was referred to the present writer for a psychiatric examination after he had broken open a gas meter in a friend's house. He was not a habitual thief, and the police making inquiries had no particular reason to suspect him, but he almost insisted on confessing. He had had a strict religious upbringing, and he explained that he felt it would be good for him to tell all. On subsequent examination, it emerged that he was feeling very worried and ashamed about some irregular sexual behaviour, and was seeking reassurance that he was 'normal'. Where the acting-out behaviour appears irrational, as in the well-to-do thief, or the sexual fetishist or exhibitionist, the neurotic basis is obvious, but when, as usually happens, the crime serves the purpose of financial gain as well as an unconscious motive, one needs to study the offender's life history and personality before reaching a conclusion. Since this is done only exceptionally, many neurotically motivated offenders may escape notice. Alexander believed such persons to be quite common among criminals, but most modern penal experts would disagree.

The following chapter sets out the results of a number of psychological studies and indicates how far they go towards confirming the existence of the anti-social and the neurotic character types among delinquents, and their relation to disturbed upbringing. Clinical experience at child guidance clinics, remand

homes and prisons leaves no room for doubt that certain delinquents manifest in extreme and unpleasant form the character
traits described, and that in many instances their life histories
run monotonously along predicted lines. On the other hand, these
problem cases are preferentially selected for psychiatric examination, so the clinician may easily build up a mistakenly bad impression of what the majority of young delinquents are like.
Many youngsters caught by the police are perfectly ordinary
characters, no different from others of their age and class. The
important question is how many delinquents display neurotic or
psychopathic patterns. Part of the answer seems to be that these
patterns are most likely to occur among the more persistent and
troublesome offenders, the ones the penal authorities find most
difficult to cope with. Such patterns may also occur among unpleasant individuals who make a lot of trouble for their families
and associates without actually committing those particular acts
which would bring them under the jurisdiction of the criminal
law.

7 Verifying the Psychological Factors in Delinquency

The clinical contribution finished in a kind of intellectual shouting match, such as one might expect if a crowd of newspapermen invaded the affairs of the laboratory. . . .

By contrast, the scientific study of personality . . . has based its theories on actual behavioural measurements. Different laboratories can repeat them and statistical and mathematical treatments of these measurements can be applied by anyone who wishes to check.

Raymond B. Cattell, *The Scientific Analysis of Personality* (1965). Penguin Books.

Maternal deprivation and criminality

Bowlby's pioneer concept

Astute clinical observers, and particularly those of the psycho-analytic school, have furnished a wealth of impressions and theories; but for the most part have left to other workers the task of collecting objective evidence to confirm, refute or modify their ideas. One way of doing this is to take some relatively simple proposition from the psychoanalytic model and see how it works out in practice when large numbers of unselected cases are surveyed. For example, if the psychoanalysts are right about the crucial importance of the early mother–child relationship in determining character, it should be possible to show that persons who have experienced a serious interruption of maternal care during a critical phase of development are specially liable to personality disturbance in later years. The psychiatrist John Bowlby [24] has become known as the great protagonist of this chain of cause and effect. In his first research on the topic, entitled *Forty-four Juvenile Thieves*, Bowlby [23] matched forty-four children, seen at a child guidance clinic and reported as stealing, with forty-four others, of the same age and sex, who, although emotionally disturbed, were not thieves. He reported that seventeen of the young thieves had been separated completely from their mothers for six months or longer during their first five years of life, whereas only two among the control group had had this experience. Furthermore, fourteen of the thieves had a serious and distinctive disturbance of personality which he called 'affectionless character', and of these all but two had experienced separation from mother. Bowlby's affectionless characters corresponded to what most people call 'psychopaths'. They showed a marked disability for close relationships with others, and a consequential lack of motivation for considerate or socially constructive behaviour.

These pioneer observations were much too neat and simple to be true of the majority of delinquents. The crudities of this first small study, and the over-ambitious conclusions it was made to support, drew sharp fire from critics such as Barbara Wootton. Nevertheless, Bowlby's work has born fruit in a mass of subsequent research, and, even if his initial views were exaggerated, the central idea, that disturbance of the mother–child relationship may sometimes produce lasting damage, has gained widespread support. As can be seen from Mary Ainsworth's excellent review [4] of the controversy, the chief points of dispute now concern questions of detail, such as how specific or how general the deleterious effects of deprivation are, how far they may be made good or reversed, how closely they are linked with delinquent behaviour, by what process they come about, what is the age at risk, and how severe the deprivation has to be.

Effects of severe deprivation

In the discussion on mental subnormality, reference has already been made to the effect of severe deprivation, especially if it occurs during the first year, in retarding intellectual growth and facility with language.* There seems little doubt that really severe deprivation, such as was studied by Goldfarb [102], leads to deep and lasting disturbance. He used a sample of babies separated at about four months of age and placed for three years in an institution which made little effort to replicate the personal quality of normal mothering. Compared with babies placed in foster homes, these children were noticeably retarded in intelligence and scholastic attainment, and most of them developed into cold, unresponsive, detached personalities, who lacked the capacity for sustained effort, and showed various kinds of difficult and wayward behaviour.

Animal studies have also demonstrated sensitive periods of development during which certain social responses have to be acquired once and for all if they are ever to be learned properly. The 'imprinting' of following responses in young birds was one of the first examples to arouse scientific interest. Normally young birds follow their mother instinctively, but if she is taken away and some other moving object, even a human being, replaces her, the instinctive response attaches itself equally

* See p. 114.

strongly and lastingly to the substitute, provided always the substitution has taken place during a brief, critical phase of development. By interference with the normal mother–offspring relationship, the subsequent social behaviour of a bird can be utterly deranged, so that the creature makes courting gestures to humans, joins flocks of another species, or tries to copulate with inanimate objects. The possible implications for human affairs emerge still more plainly in experiments with animals closer to ourselves in evolution. A homely example derives from the training of guide dogs, who are more easily educated for human needs if they have been consistently kept with humans as puppies instead of being put into kennels. More dramatic and horrifying are the experiments with monkeys, started by Harlow [113; 114], which show that artificial deprivation of mothering during infancy leads to gross social maladjustment when the monkeys become adult, particularly noticeable in inability to care for their own offspring, and absence of heterosexual responsiveness.

These observations, though fascinating in themselves, are several steps removed from delinquency research. Nowadays, very severe deprivations, like the situations studied by Goldfarb, are rare. It is important, therefore, to know the effect of the lesser degrees of deprivation which are found more commonly among delinquents. It is also important to find out what constitutes deprivation: whether, for instance, it includes neglect without actual physical separation, or separations during which an adequate mother substitute is provided. Research findings so far give the general impression that parental indifference or neglect is as damaging as separation, and that the effects of separation are greatly mitigated by substitute mothering.

Separation without deprivation not so important?

As has been mentioned in Chapter 3, surveys of young delinquents have regularly produced 'broken homes' as a contributory factor in a substantial minority of cases. Analysis of the nature of the separations involved in these cases suggests that separation from father is at least as strongly associated with delinquency as separation from mother – although perhaps for different reasons – and that separations in childhood are of significance as well as

separations in infancy. Hilda Lewis [152], in her study of children
from disrupted homes, found a very high incidence of behaviour
problems, but concluded that delinquency was linked more closely
with parental neglect than with actual separation. C. J. Wardle
[274], in a study of children attending a child guidance clinic,
found that those children who were stealing or otherwise
behaving badly came significantly more often than non-delinquents from broken homes, had a higher incidence of separation
from mother of more than six months' duration, and more
frequently had parents who themselves came from broken
homes. On the other hand, a study by Naess [197] of a less
selected group of delinquents, matched against a control group
of their own non-delinquent siblings, found no greater incidence
of separations among the delinquents. Alan Little [154] tried to
test whether, among youths in borstal, those with a history of loss
of parents or separation from parents had a greater likelihood
of re-conviction. His conclusions were almost completely
negative. Although an unexpectedly high incidence of separations
was noted (over four fifths had experienced separation from one
or both parents in childhood) no significant connexions were
found between the presence, timing or severity of the parental
deprivations and the likelihood of re-conviction or the nature of
the offences committed.

Perhaps the most satisfactory approach for the purpose of
validating scientifically the ultimate effects of events in infancy
consists of long-term follow-up studies of unselected groups,
tracing the after-lives of children observed in early years, and
comparing outcome, as regards behaviour and social adjustment,
with the individual's early history of maternal care. One such
project is the National Survey being carried out in England by
J. W. B. Douglas and his collaborators. This began as a consequence of interest taken by the Royal Commission on Population. The sample consisted of all births which took place in
Great Britain in the first week of March 1946. The original
purpose was to study the circumstances of the confinements;
but, having obtained a sample that was fully representative of
children in all types of home and in all parts of the country, the
investigators saw that they had a unique opportunity. By following these children through their school years, recording any

health and behaviour problems (and later on of convictions for delinquency), it would be possible to discover the incidence, class distribution and family background associations of various types of illness and social problems. This important project is still continuing.

One of the topics covered in the National Survey was the incidence and apparent consequences of early separations from mother. Douglas and Blomfield [49] reported that fourteen per cent of the sample had been separated from mother for a period of more than four weeks during the first six years of life. These separated children were matched against others from similar localities and types of family who had not been separated. A significantly higher incidence of nervous disorders might have been expected among the separated cases, but this was not found. However, the measures used were rather rough and ready, based upon a questionnaire to local-authority health visitors, who were asked to look out for a number of predetermined symptoms, such as bed-wetting, eating difficulties and night terrors. It may be that a more detailed inquiry, including perhaps psychological tests applied to the children themselves, would have given a different result.

The quality of maternal care most important

Setting aside the question of separation, and considering the wider issue of the quality of maternal care, clear evidence of the importance of this as a factor in future delinquency was given in the McCords' follow-up [164] of the Cambridge–Somerville Youth Study, to which reference has already been made.* The family backgrounds of 250 boys, closely studied by social workers when they were aged nine, were compared with subsequent criminal records examined after a lapse of seventeen years. The quality of mothering received in early years was one of the factors most closely associated with subsequent convictions. Most of the mothers seemed to love their children and to be actively concerned with their welfare. Only thirty-four per cent of the 174 boys with loving mothers were convicted, compared with fifty-eight per cent of the seventy-six with unloving mothers.

* See pp. 28, 71, 110, 253.

F

Sub-dividing the mothers still further, the healthiest, described as 'loving normals', who showed some zest and enjoyment in their maternal duties, produced the smallest proportion, twenty-seven per cent, of sons convicted. Over-protective mothers, who tended to restrict their boys' activities and treat them as younger than their actual age, and anxious mothers, who worried a lot when their boys participated in activities customary to their age, although they did not necessarily forbid it, were associated with a worse conviction rate – thirty-seven per cent. The worst conviction rate of all, seventy-two per cent, occurred in the boys of twenty-five neglecting mothers, who seemed totally indifferent and seldom gave their children any proper attention or sign of affection. The twenty-one 'passive' mothers, who were generally weak and ineffectual persons who couldn't be bothered about their children and left all discipline to the fathers, produced fifty-seven per cent of convicted sons. Curiously, mothers who were actively cruel, or absent altogether, had rather less convicted sons than did the passive and neglecting mothers. The correspondence between fathers' attitude and sons' conviction was similar, but less close. Ranking the parental background of the boys from 1 to 5, taking both mother and father into account, showed eighty-one per cent convicted among the offspring of the worst parents, compared with only twenty-eight per cent of those with the best parents. Other kinds of classification, for instance by family income or type of neighbourhood, corresponded much less closely with being convicted.

One may perhaps sum up the position by noting that the psychoanalytic theories have served to stimulate a great deal of productive research, most of which has tended to confirm the importance of maternal care in determining social adjustment later on. However, as a specific factor in the genesis of delinquency in the majority of cases, the analysts probably exaggerate the importance of early physical separation from mother, although deficiencies of parental care in a wider sense seem to be very important.

'Prediction studies' and their relevance to the psychology of delinquents

The prediction method of approach

The ability to predict accurately is an accepted criterion of successful science. In recent years an interest, one might say almost a craze, has developed among criminologists for trying to predict, at an early age, who will later become delinquent. The method consists in first observing the most prominent distinguishing feature in the backgrounds and histories of established delinquents compared with non-delinquents, so as to work out a list of what might be called 'warning signs'. One then applies this list to a population of youngsters, picking out all who have more 'warning signs' than, say, ninety per cent of non-delinquents. On this basis one predicts for this group a high probability of future delinquency, and with the passage of time the prediction system is either confirmed (validated) or shown to be ineffective.

Prediction systems have a number of uses, the ones most obviously appealing to administrators being the provision of estimates of the magnitude of delinquency risks in a given group of youngsters, and the selection of individuals in particular need of preventive care. In so far as the prediction systems also distinguish between known offenders with differing risks of re-conviction, they can be used as a guide in sentencing, as well as a yardstick for measuring the effectiveness of a treatment method. For example, with a particular group of delinquents submitted for scrutiny, a prediction table might indicate so bad a risk that in the ordinary course of events ninety per cent may be expected to be re-convicted. If one then applies to the group a new 'treatment', and gets an actual re-conviction rate of forty per cent, this is a considerable success, although without the prediction table it might not have been counted as such.

For present purposes, interest centres on the content of the 'warning signs', because this ought to give some clue to the things that count in the predetermination of delinquency. The relative predictive value of items relating to sociological factors, to personality characteristics, or to circumstances of upbringing must to some extent reflect the relative importance of these areas

in the causation of delinquency. However, results have to be
interpreted with great caution. A good predictive factor is not
necessarily the same thing as a potent causal factor. To give a
ridiculous illustration to point the moral, suppose it emerged
that having red hair was a powerful predictor of criminal violence.
This might be accounted for if red hair and bad temper tended
to occur together in the same person, perhaps as hereditary
qualities carried on linked genes. But it would be the bad temper
and not the red hair that caused the liability to violence.

Another difficulty about predictive factors is that they are
limited to what the investigators have chosen to examine, and
that the choice is determined by what information is available,
easily measurable, and statistically significant, rather than by
what is meaningful in terms of causal theories. Thus, in the most
famous of British prediction studies, that of Mannheim and
Wilkins [168], which concerned the prediction of the likelihood
of re-conviction of youths passing through borstals, the most
effective predictors of relapse were items concerning previous
convictions and sentences. This observation, although perfectly
valid and credible, simply tells one that the more delinquent an
individual's past has been the more delinquent his future prospects, but it gives no clue to the cause of delinquency in the first
place. In the Mannheim and Wilkins research the investigators
set out to look for predictive factors among the items which were
on record in the majority of borstal files, and they excluded items
of a subjective nature which might be difficult for lay persons to
assess in an unbiased manner. Thus, whether or not such matters
as maternal attitude or separations in infancy might have been
important as causes, they had no chance to show up in the prediction table. Apart from previous record, the factors finally taken
into account by the Mannheim–Wilkins prediction formula were
drunkenness, not living with parents, home in an industrial area,
and the longest period spent in any one job. The fact that items
such as age at first conviction, or the presence of a broken home
failed to add anything to the effectiveness of the predictions has
some relevance in causal theories. On the other hand, one can
deduce nothing about the importance, when present, of items
like illiteracy, since these were excluded from consideration on
grounds of statistical infrequency.

The Gluecks' system

The prediction studies carried out by Sheldon and Eleanor Glueck [95; 98] have greater relevance to theoretical discussions because the scope of their inquiries was wider. In their great work *Unravelling Juvenile Delinquency*, to which reference has already been made,* they compared, for some 400 items of information, 500 seriously delinquent boys in reform schools and 500 non-delinquent 'controls' of similar age, intelligence, ethnic origin and social class. The items covered social background, family circumstances, parental attitudes, bodily configuration, health, psychological characteristics, as well as observations obtained by psychiatric examination and by the Rorschach (inkblot) personality test. This monumental research represents without doubt the most comprehensive survey of delinquents that has ever been carried out, and the information they unearthed has relevance far beyond the topic of prediction studies. Out of this enormous wealth of comparative material, the Gluecks selected a range of items, ascertainable at age six, which distinguished delinquents from non-delinquents, and which could be used as predictors. Here, at the outset, a number of causal influences was excluded. Gang affiliations, running away from home, reaction to school discipline, and a host of other items that had actually been found to correlate highly with delinquency were eliminated because they did not apply to the very young.

The items finally used by the Gluecks for compiling a prediction table related to five topics; discipline by father, supervision by mother, affection from father, affection from mother, and cohesiveness of the family, that is mutual dependence, trust and loyalty. In some later studies they have dropped the variables concerning father and affection because of difficulties in making ratings, 'affection' being a somewhat complex and subjective assessment, and father being absent in an important minority of cases. Now, in spite of the artificial way in which these factors were arrived at, it would still be of great theoretical and practical importance if it proved to be correct, as the Gluecks now claim, that the quality of maternal supervision and discipline, and the

* See pp. 72, 118.

cohesiveness of the family, observed at age six, or even earlier, serve to predict efficiently the presence or absence of delinquency at adolescence or later. This claim dovetails nicely with the psychoanalytic theory that the salient determining factors in delinquency are well established during infancy and have to do with the emotional tone of the family and especially the attitude of the mother. If delinquency is largely predestined from family circumstances during infancy, little importance can be attributed to those wider neighbourhood and social factors which come into operation at a later age. But is this really so?

Although similar in principle, the claims made for prediction devices, and especially that of the Gluecks, differ in one essential respect from the attempts made by workers like Hathaway and Monachesi, or Kvaraceus, to relate present personality traits to future delinquency. These authorities have commented quite explicitly on the disappointingly small correlations between personality measures and delinquent-proneness emerging from their work. Although such slight correlations have theoretical importance, their practical value as predictors in any individual case is minimal, and they leave plenty of room for the operation of other factors. The Gluecks, however, claim that 'a few *relevant* predictive factors, operating cumulatively, do in fact serve adequately to forecast behaviour'. In their system, supervision of the boy by his mother appeared to over-ride most other things. Thus, '83.2 per cent of the cases in which maternal over-sight had been unsuitable ... proved to be delinquents compared with 9.9 per cent in which it was suitable' [94].

The validity of the Gluecks' claims has been challenged by other authorities on a number of technical grounds, which are too complex to go into in any detail [267]. One major controversial issue concerns the doubtful applicability of the sharp contrasts between extreme delinquents and non-delinquents to a normal school population, which must include a large 'undistributed middle' of individuals who have a fifty-fifty chance of delinquency. Another issue concerns the statistical significance of predictive successes, which are generally less impressive with populations containing only a small minority of delinquents. Another reason for doubt is that the predictions sometimes appear to be more effective than the initial ratings on which they were based. The controversy still rages, and only time will tell who is right. The Glueck prediction system is now being tried in a number of important prospective studies. If it should prove even half as efficient as is claimed, the theoretical implications outlined above will have to be faced.

Personality measures applied to delinquents

Early signs of instability in future delinquents

According to psychoanalytic theories, the anti-social character traits or neurotic features of serious delinquents become manifest at a tender age. If so, it should be possible, by means of appropriate personality measures applied to children, to identify an unstable and delinquent-prone minority whose subsequent histories will reveal a significantly greater than average incidence of convictions. In the National Survey carried out by J.W.B. Douglas and others, to which reference has been made earlier in this chapter in connexion with the effect of separations from mother, something of the sort was tried [194]. At age six, and again at eleven, the mothers of the 5,000 children in the survey were asked about various nervous symptoms, such as stammering, nail-biting, bed-wetting, night terrors and nervous habits. At age thirteen, the children's teachers were given questionnaires on which they reported traits of nervousness or aggressive maladjustment. The latter was indicated by such items as disobedience in class, resentment at criticism, quarrelsomeness with other children, being rough in the playground, lying to evade trouble, and playing truant. Juvenile court appearances of the survey children were obtained up to age sixteen. No significant connexion was discovered between the incidence of nervous symptoms reported by mothers at an early age and the records of subsequent delinquency. On the other hand, the children identified by teachers as 'aggressively disturbed' at thirteen had a significantly raised incidence of juvenile convictions. This was not due to the teachers giving unfavourable ratings to those known to have had convictions, since the relationship was just as close in the case of children who were first convicted after age thirteen. The children picked out by teachers as being 'nervous' did not have any more delinquent records than the average. Similar results emerged from the work of D. H. Stott [253; 254], who devised a questionnaire for teachers known as the Bristol Social Adjustment Guide, which proved quite efficient in distinguishing delinquent children on the basis of their unstable behaviour in class. The questionnaire sought to detect all types of maladjustment, although some forms, notably unforthcomingness (i.e. lack of confidence with people and in new situations) and depression (i.e. listlessness, depressive moods), were not common in delinquents. A hostile or unfriendly attitude to adults, quarrelsomeness with other children, as well as some symptoms of emotional tension, were distinctly commoner among delinquents.

Stott compared children who were put on probation in Glasgow with a control group of other children of the same age and from the same schools. Forty-six per cent of the young probationers, compared with only seven per cent of the non-delinquents, were rated 'maladjusted' on the teachers' questionnaire. The validity of this result has been questioned on several grounds. Perhaps the juvenile courts selected the more disturbed children for putting on probation. However, on applying the questionnaire to all convicted children, those put on probation had much the same scores as those fined or admonished. Perhaps the teachers had a bias against known delinquents, and so gave them worse ratings. If so, this would not explain the predictive value of their ratings. Of the probationers rated maladjusted by teachers, nearly a half relapsed during their period of supervision, whereas of those rated stable less than a quarter relapsed. Perhaps the poorer classroom behaviour of delinquents had no connexion with their offences but was a reflection of the bad habits and attitudes of the low social class from which they came. In another study, Stott compared the scores of boy truants with a series of boys from the same school chosen because they lived nearest to the truants, and hence presumably belonged to much the same social class. The truants scored very much worse than their neighbours. This observation has some importance in view of the criticism that predictions from teachers' ratings work only by virtue of the unfavourable scores given to lower-class children.

Rebellious attitudes precede actual delinquency

In the United States, A. J. Reiss at Chicago [218] also found that school reports describing 'poor deportment' or 'frequent truancy' were statistically very effective predictors of whether or not delinquents put on probation would relapse during their period of supervision. Also in the United States, W. C. Kvaraceus [151] worked on rather similar lines, but using questionnaires and tests addressed to the children as well as to their teachers. He found, as have others, that teachers' assessments correlated more closely with future delinquency than did the children's own test responses, a fact which, as he wryly commented, supports the idea that 'nothing predicts behaviour like behaviour'. Nevertheless, both verbal and non-verbal tests of attitude and personality, as well as measures of retardation in reading (although not in intelligence), did bear some significant relationship to future delinquency, although not enough to allow practically useful prognostications in individual cases.

These researches receive further support from the work of Hathaway and Monachesi [118], to which reference has already been made. Using the personality questionnaire known as the Minnesota Multiphasic Personality Inventory, they found that children with the classic clinical signs of neurosis (anxiety and depression) were not particularly prone to delinquency in later years. On the other hand, in their survey, as well as in numerous other surveys of samples of established delinquents, such as that of borstal youths by Gibbens [82] it was shown that delinquents tend to score unusually high on the so-called psychopathic deviate scale of the M.M.P.I. This significant difference in the pattern of delinquent responses implies some kind of difference in the personality of delinquents as a group, and the kind of peculiarity displayed falls in line with the stereotype of the aggressive, anti-social character formation described by clinical workers. Thus, at face value, many of the questionnaire responses typical of delinquents suggest a resentful, rebellious attitude. For instance, Gibbens reported that borstal youths tended to reply 'yes' to the statements 'I know who is responsible for most of my troubles' and 'If people had not had it in for me I would have been much more successful', and to say 'no' to the statement 'I am always disgusted with the law when a criminal is freed through the arguments of a smart lawyer'.

Hathaway and Monachesi [117] showed that the personality traits typified by such responses precede the onset of official delinquency, and so could not be due to attitudes developed as a result of being caught and subjected to penal action. When the M.M.P.I. is given to different categories of young offenders after conviction, it is the more persistent delinquents, and those whose immature and anti-social attitudes are apparent to those around them, who produce the highest scores on the 'psychopathic' scale [245].

Anti-social character traits identifiable by tests

Sociologists have been understandably reluctant to admit systematic personality differences between delinquents and non-delinquents, and their scepticism has been fed by the inconsistency and unreliability of much of the results from personality-testing of delinquents. The American sociologists Schuessler and Cressey [230] made a devastating survey of 113 studies published up to that time, showing that where apparent differences between delinquents and non-delinquents had been reported they could often be explained by the way the samples had been selected, or by other fallacies of method. Furthermore, between one study and another, the claimed differences were thoroughly inconsistent and sometimes contradictory.

Such harsh strictures would not be so well justified today. A more recent and comprehensive review by M. Argyle [11] concluded that established delinquents had frequently been shown to differ from non-delinquents on several important traits. The most striking were the well-known features of the anti-social or psychopathic character, and included cruelty, aggressiveness, lack of perceptiveness of the feelings of others, impulsiveness, and rejection of authority.

Argyle suggested that the most distinctive of delinquent characteristics fell into four categories, and that each of these was related to specific features of the background of offenders. First, he noted the 'lack of sympathy' displayed by many delinquents, that is their relative callousness and aggressiveness, and their insensitiveness to other people's feelings. Evidence collected by such workers as Loban [158], who used the Hawthorne test for rating 430 adolescents on a scale varying from cruel to compassionate, suggests that cruelty and social insensitivity stem from fear of rejection, and are related to early experience of cruelty or neglect by one's parents. A more recent investigation in Iowa [63] demonstrated very neatly and conclusively that those children ranked by their school-fellows as the most aggressive in the class (on a questionnaire listing a variety of items of aggressive and spiteful behaviour and asking who among the class does this) were most likely to have had severer punishments at home (as judged from independent ratings obtained from interviews with parents).

The second characteristic quoted by Argyle, lack of conscience or weak super-ego, was apparent in the low scores attained by delinquents on questionnaires about moral values and moral choices, their liability to lying and cheating in tests, and their tendency to extra-punitiveness – that is projecting blame on to others. Research surveys generally yield results supporting the psychoanalytic contention that parental discipline that lacks warmth and consistency tends to lead to this type of character defect [236]. Thirdly, there was the characteristic which Argyle called impulsiveness or lack of ego control. This revealed itself in impatient, careless performance on psychomotor tests,* poor scores on tests of perseverance (such as measuring how long the subject can sit with one leg stretched out and raised from the floor), and a preoccupation with immediate satisfaction rather than long-term goals (which was apparent in their choice of themes in projection tests involving completing unfinished sentences or inventing stories). It is not altogether clear how this differs from the weak super-ego type, especially as both appear to be related to similar inadequacies of child training. Perhaps there is a greater consitutional element in impulsiveness due to strong instinctual drives than in impulsiveness due to lack of acquired restraint. Finally, Argyle noted the tendency of some delinquents to identify themselves with an anti-social scale of values, to show resentment and rejection of controlling authorities such as police, teachers and fathers, and to seek leadership from

* See p. 137.

among the more rebellious of their own age group. Apart from these attitudes such delinquents were not psychologically abnormal.

The first three of Argyle's delinquent characteristics, which sum up a large number of research results, correspond quite closely, both in immediate features and in background influences, to psychoanalytic impressions of the anti-social character type. His last group corresponds more closely to the delinquent model suggested by sociological theories.

The neurotic type identifiable by tests?

The evidence quoted so far tends to confirm the existence of psychopathic character traits, both as a frequent concomitant of persistent delinquency, and as a significant precursor of delinquency in general. The 'neurotic' type, on the other hand, fails to stand out in these statistical surveys, in spite of the prominence of such persons in clinical studies of persistent offenders. A probable explanation for this is that the total population of 'neurotics' includes groups of opposite tendencies. The introverted anxiety neurotic, who tortures himself more than other people, is probably less likely than the average person to become delinquent. The type identified by Alexander as the 'acting-out neurotic', a tense, conflict-ridden person who relieves himself in action, is probably more delinquent-prone. He is also probably more likely to be an extravert and to fall into the category of 'unstable extraverts' on the personality dimensions believed by Professor Eysenck. In surveys of schoolchildren, he is likely to be superficially indistinguishable from the troublesome boy of 'psychopathic' disposition, and hence to be so classified by teachers. In more refined psychological inquiries, he has a better chance of coming to light. Thus, the Americans D. R. Peterson and H. C. Quay [203], applying the statistical techniques of factor analysis to the questionnaire responses that distinguish delinquents and non-delinquents, demonstrated that the delinquents did not produce a homogeneous pattern. One group of delinquents might respond similarly to one cluster of items, whereas another group might pick upon a different cluster. Among juvenile delinquents they identified two distinct factors. One consisted of a response pattern indicative of a 'psychopathic' or amoral and rebellious attitude, typified by endorsement of such items as 'I do what I want to, whether anybody likes it or not'. The other factor was apparently indicative of low self-esteem coupled with moodiness and emotional tension, in other words 'neuroticism'. This was typified by endorsement of items like the following: 'I seem to do things I regret more often than other people do'; 'It is hard for me to act natural when I am with new people'; 'People often talk about me behind my back'.

In a later attempt to confirm these observations, Quay [213] applied a similar factor analysis to the inter-correlations of the behavioural characteristics of youths in a reform school, as per-ceived and rated by the correctional officers. Two of the domi-nant factors or patterns which emerged corresponded rather well with what had been found by questionnaires. The first pattern was one of overtly aggressive behaviour with a generally hostile demeanour and a rebellious attitude towards authority and dis-cipline. The second pattern was again one of 'neuroticism' with items like timidity, social withdrawal, depression, anxiety and over-sensitiveness all prominently featured. Such results tend to confirm the theory that among the total population of delinquents psychologically distinctive sub-groups of 'psychopathic' and 'neurotic' types can be identified.

Classifying delinquents on a psychological basis

The Hewitt and Jenkins classification

Sufficient information is now available, both practical and theoretical, to begin to identify sub-groups of delinquents in a fairly objective manner, and in a way that has some relevance to causation, and hence to treatment. One of the earliest and simplest classificatory systems, but still one of the best, arose out of some empirical surveys of young delinquents by Hewitt and Jenkins [120]. They collected evidence as to the relative proportions of young delinquents falling into the categories of 'neurotic' and 'anti-social character' types. They began with a study of badly behaved children seen at the Michigan Child Guidance Institute, and found that the 'symptoms' tended to fall into one or other of three more or less distinct groupings or clusters. The 'unsocialized aggressives' were prone to cruelty, violence and revengefulness, to initiating fights, to malicious mischief and destructiveness, and to open defiance of authority. In addition they were bitter and disgruntled in attitude and noticeably lacking in remorse. The 'over-inhibited', or neurotic, boys, in spite of their transgressions, were generally submissive and over-sensitive, prone to worry, depression and shyness, seclusive in habits and lacking in interest or energy. The 'socialized' or 'pseudo-socialized' delinquents, on the other hand, were more prone to furtive stealing and to association with gangs and bad companions, but were less overtly aggressive and uncooperative. A later survey of the population of a training school for delinquent boys confirmed that the majority of inmates fell into one or other of these three groupings, and that the 'socialized delinquents' were rather commoner than the other two types. The chief interest of this classification (apart from the fact that it was built up by statistical analysis of items of behaviour rather than by impressionistic judgements) arose from the correspondence between present reactions and previous background and upbringing. The great majority of the unsocialized aggressives had experienced active rejection by their parents; whereas the over-inhibited had more often experienced a repressive upbringing in a family atmosphere of tension and uncertainty. The pseudo-socialized delinquents, on the other hand, had experienced parental rejection less often than parental neglect, with laxity of supervision and routine, and consequent exposure to delinquent influences in the neighbourhood.

This threefold division of young delinquents corresponds rather well to theoretical types that have been so far described. The 'unsocialized aggressives' correspond very nicely to the 'anti-social character type' described by Friedlander, namely, individuals whose personality has been badly warped, often as a result of severe emotional rejection. The same type of person, when he grows a little older, and if his character deficiencies remain sufficiently well-marked and unpleasant, would be called by most authorities a psychopath. The pseudo-socialized delinquents have a lesser degree of character deformity, and can fit in among peer groups of similar type, although not among the wider society. The neurotic-inhibited delinquents resemble the conflict-ridden neurotic types described by Alexander and other psychoanalysts.

A similar classification of juvenile delinquents emerged in the work of A. J. Reiss [219] in Chicago, who analysed the records of 1,110 white male probationers from the juvenile court of Cook County. On the basis of psychiatric workers' reports they were allocated to three groups, normals, social delinquents, and the maladjusted – the last named consisting of boys of either neurotic or psychopathic tendency.* The normals had no obvious peculiarity of attitude or personality. They had no representation in the Hewitt and Jenkins classification since these investigators were concerned with serious social deviants in institutions. The social delinquents were boys who had failed to internalize certain middle-class standards; they identified themselves with rebellious peer groups, and experienced little guilt about their transgressions. The third group were impulsive, weak in self-control, and either highly aggressive or miserably insecure and anxious, with a lot of internal conflict about their delinquencies. In Hewitt and Jenkins's terms this must have included both unsocialized aggressives and neurotic inhibited types.

As in the Hewitt and Jenkins investigation, significant differences emerged between the backgrounds typical of the various sub-groups of delinquents. Those classed as 'maladjusted' were found less often than the other groups to have come from poor neighbourhoods or areas of high delinquency, to have left school prematurely, or to be the last child of a large family, or to be the offspring of foreign-born parents. That is to say, in social circumstances, they were relatively favoured, although in behaviour they were worse than the social delinquents, being more often incorrigible and destructive, and commencing their official delinquent careers at an earlier age. They were also much more often lone offenders who did not participate with peers in either legitimate or delinquent activities. The 'normal' offenders, on the other hand, differed from both the 'social' and the 'maladjusted' groups in being better behaved at school,

* For the sake of clarity, the terminology actually used by Reiss has been rather freely adapted.

truanting less, being better scholars, and more often having parents free from severe marital discord. The social delinquents, more often than the other groups, came from large families, had delinquent siblings, and had parents who were lacking in moral example or discipline. It would seem that a good home in a bad social environment produces the occasional, non-serious delinquent or normal personality who may be expected to reform very quickly, while the lax home in a bad neighbourhood encourages the development of the 'socialized delinquent' who rejects conventional standards, and at adolescence is liable to become an official delinquent. Conflict-ridden homes, on the other hand, even in relatively good neighbourhoods, are liable to produce more serious misfits, especially among only and eldest children, upon whom parental disharmony impinges most acutely. Such children, if they become offenders, are liable to be particularly wild and incorrigible and to take to lone delinquencies from an early age.

Uses and limitations of classification

The rough classification of delinquents into the groups of 'normal', 'neurotic' and anti-social ('psychopathic') character types represents in convenient although over-simplified form the views of many authorities on criminal psychology. The classification has some practical value, since it relates both to the causes which predominate in a particular case and to the most suitable lines of treatment. For the inhibited neurotics, a permissive approach calculated to 'bring them out of themselves' seems appropriate, but for the psychopaths a similar policy might prove disastrous. The disadvantage of this, as indeed of all other systems of classification on psychological principles, is that it cannot take fully into account the complexities of an individual case, particularly in regard to the coexistence in one and the same person of seemingly contradictory psychological mechanisms. By counting up how many features of behaviour fall into each class, it may be possible to allocate most psychologically peculiar delinquents to either the 'neurotic' or the 'psychopathic' group, but this conceals a considerable overlap. In practice, some offenders display an undoubtedly 'psychopathic' absence of conscience and incapacity for love, and at the same time suffer from anxiety, depression, hypochondria and other marks of 'neurotic' reaction. Furthermore, the absence of super-ego and a callous indifference to other people's feelings can be very conspicuous in certain areas, in relationships with authorities for example, whereas the same man, in his dealings with a younger brother perhaps, may display an unsuspected altruistic facet to his personality. The use of abstractions like conscience or super-ego obscures the elementary point that learning can proceed unevenly, so that some aspects of morality are absorbed quite well, while in others the individual remains immature or psychopathic. Then again, the borderline between psychologically 'normal' offenders and those to be called 'neurotic' or 'psychopathic' defies exact delineation. Variations are a matter of degree, and, depending upon one's standards of conformity, different proportions of the offender population fall beyond the borderline of normality.

On anything like a strict standard, many of the predominantly 'normal' delinquents share with the 'psychopaths' a sufficient number of undesirable personality traits to make their classification doubtful. Finally, the rough and ready division between 'neurotic' and 'psychopathic' types reveals very little of the detailed dynamics of the individual case. Thus, of four young rebels, one may be unconsciously courting disaster, on Freudian lines, while another is fighting to get free from a dominating mother who crushes his masculine aspirations, a third boy is over-compensating for a secret feeling of inadequacy, and a fourth is displacing on to innocent adults the hatred he has built up against a cruel father before whom he dare not reveal his feelings. Any one of these reactions to stress might occur in a 'normal', 'neurotic' or 'psychopathic' personality, the classification depending upon the quality, severity, and persistence of the reaction, as well as upon the presence or absence of other marks of instability. In short, useful as it is for analytic purposes and as a starting point for research into causes, neither this nor any other simple sub-division of delinquents can be expected to provide much of a picture of the rich variation of delinquent characters encountered in real life.

Classifying delinquents by their moral development

The amorality of delinquents

Grouping delinquents according to whether their disturbance is primarily individual (i.e. neurotic or psychopathic) or socially conditioned (by identification with an undesirable sub-culture) is useful up to a point, but does not help much in the large number of cases in which anti-social attitudes arise from a mixture of personal difficulties and social circumstances. In assessing delinquents for treatment purposes, one needs some measure of the depths or severity of personal handicap. A possible yardstick for this purpose is the stage of emotional maturity the delinquent has reached. In this context, what psychologists call emotional maturity might just as well be called moral development. It reveals itself in such old-fashioned virtues as sympathy, cooperation, tolerance, love, trust and altruism, all of which are descriptions of the quality of a person's relationships with others. These capacities are conspicuously lacking in the psychopathic character, only fitfully displayed by the neurotic, and when present in the socialized delinquent tend to be limited to dealings with his own special cronies.

The idea of assessing people according to their state of moral development bristles with dangers. Psychologists and social scientists have long struggled to remain neutral and uncondemning in their descriptions of humanity, and to avoid value judgements, but this stance becomes difficult to maintain when the measuring scale itself consists of points of virtue ranked on a progression reflecting an accepted system of values. The topic of moral development hardly creates the problem, it merely brings into sharper focus an ever-present and inescapable difficulty in working with labels like 'delinquent' and 'psychopathic' which carry censorious implications. Although the use of moral terminology may seem to add to the opprobrium attached to delinquents, the effect of bringing moral qualities under scientific observation may be to reduce the scope for righteous indignation. An individual whose moral development has been stunted by a bad upbringing has in his own way as much claim to sympathy as the stupid person whose limitations arise from inferior brain power. Another danger lies in the tempting suppositions that criminal habits necessarily go with moral turpitude in other respects, or that criminals are the chief exemplars of wickedness in society. Criminals sometimes refer to themselves picturesquely as villains, and undoubtedly some of them are very low on the scale of moral development, but so indeed are many others whose selfishness and lack of concern for other people is manifested in domestic tyranny, neglect of parental obligations, ruthlessness in business and a thousand and one other abuses not listed in the criminal code.

Moral development has obvious relevance to delinquency research, but ever since the exhaustive Character and Education Inquiry of Hartshorne, May and Shuttleworth,* psychologists have doubted whether moral behaviour exists as a stable and consistent character trait, since so much seems to depend on the situation of the moment. However, the Hartshorne and May conclusions were based upon very simple and relatively harmless situations which gave scope for dishonesty. It could be that more deep-seated dispositions towards anti-social reactions would have been identified in some persons by observation of a wider range of behaviour, especially behaviour that visibly hurts friends and acquaintances.

Stages in moral development

The Swiss psychologist Jean Piaget [205] is the most famous exponent of the view that moral development proceeds in recognizable stages through infancy and childhood. He and his collaborators told children stories setting out hypothetical situations calling for a moral judgement. For example, in one story, a boy stole some bread to give to a hungry friend and a girl took a ribbon to decorate her dress. The children were asked if one character was naughtier than the other, and how they should be punished. In their early years up to about eight, Piaget believes that children display a predominantly heteronomous concept of morality, in which rules are viewed as absolutely fixed and outside their personal control, like the laws of gravity. At this stage, the child thinks rules are there to be obeyed without reasoning or questioning, and punishments are the natural consequence of

* See p. 43.

transgression, regardless of extenuating circumstances. For example, one child of this age said, in response to the story quoted above, that the boy deserved the greater punishment since the bread he took was bigger than the ribbon. An action is perceived as bad if it provokes punishment. To hit a big boy is worse than to hit a small boy because in the former case the 'punishment' is liable to be more severe. As the child's ability to distinguish between his own and other people's viewpoints develops, so he comes to appreciate ideas of justice and fair play. Morality is no longer governed by external rules but by internalized principles, based upon ideas of cooperation and respect for other people.

Later studies, notably those of Lawrence Kohlberg [150], confirm Piaget's general concept of a progressive sophistication in moral values with increasing age, but do not always tally on points of detail, and on the whole make the picture more complicated. For instance, the development of moral ideology is not an exclusively individual phenomenon, it may be speeded or retarded according to the attitudes of the culture in which the child lives, the social class he belongs to, and the disciplinary techniques to which he has been subjected. Transition from one stage to another is not clear-cut, and the same child may apply primitive values in one situation, more mature ones in another. More important, the correlation between actual behaviour and the child's understanding of moral principles may be quite slight.

Peck and Havinghurst's classification by moral development

An attempt to identify stages of moral development by observing actual behaviour, as well as by applying psychological tests, has been reported by Peck and Havinghurst [201]. They used a five-point classification, as follows. The *amoral* type follows his whims and impulses without regard to how this affects others. He has no internalized moral principles and feels under no obligation to curb his impulses. This is the normal state of affairs in early infancy, and a tendency to react at times in this infantile fashion is the most constant characteristic of the severe psychopath. The *expedient* type perceives and considers how he affects others, but only for the purpose of gaining his own ends.

He will be honest and avoid hurting others if that seems to be the best rewarded policy, but he will deceive or hit out if he thinks he can get away with it or come out on top. He has no internal conscience to restrain him, only the forces of social disapproval. This stage is typical of the very young child who has learned to conform to rules only when an adult is around to see and punish his misdeeds. The *conforming* type has no strong individual conscience, but feels shame if he deviates from what is expected by his friends. He follows a consistent line of conduct, but his moral horizon is restricted by what happens to be in vogue among his group. Some of the worst atrocities against persecuted minorities, as well as many marauding crimes of sub-cultural delinquents, are committed by persons who are conformists to their own milieu. The *irrational conscientious* type has a strongly developed conscience, and feels guilt if he breaks his own rules, but his standards are rigid and blind to possible detrimental consequences. This is the classic state of affairs depicted by psychoanalysis in the case of neurotics overwhelmed by inhibiting and punitive super-ego. Those at the highest level, described by Peck as the *rational-altruistic type*, have a stable set of moral principles, but are rational and flexible in applying them to particular situations, and fully capable of perceiving and taking into account other people's needs, whoever they may be. They behave well, not because they are frightened, or just because people expect it of them, but because they like to do so.

These types were said to be distinguished not only by their likely reaction in situations calling for moral decisions, but in a wide range of personality traits. Thus the *amoral* types were fundamentally distrustful, hostile people lacking the perceptiveness or the motivation necessary to achieve control over their impulses or maintain stable relationships with others. The *expedient* types, motivated by a self-centred preoccupation with getting things, were also hostile, suspicious persons, and laboured under a chronic sense of frustration on account of the unsatisfactory and temporary quality of their goals. Only the *rational-altruistic* types seemed to be happy, well-integrated persons capable of facing reality without fear or defensive denial, and capable of using their talents to the full. The progressive improvement in personality concomitant with the stages of moral development justifies the use of these stages as an index of general emotional maturity. A surprising degree of constancy of moral reactions over years was reported by Peck, so that some adolescents were seen to have been stuck for years at a primitive level, and would probably remain so indefinitely.

The evidence for these conclusions consisted of very high correlations between different methods of assessment of the same children. For instance, those rated emotionally mature on psychological tests were also rated rational-altruistic by clinical observation, and were reported as well behaved and morally reputable by peers and adults in contact with them in the community. Unfortunately, this study was based on a very small sample; raters could have been biased by knowledge of information from other sources, and other researchers have not been able to reproduce the high correlations reported. Nevertheless, it has been mentioned here because the idea behind this kind of research seems promising. An actual example of the results of treating delinquents in different ways according to their level of maturity will be described later.* The findings of this kind of research dovetail rather nicely with evidence on the one hand that many delinquents are distinguished by low levels of moral development, and on the other that the levels attained by individuals are in large part the consequence of their upbringing. The interpolation of the concept of level of maturity between the faulty upbringing and the delinquent outcome helps to supply a causal link. It also helps to explain why delinquent behaviour is not a necessary or invariable outcome, since it is only one of many ways in which the difficulties of the emotionally immature may manifest themselves.

* See p. 284.

8 Girls, Sex, Drugs and Violence

I am going to talk about teenagers and that means, almost inevitably, that I am going to talk about violence and sex.

Professor G. M. Carstairs, *This Island Now* (B.B.C. Reith Lectures for 1962). Penguin Books (1964). p. 43.

Drugs

The variety of addictive substances

As was said at the outset, most generalizations about offenders refer to the men and boys who commit the common indictable crimes against property. More unusual phenomena, such as sexual assaults, crimes by females, drug abuse and serious acts of violence present very different pictures. Each must be considered as a separate problem.

Addiction means persistent and excessive consumption of some chosen substance to the detriment of physical health or social welfare. Anything which gives gratifying sensations or a feeling of euphoria is liable to produce addiction, including sweets, coffee, tobacco, alcohol, barbiturate sedatives, amphetamines and other stimulants (e.g. purple hearts), as well as the traditional narcotics like morphine (opium), cannabis (marijuana, reefers), heroin or cocaine, and the more recently fashionable hallucinogens (mescalin, L.S.D.). Some of these, if taken to excess over a long period, have deleterious physical effects. Excess of carbohydrates may lead to obesity and possible heart disease, heavy smoking to lung cancer, alcohol may produce liver disease and cerebral degeneration. Some of them are also potentially dangerous in their immediate intoxicating effects, rendering the consumer temporarily confused, incoordinate, reckless or aggressive.

In any given place or time, the substances singled out as immoral or illegal and the ones regarded as socially acceptable are determined much more by custom and prejudice than by any objective weighing-up of their relative dangerousness. Thus, in terms of the risk of serious poisoning effects, of the build-up of physical dependence, and of the release of dangerous impulses during periods of intoxication, alcohol is probably more undesirable than marijuana, although in Western countries the latter has long been classed with more powerful narcotics as a dangerous and prohibited drug [246]. In Moslem cultures, however, imbibing alcohol was for long considered sinful and harmful, whereas smoking marijuana was socially accepted. At one time opiates were widely used in the West in patent medicines, and in the medical treatment of all kinds of chronic illness.

Physical dependence

Certain drugs are considered especially dangerous because of the phenomenon of physical tolerance – dependence. Repeated doses induce a bodily resistance, so that larger and larger amounts are needed to produce the same degree of gratification. This leads in turn to a physical dependence, since sudden interruption of the customary dose produces highly unpleasant or dangerous withdrawal symptoms. Once 'hooked' in this way, an addict cannot usually discontinue of his own unaided volition. Morphine and heroin show this characteristic very strongly, but to some extent it is also shared by barbiturates, amphetamines, and alcohol. If dosage is suddenly interrupted, the barbiturate addict is liable to epileptic fits, the amphetamine addict to depression and to changes visible on the electro-encephalograph, and the chronic alcoholic to delirium tremens.

The seriousness of these complications is often exaggerated. They can quite easily be avoided by a gradual reduction in dosage or a substitution of tranquillizers for the addictive drug. But heroin and morphine carry other risks. The former is much the more powerful and also the more widely abused. It can be mixed with other things and taken by mouth, or inhaled as snuff, or injected. Use of impure products in imprecise quantities can result in dangerous overdosage. Since injection into a vein produces euphoria more swiftly and completely than other means, this presents a strong temptation to addicts, in spite of the risks of respiratory collapse or serious infection which this procedure entails. Anti-social characters, whose reckless misuse of drugs has led to a strong addiction, have little compunction in selling surplus supplies in order to finance their own further consumption, thereby spreading the habit to others.

Psychological dependence

Addiction is usually a state of mind more than a physically determined condition. The alcohol or narcotic addict who has been taken through the withdrawal phase in hospital, and thus freed from physical compulsion, nevertheless all too often resumes the habit as soon as he is released. On the other hand, where a particular drug is socially accepted, and the setting and amount of its consumption are regulated by custom, serious abuse is relatively uncommon. Opium smoking among the Chinese was a case in point. On the other hand, the introduction of European alcohol to African and Red Indian tribes who were unaccustomed to it often had disastrously disruptive effects. In any culture, however, there are some susceptible individuals who, once having found means of relief or oblivion from their anxieties and frustrations through intoxicants, crave this relief in all subsequent situations of stress. Excessive drinking, beyond the bounds of accepted custom, and abuse of drugs, especially those drugs made more attractive by being legally forbidden, is also common behaviour among anti-social (psychopathic) characters, who are by definition defiant of social restraints. Among some of the criminal sub-cultures and gangs in American cities, use of narcotics has become a part of the young delinquent's way of life, a kind of inverted status symbol [33]. This kind of social support enables some young people to identify themselves with the class of drug users, just as other youngsters might be proud to count themselves among the ranks of drinking and smoking men.

Young drug takers

In England, narcotic addiction used to be a vice of older people, especially those who had been introduced to drugs during illness, or of hospital workers and pharmacists, who had access to narcotics in the course of their professional duties; but recently narcotic addiction has made an appearance among the young, and especially among delinquents [19]. However, officially known cases are still limited to a few hundred addicts. In 1964, of a total of 456 Home Office registered narcotic addicts, only forty were under twenty years of age. This is infinitesimal compared with the prevalence of addiction in the United States, where 20,000 heroin addicts have been reported in New York alone [247]. Illicit production and distribution of narcotics is less effectively controlled in America, but the situation in England could develop if access to heroin became too easy [182].

A more pressing problem at present is the juvenile craze for 'pep' pills, usually amphetamine derivatives. These are useful medicines in psychiatric practice, since they impart a feeling of wellbeing and self-confidence in otherwise depressed and over-anxious persons. As a euphoriant for social purposes they have the disadvantage that overdosage is all too easy and may lead to alarming hallucinations, or reckless behaviour, to sudden physical collapse, or even to attacks of madness [42]. That the habit has become widespread among delinquent adolescents was revealed by a recent study by Scott and Willcox [235]. Analysis of urine from unselected samples of youths in a London remand home showed that some seventeen per cent had been taking amphetamines.

Some of the boys who admitted using the drug said it made them enjoy things better, talk better, and gave them extra vitality. Some consciously adopted the practice as a cheap substitute for alcohol. It was customary to take the drugs mostly at weekends for adding zest to parties. Amphetamines were found just as frequently in the urine of delinquents in the remand home for girls. How common drug-taking has become among non-delinquent youngsters is unknown. A questionnaire sent to Oxford students by the magazine *Isis* revealed that 500 of them were smoking marijuana. Dr Arnold Linken of the student health service at London University estimated that in 1964 about four per cent of students were constantly using marijuana, while about ten per cent had used it occasionally. Among the delinquents, amphetamine-taking was not significantly associated with any particular type or seriousness of offence, or any noteworthy feature of personality or background. Instances of extreme misuse, however, involving persistent gross overdosage, episodes of delirium, loss of efficiency at work, and reckless or aggressive misconduct during intoxication, were found only among boys whose personalities were inadequate or anti-social before ever they started drug-taking. Temporary overdosage produced confusion and loss of awareness of surroundings, with nonsensical rambling speech and inappropriate behaviour, such as masturbation in public or impulsive aggressiveness, followed by memory loss for all that happened during the period of intoxication. In England, the Misuse of Drugs Act, 1964, made unauthorized possession of amphetamines an offence punishable by imprisonment, as had long been the case with marijuana, opium and heroin. Convictions are secured, not by evidence of intoxication, but by the police finding tablets in a suspected person's pockets or belongings.

The connexion with crime

The consumption of intoxicants bears a complicated relation to the commission of crimes. Heavy drinking habits, as well as the use of prohibited drugs, are rather common among the anti-social characters who find their way into penal institutions. Similar habits are also found among individuals who are in no way anti-social, but who suffer from personal problems or neurotic tendencies, or who have had the bad luck to get caught up in a group where heavy drinking is customary. These people are hardly likely to go in for crimes as a result of their habits – except perhaps for motoring offences – unless they become so uncontrollably addicted that they must resort to dishonesty, or to association with criminals, in order to maintain their supply of intoxicants. The anti-social characters, on the other hand, may take a stiff drink or a dose of stimulant for the express purpose of bolstering up their courage when out to commit an offence. Most intoxicants, and especially alcohol, have a disinhibiting effect upon many people. Since anti-social characters generally have poor control over their aggressiveness to begin with, once intoxicated some of them are peculiarly liable to impulsive violence, and it is a well-known criminological observation that murders, woundings, rapes and assaults are frequently committed when offender or victim or both are to some degree intoxicated.

Chronic abuse of alcohol or other drugs calls for medico-psychological treatment, first to deal with any physical dependence that may be present, second to treat the underlying personality problems [146]. In so far as the problems are those of the anti-social character, treatment will run along much the same lines as the therapeutic communities for persistent offenders described in Chapter 11. In some cases compulsion may be necessary to secure cooperation at first. In the form of the self-help groups known as Alcoholics Anonymous and Synanon, this community approach has been found to be about the most effective means of rehabilitating both alcohol and drug addicts [29]. Synanon, a society for narcotic addicts started in California, requires its members to participate in soul-searching group discussions in the course of which self-deceptions and rationalizations are determinedly stripped away, and the addict is made to recognize his own weaknesses and deal with them in other ways than by looking for a 'fix'.

Methods of control

Drug-taking, especially among the young, readily arouses public concern owing to the popular idea that it leads inevitably to moral degradation and hopeless addiction. Actually, the majority of students and others who try out reefers or pep pills suffer no obvious harm. It is the weaker characters with personality problems who are liable to become malignantly addicted, and who stand most in need of protection from their own foolhardiness and lack of control. No one feels pleased at the spectacle of teenagers emerging from notorious cafés glazed-eyed and 'high', but is it any sadder than the sight of older age groups rolling home drunk when the bars close? The public have a curious double standard in regard to alcohol compared with other intoxicants. In the case of alcohol, there is scant support for prohibition of the pleasure of the majority for the sake of preventing abuse and disaster among a minority. In the case of less familiar intoxicants, a strong body of opinion favours extending the legal prohibitions and introducing harsher penalties. In the present writer's opinion, such a policy would be unwise. In America, where the laws are already much harsher, the fact that addicts are punished and dealt with as criminals thrusts them back into a criminal milieu, surrounds drug-taking and drug trafficking with the glamour of dangerous illegality, and greatly hinders rehabilitation of the individuals affected.

Indirect control by stricter regulation of the manufacture and sale of certain drugs is preferable. For instance, drinamyl pills, the famous purple hearts, are now made in plain, undistinguished looking tablets. But this cannot solve the problem completely. Persons bent upon abuse of intoxicants can always find some-thing, by swallowing tablets meant as pain-killers or to relieve obesity, by sniffing glue, gasoline or cleaning solvents, by taking seeds from Morning Glory, by drinking certain cough mixtures, by swallowing methylated spirits, or finally by getting drunk in the orthodox legal manner with ethyl alcohol. It would be impossible to control all potential intoxicants in the same way as the drugs now scheduled as dangerous. Education and example may help to dissuade young people from making un-desirable experiments, but since so many adults feel the need to use hypnotics or tranquillizers, the pill-taking habit is not likely to disappear.

The English law has already powerful means of control. Except in special offences requiring a specific malicious intent (which might be difficult to establish in a severely intoxicated person) anyone who breaks the law while intoxicated can be fully punished for what he has done, and indeed the fact of having taken an intoxicant can be considered an aggravating circum-stance warranting a more severe sentence. Furthermore, a con-victed offender known to be addicted to alcohol or drugs can be committed to hospital for treatment, either semi-voluntarily, as a requirement of probation, or compulsorily, under the Mental Health Act, 1959, if certified as being of psychopathic personality. At present, to be found in a public place drunk and incapable from alcohol intoxication constitutes a minor non-indictable offence. Public intoxication of any kind could be made a criminal offence, with liability to compulsory detention in hospital for observation. The necessary treatment centres would have to be made available under the National Health Service.

Young sex offenders

Types of sex offenders

From the physiological standpoint, sexual urges are at their strongest and most continuously pressing in young post-adolescents, and yet among convicted sex offenders there is not such a high proportion of young males as there is among convicted thieves. In the age range fourteen to twenty-one, only 2.4 per cent of the indictable offences of convicted males are classed as sexual crimes, in the age range twenty-one to thirty it is 2.6 per cent, for those of thirty and over it is 5.3 per cent. Mature men of twenty-one to fifty years are liable to be convicted of indictable homosexual offences almost as often as youths of seventeen to twenty-one. The seventeen to twenty-one age range is particularly prone to conviction for rape or indecent assaults on females. After twenty-one the liability to such convictions is less, but no further striking decrease occurs until the late forties [129]. The comparative ease with which young adults can find sexual outlets – even deviant outlets – without resorting to assaults or importuning may go some way to explain why they do not make a greater contribution to the statistics of sexual crime.

Sex offenders include a wide variety of persons, both young and old. The prevalence of habits of sexual licence in delinquent sub-cultures has often been remarked upon, and may in part explain the significant overlap of convictions for sexual and non-sexual crimes. Many more persons have convictions for both sexual and non-sexual offences than would be the case if the two phenomena were unrelated. Michael Schofield [228], in his survey of sexual behaviour of English teenagers, found a significant positive association in both boys and girls between experience of appearance at court (or admitted law-breaking) and experience of sexual intercourse. He found that in boys, early experience of sex was associated with 'out-going' activities, such as dancing, going to parties, and visiting coffee bars; so of course is delinquency. Youths brought before the court for sexual misconduct are often referred for psychiatric examination, and one of the commonest characteristics to be found in them is a reckless defiance of restraint and authority, similar to that of the confirmed non-sexual delinquent. This is especially evident among those convicted of heterosexual assaults, although it may also be found in boys who experiment with a variety of deviant activities, perhaps one time stealing women's underwear, another time spying on women's lavatories or changing-rooms, or another time exposing themselves indecently.

Of course many young sex offenders are quite normal psychologically. A youth whose only offence consists in having been intimate with a girl under age, although she may have been as physically mature and as eager for the experience as himself, is often no different sexually or socially from many of his peers. On the other hand, many of the men who offend by making unwanted or aggressive sexual approaches to strange women, although not abnormal in the nature of their sexual inclinations, are often to some extent psychopathic, lacking in self-control in many other ways, and possibly unwilling or unable to submit to the constraints of marriage and family life. Some of them, on the other hand, may be shy, inadequate personalities who find difficulty in striking up normal social relationships with the opposite sex, and so feel sexually frustrated. Over half the males who come before the courts for sexual offences have committed sexually deviant acts, shocking women by a ritualistic display of the genitals (exhibitionists), indulging in sex play with pre-pubertal children (paedophiles), taking part in or proposing sexual acts with other males (homosexuals), or making obscene suggestions by telephone.

These deviant offenders are not all of them perverse to the extent of being unable to obtain sexual satisfaction normally. Some are young, immature characters groping their way by crude experiment towards a more realistic pattern. In the human species the sexual instinct has to be channelled in the right direction by learning, and although ideally this process should be completed by adolescence, it isn't always so. For instance, a certain amount of homosexual interest occurs so commonly at adolescence it is widely regarded as normal, and Kinsey's surveys [148] have shown that many young men of predominantly homosexual habits in early adult life develop later into well-adjusted heterosexuals. Some delinquent youths take advantage of their homosexual propensities and either prostitute themselves for money or social gain, or else entice older men into compromising situations in which robbery, blackmail or extortion can be practised with relative impunity.

Prospects of re-conviction

Sex offenders, particularly young ones, should be handled sympathetically, since the expectation of future re-conviction is much smaller than in the case of thieves, and one does not want to do anything that will hinder socio-sexual learning and development still further. In the Cambridge survey of a sample of 2,000 convicted sex offenders [217], 82.7 per cent had never before been convicted of a sexual offence, and 84.5 per cent were not subsequently convicted of sexual crime during a follow-up period of four years in freedom. This surprisingly optimistic outlook has been confirmed by researches in other countries. In a twenty-year follow-up of 2,000 Danish sex offenders, Sturup [256] showed that only ten per cent were re-convicted of sexual crime. Nevertheless, some categories of sex offenders do have a higher re-conviction rate. The Cambridge survey showed that as many as twenty-seven per cent of men convicted of homosexual offences with boys under sixteen were re-convicted. By the end of the follow-up period, five per cent of the sample were recidivists with four or more convictions for sexual offences. This minority were mostly confirmed paedophiles, exhibitionists, or homosexuals addicted to importuning in public lavatories. They were a particularly abnormal group; for the most part they were men of mature age (forty per cent being over thirty when first convicted of a sexual offence), and over half of them had convictions for non-sexual offences as well.

Sexual assaults on children

Child-molesters or paedophiles, particularly homosexual paedophiles, arouse great disgust among parents, prisoners and judges, as well as fear for the harm they may do to the children by shocking and terrifying them, or by awaking in boys a taste for deviant sexuality. Actually, the dangers to children are less than popularly supposed. Most paedophiles are childish in their approaches, and go no further than the mutual display and fondling which small children might indulge in among themselves. Although this does not make the offence any less obnoxious, the fact is that the victims are not infrequently seductive, attention-seeking children who try to elicit interest from neighbours, relatives or strangers where they have not been able to get it from their own parents. A survey of a sample of child victims in London showed that two thirds of them had been sufficiently willing participants to cooperate in assaults more than once or by more than one assailant. The assailants were mostly relatives or neighbours, less commonly strangers [87]. Given a normal background, the experience itself is not likely to impair a child's emotional development [16], although the fuss and distress of subsequent court appearances can be harmful. In Schofield's recent study of homosexuals and a control group [229], neither in his own samples nor in his survey of other researches did he find any evidence that casual homosexual contacts with adults were liable to turn boys towards a homosexual orientation in later years. Indeed, the very fixed type of exclusive homosexual deviant, who has an ineradicable aversion to heterosexual contacts, is likely to have been sexually inhibited and inexperienced in his early years.

J. W. Mohr [183], in a careful study of paedophiles in Canada, found that these offenders tended to cluster into three age groups, with peaks of incidence at adolescence, at thirty-five, and again at about sixty years. Many of the first group were shy and socially retarded youngsters who might be expected to develop normally in time, given the right encouragement and opportunity. Among the older offenders, many had slowly developed a precarious sexual adjustment, which later gave way in the face of the stress of family or marital problems, or the feelings of loneliness and failing powers experienced at the onset of old age. Only a minority were sufficiently compulsive and persistent in their practices to warrant detention in close custody.

As has been shown by Schofield and other investigators, ordinary homosexuals do not go in for child-molestation, and are very different from the paedophiles in background and attitude. On the other hand, some homosexuals, although they have no interest in pre-pubertal children, have little scruple about activities with post-adolescent youths. Since the majority of the homosexual incidents which actually come to courts concern importuning or indecency in public places, or activities with youths, it is doubtful if the proposed reform of the law would result in any great change in the criminal statistics. There is no evidence of any increase in homosexual tendencies among young persons. In so far as homosexual fixations are based upon fears and inhibitions against normal sexuality instilled by a repressive upbringing, one would expect some decrease in incidence as a result of the more open and matter-of-fact approach to sex that has developed in recent years.

Sexual maladjustment can spoil all prospects of a happy life, or, by the ruin of an established marriage, damage the emotional development of children of the next generation. The courts are therefore performing a very useful social service if they see to it that young sexual deviants whose behaviour has come to light through police action are seen and treated psychiatrically whenever possible.

Girl delinquents

Why are girls less often delinquent than boys?

Various reasons have been put forward why crime is not a typically feminine habit. Perhaps it is partly a matter of opportunity. Men go out and about more, frequent bars more, and so have more chance to thieve at work, to commit business frauds, and to learn about criminal ways and means. In countries where, by tradition, women were kept to a purely domestic role, playing no part in the wider social and economic life, their crime rate was correspondingly tiny. It seems to be a general rule that, as women become emancipated, so the proportion of women among convicted persons increases. N. Walker [271] has contrasted the ratios of men to women among adults convicted of various offences in England. In larceny from unattended vehicles it is eighty to one, in assaults and woundings it is four to one, in drunkenness and disorderly behaviour it is fourteen to one, in larceny from shops it is one to two. Shop-lifting is a more typically feminine crime presumably because women have more opportunity for it.

Pollak [207] has suggested that the difference in crime rates between the sexes is exaggerated by a policy of not pursuing inquiries or pressing charges against women. Another suggestion is that women in our culture are brought up to be more passive and conformist than men, and so they are more likely to support morality and the *status quo*, and avoid crime. Men are expected to be more assertive, to compete, and to provide, and are therefore under greater temptation to dishonesty.

The misconduct of juveniles shows marked sex characteristics long before the age when economic pressures, or even differences in physical strength and agility, could plausibly account for it. School-teachers find girls more amenable, parents less often take their daughters to child-guidance clinics, and the number of places in remand homes or approved schools occupied by pre-pubertal girls is very small indeed. As the psychiatrist T.C.N. Gibbens [81] once said of girls:

... environmental stress is much more likely to produce shyness, timidity and inhibited neurotic behaviour of a sort which is less often complained of by parents because it causes less nuisance and more easily passes for normal. It is only a small proportion of girls who 'act out' their troubles by wayward, aggressive and defiant behaviour ...

Wayward girls are worse than delinquent boys

The small minority of girls who do become actively wayward generally present more difficult problems than boy delinquents, and they more often come from very disordered or conflict-ridden homes. Using data from the Flint, Michigan Youth Study,* Ruth Morris [186] compared matching groups of delinquent and non-delinquent boys and girls. She found that, to a significant extent, the delinquent girls had the highest incidence of broken homes, or of homes beset by quarrels and tensions, and they were more often untidy and neglected in personal appearance. Male delinquents often appear to be boisterous, exuberant boys who have found satisfaction among their more rebellious peers, but wayward girls are more often unhappy

* See p. 57.

misfits. Although admitted on the fringes of male gangs, girls have nothing like the same support from the delinquent subculture that boys can find.

Another big difference appears at puberty. Whereas the wayward boy usually takes to stealing and breaking-in, and only exceptionally to sex offences, the wayward girl more often takes to sexual misconduct. The promiscuity of wayward girls serves as an effectively upsetting form of protest against the attitudes and restrictions of older relatives. Often, it also seems a way of searching for the affection which was wanting in an unhappy parental home. It would be wrong to suppose that all young girls who run away from unhappy homes into the arms of a lover are promiscuous. Some of them form emotional attachments as strong as they are unsuitable. As Gibbens [81] pointed out, even promiscuous girls are not necessarily bound for a career of professional prostitution. In his sample of 400 girls passing through a London remand home only about five per cent became prostitutes.

Girl thieves are often, but not always, sexual rebels. The two forms of behaviour are perhaps influenced by different factors. In a study of a sample of girls at an English approved school, the psychologist Elizabeth O'Kelly [199] contrasted the background of thieves and sexual delinquents. While both groups came mostly from disturbed homes, the thieves had more often suffered separation from or rejection by parents, while the sexual delinquents more frequently had difficult relations with fathers, and mothers who were conjugally unstable.

Such surveys as have been done on older girls in borstal, who are mostly convicted for offences against property, or disciplinary offences, such as running away from approved schools or breaking the conditions of probation, demonstrate very clearly the highly unstable character of the girls concerned, much worse than boys in borstals, and the continuance of problems of sexual promiscuity. Dr Epps [61], who studied 300 borstal girls of average age nineteen, found that thirty-seven per cent required treatment for syphilis or gonorrhoea or both, which was many times the rate of venereal infection among youths in borstals. About a third had experience of prostitution. Unhealthy homoerotic behaviour was also a problem, not necessarily indicative of a real fixation, but due, Dr Epps thought, to the segregated environment and the instability of the inmate group. The incidence of neurotic symptoms, psychopathic traits and disordered homes was all greatly in excess of what has been reported of borstal youths.

Legal control of promiscuous girls

The methods of dealing with troublesome girls are complicated by the double standard adopted by society, and by those who enforce the law, to the sexual behaviour of boys and girls. Staying out late in the company of the opposite sex, and actual or suspected sexual promiscuity are taken more seriously in girls, partly because of the risk of pregnancy, partly because it is considered particularly unseemly, leading as it does to loss of social status and to prostitution. Although, technically, it is the boy or man who commits an offence by having intercourse with a girl under sixteen, it is the girl who is the more likely to lose her liberty as a result. In England, juveniles up to the age of seventeen may be brought to court and dealt with as 'in need of care, protection or control' if they are 'falling into bad associations' or 'exposed to moral danger' or have been the victim of a sexual offence or are members of the household of a person convicted of a sexual offence against a child.* Alternatively, the parents may complain to the children's officer that they cannot control her conduct. In either case, the court frequently puts the girl under the care of the local authority, but may order supervision by a probation officer or commit her to an approved school. The population of approved-school girls has more 'protection' cases than official offenders.

According to the letter of the law, juveniles of either sex may be brought before the court on these grounds. In practice, boys who stay out late or get into bad company are not usually apprehended, but women police frequently take girls into custody if they are found in night clubs, or in the company of known prostitutes, or after running away from home with a lover. However, after reaching the age of seventeen, except if already under supervision, the girl can no longer be compulsorily

* Children and Young Persons Act, 1963, s.2.

controlled in this way unless she breaks the law, and in England prostitution itself (as opposed to soliciting in a public place, or benefiting from the prostitution of others) is not an offence.

The system whereby girls can be compulsorily segregated, and processed as if they were criminals, for sexual behaviour which is not in itself defined as illegal naturally produces resentment. Those committed to institutions, though protected temporarily from becoming pregnant, are exposed to the influences of an unstable and anti-social peer group, and are prevented from coming to terms with a normal social environment. On the other hand, if such girls are allowed to live outside, and then become pregnant, the consequences, both to themselves and others, can be still more distressing.

Youthful violence

Age and type of offence

Contrary to popular belief, there is a smaller proportion of youthful offenders among persons convicted of violence than among persons convicted of larceny or of breaking and entering. In the *Criminal Statistics, England and Wales, 1965*, fifty-eight per cent of those convicted of indictable crimes of violence against the person were aged twenty-one or more, compared with only twenty-nine per cent of those convicted of breaking and entering. Convictions for violence are uncommon under fourteen years of age, but quite common from fourteen to seventeen, and twice as common again from seventeen to twenty-one. It seems that adolescence is the time when some delinquent boys first begin to add violence to their repertoire of infractions. Up till then, their aggressive acts are usually limited to fighting among themselves in playgrounds and similar places, where such behaviour is widely tolerated, provided no one gets badly hurt. Occasionally, however, some police action is taken, as in a case recounted to me by a probation officer who was put in charge of four small boys, all aged under ten, after they had been convicted of robbery with violence. They had knocked down a school-mate, and then taken from him sixpence wrapped up in a handkerchief, thus transforming an incident of petty bullying into a grave criminal act.

The aggressive youth begins to appear in the criminal statistics when he gets involved in fights over girls at dance-halls, or teams up with a gang bent upon spoiling some rival social function, or gets quarrelsome after taking drink, or forces himself upon girls. As was shown in the study of violence in London by F.H. McClintock [162], relatively few of the incidents leading to indictable convictions involve serious injury, or the use of knives or guns, or are committed in connexion with other crimes, such as robbery, or resisting arrest. The typical act of youthful violence is one of quarrelsomeness or hooliganism, involving a punching attack in a pub, café, or in the streets, perpetrated in the heat of the moment, usually in a low-class neighbourhood by a low-class assailant against a person known to him. Although old ladies or other respectable and unprovocative citizens have been waylaid on the streets, this is a very uncommon event in England. The proportion of youths convicted for the first time for violence who have a previous record of conviction for an offence against property is much higher than the average for their age and sex, which confirms the common-sense view that delinquents are more prone to violence than non-delinquents.

More than most crimes, offences of violence are typically committed by lower-class persons. The lower-class culture affords the young male comparative freedom to express his aggressive feelings physically. Unfortunately many persistent delinquents seem to have an inordinate amount of aggression to express; indeed aggressiveness has always been thought one of the hall-marks of the psychopath. Middle-class people are much more restrained in their aggressiveness; but at the same time probably more effective in verbal attacks and in fighting through solicitors or by complaints to officials. The fact that girls are comparatively non-violent is probably due as much to cultural restraints as to physical incapacity. Females who have committed personal violence are not uncommon among borstal girls, and, as Wolfgang and Ferracuti [288] have pointed out, in Philadelphia coloured females have a homicide rate two to four times that of white males. These investigators have set out to demonstrate, in a study carried out at the University of Puerto Rico, that open violence in particular circumstances can be normal, socially supported behaviour in some sub-cultures. Where this state of affairs is well established it will be reflected in the attitudes and personalities of the people, and in the absence of guilt feelings following acts of violence. The fact that the use of violence may be restricted to one sex, or to a particular age group, may be itself a cultural expectation rather than a biological phenomenon. Among some aggressive American gangs, acts of violence help individuals to prove 'heart' or to acquire 'rep', but even among the wildest groups there are always some limits to the acceptable degree or frequency of violence.

Origins of violence

According to some psychologists, aggressiveness results from chronic frustration of instinctual satisfactions [18]. The child deprived of parental love, the low-class person who is bossed around and given small reward for any effort he may make, the youngster who can only get what he needs at the risk of brutal punishment, are so sensitized by their frustrating experiences that the slightest provocation serves to elicit an aggressive re-action. If the frustrating agents are parents or vaguely identified authorities responsible for social injustice, they are often too powerful or too remote for direct attack, and then the aggression tends to get displaced on to substitutes. Hence the popularity of scapegoats, especially members of racial minorities, as targets for seemingly wanton bullying.

Acts of malicious destruction may provide one substitute out-let for aggression against people. While it is inconvenient to have one's car tyres cut with a razor, it is less so than having one's face so treated. J. M. Martin [171], in a study of juvenile vandalism in New York, came to the conclusion that such offenders were more predominantly male, rather younger, and more prone to offend in groups than the general run of young delinquents. He found that some of these offenders were normal and usually law-abiding boys who had been accidentally caught up in group exploits, but more often they were either seriously disturbed individuals, using the opportunity to hit out blindly, or else they were mem-bers of an aggressive sub-culture, living in bad neighbourhoods, and participating in the marauding activities of local gangs. Some vandalism has a crude economic element, like tearing fixtures off walls and then selling them, and some is actuated by spite against the owner of the property, but more often vandalism is simply a satisfyingly aggressive mode of demonstrating delinquent prowess and contempt for authority. Many youngsters who take part in such destructive exploits have little experience in caring for property of their own and little appreciation of the consequences of their acts.

Violent tendencies in young men are not necessarily indicative of a poor outlook for the future. The spiritedly aggressive youth probably has a better potential for adjustment later on than the passive, discouraged type. T. C. N. Gibbens [85], in his survey of borstal lads, remarked that 'the outlook for rehabilitation often seems unusually good' in the case of those convicted for violence. On the other hand, a more diffuse kind of aggressiveness (corresponding to the Hewitt and Jenkins description of unsocialized aggressiveness), erupting in inappropriate situations, and manifest quite early in childhood, appears to be a bad sign. H. H. Morris *et al.* [185] followed up a group of children seen by psychiatrists on account of cruelty, destructiveness, defiance, tantrums or other aggressive behaviour. Open rejection by parents, and a high incidence of criminality and personality disorders among the parents were typical of the histories of these children. By the time they were young adults, only one fifth of this group had achieved a satisfactory adjustment. Some had become chronic mental cases, others were criminals, and a majority were leading irregular and disordered social lives.

Clinical examination of young men convicted of violence suggests no simple solution. A very few have identifiable neurological conditions, epilepsy, or mental subnormality, which might contribute to their aggressiveness. A minority are violent only when intoxicated, so that control of their drinking habits is the primary concern. Most of them present a mixture of individual character defects and low social standards. Except in some extremely volatile cases, tranquillizing drugs are not particularly successful. It appears that with this type of offender, as with many persistent offenders against property, there is no substitute for a thorough inquiry into the individual history and personal characteristics followed by a slow process of personal and social training.

The influence of television

It has been said that members of delinquent sub-cultures derive their deviant scale of values by selecting and exaggerating trends apparent in society as a whole. Delinquents need not look very far to find models for the violent anti-hero; he appears in comics, on television, in the cinema and in the popular press. Many commentators have criticized the mass-media, and especially the television authorities, for depicting crime and violence so much larger than life. It is claimed that by making criminal activity 'news', and by using crime as a recurrent theme for popular plays and films, journalists and broadcasters are holding up exaggerated models and distorted values which young people may emulate, and are diffusing information about criminal activities which some of them may then decide to try for themselves [285].

The long-term effects upon society of persistent exposure to spectacles of violence and crime are almost impossible to assess. However, the Television Research Committee, appointed in 1963 by the Home Secretary, found no direct evidence of a general increase of violence as a result of young people viewing television. On the other hand, evidence was forthcoming that potentially aggressive and maladjusted youngsters find violence on the screen particularly fascinating, but instead of obtaining vicarious satisfaction they are more likely rather than less likely to respond to a situation aggressively afterwards [111]. Just what ought to be done on the basis of such a finding is far from obvious. It is the old problem, which is common to the regulation of alcohol, pornography, loans, gambling, etc., whether to apply rigorous prohibitions to everyone for the sake of trying to shield the susceptible few.

9 The Penal System

Penal legislation hitherto has resembled what the science of physic must have been when physicians did not know the properties and effects of medicines they administered.

Sir Samuel Romilly (1811), quoted by L. Radzinowicz in *A History of the English Criminal Law* (1948). Stevens & Sons. Vol. 1, p. 396.

Every act of authority of one man over another, for which there is not an absolute necessity, is tyrannical.

Cesare Bonesana, Marchese de Beccaria, *Essay on Crimes and Punishment* (1764). (First American edition, New York, 1809, p. 12.)

Sentences for the young

Nineteenth-century reforms

Use of the grand title 'penology', or the euphemistic label 'treatment', cannot disguise the fact that the things done to offenders have scant scientific basis. If the causes of deviant behaviour are diverse and little understood, the means of controlling it have hardly reached the point where scientific scrutiny can begin. What happens to offenders in practice is an uneasy mixture of traditional punishment, segregation and discipline, diluted by humanitarian and psychological ideas about the importance of the sympathetic, personal approach.

Descriptions of the English penal system in operation, and of the laws which govern it, will be found in more authoritative works [77; 224; 268]. In England, rapid legislation and continuous political argument have put the contemporary system, at least in so far as it applies to young offenders, into such a state of flux that any detailed statement would soon be out of date. The brief sketch which follows is intended merely to give a little practical orientation so that it may be seen how far theories and proposals about treatment are just pie in the sky.

On the scale of history, methods of disposal of convicted offenders of any age other than by death, flogging or imprisonment under highly deprived conditions are quite recent developments. The hanging of small children used to be 'by no means unusual' in England [46]. In 1816, Samuel Romilly, in pleading unsuccessfully before the House of Commons for the abolition of hanging as a penalty for shop-lifting, mentioned the case of a ten-year-old boy at that very moment in Newgate Prison under sentence of death. In fact, since crime has always been a youthful activity, most of those hanged in the days when thieves were liable to execution were youngsters. The English Solicitor General, in 1785, noted that nine out of ten offenders hanged at that time were under twenty-one [214].

In the first part of the nineteenth century, in England as in most other countries children and young persons, both those convicted and those awaiting trial, were sent to the same appalling prisons as adults, where no doubt they were quickly depraved and brutalized by their experience. In 1817, the *Second Report of the House of Commons Committee on the State of the Police in the Metropolis*, reported that in the previous year the new prison at Clerkenwell had received 399 felons aged from nine to nineteen, and that young and old were mixed indiscriminately, regardless of the nature or gravity of their offences. The report went on to describe how petty street pilferers, many of whom might be boys just starting a career of crime, were 'usually committed for a short time to prison, sometimes severely flogged, and then, without a shilling in their pockets, turned loose upon the world more hardened in character than ever'. Sir Edmund Du Cane [51], writing of the same period, 1816, noted that of the 3,000 prisoners in London aged under twenty a half were juveniles under seventeen.

Separate arrangements for young prisoners were made for the first time following the report of a Select Committee of the House of Lords set up in 1835 to inquire into the state of the jails. One of their recommendations was to open a penitentiary for juveniles. At that time, prisoners awaiting transportation were confined aboard the famous convict hulks so vividly portrayed by Charles Dickens. Since boys could not be transported until they reached fourteen years of age, some of them had to remain as much as five years on the hulks. On 21 July 1831, John Capper, Superintendent of the Convict Establishment, that is the hulks, giving evidence before the Select Committee on Secondary Punishments, explained that the youngest of his charges was 'nine years old and deemed incorrigible' and that 'it is quite melancholy to see some of them; they can barely put on their clothes'. He thought solitary confinement a more efficient punishment for boys than whipping. Under the Parkhurst Act, 1838, an old military hospital on the Isle of Wight (still one of our most famous prisons) became for the next twenty-five years a prison which received boys from ten to eighteen years of age. This institution was criticized by the militant reformer Mary Carpenter, who preferred to see schools for delinquents privately run by religious bodies [27]. She claimed that the use of leg irons, armed guards, whipping, solitary confinement and a generally tyrannical régime kept the boys in a desperate and unreformed condition, ready to break out, plunder and kill if ever they got the chance. Although certainly very harsh by modern standards, the Parkhurst experiment represented an advance on the previous system, and some of the men who ran the prison were at least as enlightened in their understanding of juvenile troubles as the staff at the private reformatories, at some of which whippings were excessively frequent. The Youthful Offenders Act, 1854, authorized the establishment of Reformatory Schools run by voluntary agencies under the supervision of the Home Secretary, as an alternative form of detention for juveniles, although they had first to serve a short time in prison. The boys' prison at Parkhurst finally closed in 1864.

The development of approved schools and borstals

The numbers of juveniles incarcerated in prisons with adults gradually decreased, until the Children's Act of 1908 finally abolished imprisonment for those under fourteen, and placed restrictions on the imprisonment of those in the fourteen to sixteen age group. The reform schools in England, and the houses of refuge in the U.S.A., served to rescue young people from the adult jails, and to give young paupers and criminals (at that time these categories were scarcely distinguishable) a chance to learn a job and earn their bread. These schools long preceded the establishment of compulsory school attendance. They were the precursors of the present-day approved schools, which are institutions run by local authorities or private persons, 'approved' and inspected by the Home Office. They receive delinquents sent to them as compulsory boarders by order of the courts. At present children aged ten and under seventeen may be sent to approved schools, where they may be detained for up to three years, but not after reaching the age of nineteen. For the two years following release, but not after reaching the age of twenty-one, they are legally under supervision, and can be recalled for bad behaviour. The juvenile courts may also make Fit Person Orders in respect of offenders, which have the effect of transferring parental rights and responsibilities to a guardian, usually the local authority. The juvenile may then be sent to foster parents, a children's home, a boarding school for maladjusted children, or an approved school, according to his particular needs.

The institution of reformatories for children still left a large number of adolescent offenders mixed up with old lags in adult prisons. It was not until the end of the nineteenth century that some small-scale experiments with institutions specially designed for slightly older youths led to the development of the English system of borstals. Borstal detention (now called training) was first formally instituted in the Prevention of Crime Act, 1908, which provided a system of separate incarceration and training, as an alternative to imprisonment, for young persons. At present, delinquents aged fifteen and under twenty-one may be committed for borstal training for the same range of offences as adults may be imprisoned. The period of detention is from six months to two years, with a further two years under the supervision of a probation officer following release, during which time the offender may be recalled for another six months if he misbehaves.

In spite of the coming into existence of the borstal system, it was a long time before the idea became accepted that the majority of youngsters could be dealt with outside of the adult prison system. However, under s.3 of the Criminal Justice Act, 1961, no one under twenty-one should be committed to prison unless his offence warrants detention for three years or longer. A special section of the prison at Wakefield is reserved for youths serving long sentences.

Borstals differ from prisons not so much in the security precautions against escape (indeed the majority of borstals are 'closed' institutions) as in the comparative freedom and mobility of the offenders within the institution, in the assumption by the staff of a teaching and training role which brings them into constant functional contact with inmates, and in the concentration upon learning a job and using time constructively. In theory, at least, borstal training 'seeks the all-round development of character and capacities – moral, mental, physical and vocational'. In the case of 'young offenders for whom a long period of residential training away from home is not yet necessary, but who cannot be taught respect for the law by such measures as fines and probation' [126], the Criminal Justice Act, 1948, provided for the setting up of detention centres. These now receive offenders from fifteen up to twenty-one years of age, for a stay of three to six months, in 'secure establishments with strict control' where the régime is 'brisk and firm' with 'a strong emphasis on hard work' [132]. The intention is primarily deterrent, and the system was at first described as 'a short, sharp shock'. For boys, the medicine consists of an unremitting sequence of square bashing, P.T., and manual labour mostly performed at the double. It is said to be 'unsuited to those are are seriously handicapped physically or mentally'. Prisons, borstals and detention centres are at present all run by the Prison Department of the Home Office.

The *Report of the Departmental Committee on Corporal Punishment*, 1938, recommended the abolition of this penalty for both juveniles and adults, and in fact it came to an end with the Criminal Justice Act, 1948. It is retained in England (but not in Scotland) for male prisoners guilty of serious violence against a prison officer, although the 'cat-o'-nine tails' may not be used for the purpose on those under twenty-one. It is not permitted in detention centres, or borstals, but it is used to a limited extent in approved schools and remand homes. To all intents and purposes, however, torture by flagellation, once the most frequently used and highly regarded of English penal treatments, and stoutly defended by judges as a necessity for the protection of society, has now passed into disuse, and this in spite of an important and vocal section of public opinion still in favour of it. Flogging always had serious practical disadvantages. The tough young thug, well used to personal violence, was probably made still tougher and more determined to retaliate. More timid types, who might have been put off by it (the middle-aged shop-lifters for instance), were rarely considered suitable subjects. This leaves committal to a detention centre as the most overtly punitive of the measures open to the courts for most young offenders.

Non-custodial sentences

Attendance centres form a less important part of the penal establishments [161]. They also came into being with the Criminal

Justice Act, 1948. They are usually run by the police and serve offenders aged ten up to twenty-one, who are required to attend for hourly or two-hourly periods up to a maximum of twenty-four hours, during what would normally be their free time, usually Saturday afternoons. This punishment can be combined with probation or a fine if more than one offence has been committed, and it can be given for failure to comply with the requirements of probation. It is not meant for the more serious delinquents, and those previously sentenced to penal custody are not eligible. The régime consists of inspection for tidy appearance, P.T., 'chores' and instruction in carpentry or other useful skills.

Apart from attendance centres, the non-custodial measures for young offenders are much the same as for adults, namely, police cautions, conditional or absolute discharges, fines and probation orders. In the case of children the maximum fine is £10, or £50 for young persons under seventeen. It is the parent who must pay a child's fine, and a parent may be ordered to pay a young person's fine. Probation orders place the offender under supervision for a period of up to three years, during which he must comply with the requirement to report to, and receive visits from, the officer as directed, to lead a regular and industrious life, and to abide by any additional special requirements that may be written into the order, such as residing with a particular relative, staying at a special hostel for probationers, or undergoing psychiatric treatment. A breach of the requirements renders him liable to sentencing for the original offence, or he may be fined or sent to an attendance centre while the probation supervision continues. As with adults, a further conviction while on probation renders him liable to two separate sentences, one for the original offence, another for the latest offence. Since probation is technically non-punitive, with a possible sentence in abeyance, it cannot be combined with other penal measures. In respect of any one conviction, the offender who has paid a fine or gone to a detention centre cannot then have the benefit of probation. Those given probation or a conditional discharge can be ordered to pay for damages or compensation to victims.

Except in the case of certain serious crimes which must be

reported to the Director of Public Prosecutions, the English police exercise a discretion whether to bring an offender to court, or to dispose of the matter with an informal or formal caution, the latter being entered in their records. Something like a quarter of a million formal cautions are administered annually to traffic offenders. Formal cautioning is also very commonly used with juveniles, especially younger juveniles and first offenders, but practice varies from one police district to another, some forces hardly using the procedure at all, others applying it to nearly half the children apprehended.

In some areas, of which Liverpool is perhaps the best known, a system of police juvenile liaison has developed, whereby, with the consent of their parents, juvenile offenders who have been cautioned are subsequently visited in their homes by plain-clothes policemen, who talk to their parents, inquire after their welfare, and issue authoritative advice and warnings, after the manner of some probation officers. The police also attempt prevention, by visiting and advising children who have not got so far as to commit crimes under circumstances in which they could be convicted, but who are known to them for truancy, disorderly behaviour or keeping bad company. Judging by the low re-conviction rates of juveniles who have committed indictable offences but have been dealt with by the liaison officers, the scheme seems to have had a good effect. However, professional social workers tend to criticize the encroachment of amateurs on to their domain, and some legal authorities feel the system usurps the decision-making powers of the courts. The important issue is whether it really works, not whether a few sensitive toes may be stepped upon in the process [175].

The annual criminal statistics for England and Wales give data on the use made by the courts of the different sentences or orders available. In 1965, 25, 37 and 39 thousand persons were found guilty by magistrates courts of indictable offences in the age ranges ten to thirteen, fourteen to sixteen, and seventeen to twenty respectively. Taking the age groups in this order, fines were given to 18.5 per cent, 31.6 per cent and 53.5 per cent of offenders, probation to 33.3 per cent, 29.2 per cent and 17.4 per cent, and some form of detention to 5.4 per cent, 9.0 per cent and 10.0 per cent [128]. The increasing use of detention and of fines, and the decreasing use of probation continue after the age of twenty-one. For non-indictable offences, the great majority, in all age ranges, were fined.

Courts for the young

Special features of juvenile courts

Save in exceptional circumstances (as when a juvenile has been involved together with an adult in committing an offence) all persons under seventeen are tried summarily in special magistrates' courts for juveniles. At these courts, the magistrates, who must include both a man and a woman at every session, are supposed to be specially qualified for dealing with children. The convictions and sentences they record are officially known as 'findings of guilt' and 'court orders', which technically do not rank the same as criminal convictions. Unlike the ordinary courts, they have a statutory duty, when making decisions, to have regard to the welfare of the offender and when necessary to take steps to remove him from undesirable surroundings and secure a proper education and training, and they are obliged to obtain reports on the social background of the offender. These are usually furnished by the probation officers or by representatives of the local authority children's department, and by the child's school. The juvenile courts can postpone their decision, following a finding of guilt, and in the meantime send the offender for a few weeks to a remand home, where he is kept in custody and under observation while social reports on his background and behaviour (and also psychiatric reports, if requested) are being prepared. Although theoretically not intended as punishment, a belief in the salutary effect of a short spell in a remand home may not be without influence when magistrates decide upon this course in preference to obtaining reports from probation officers or clinics while the child is at liberty. On the other hand, it must in fairness be pointed out that remand homes are geared to producing psychological and medical reports for courts, when these are needed, more swiftly and efficiently than most outside clinics. Incidentally, the police use remand homes in place of station cells when they do not think it wise to allow a juvenile to go home after he has been apprehended.

The juvenile courts are meant to be welfare agencies as well as dispensers of punishment, and they do in fact take into account a great deal more than just the nature of the offence that has brought a child before them. However, the most casual scrutiny of their decisions suffices to show that tariff justice remains a most potent consideration, so that trivial first offences usually lead to a fine or discharge, and subsequent or more serious offences to probation or custody. Presumably anything departing too far from this routine would shock the sense of justice of parent, child and magistrate alike.

In the juvenile courts certain rules that have to be followed in adult courts are waived. For example, although press representatives have to be allowed in, members of the public are not permitted to attend as casual observers, and the juvenile must not be identified by name in any report that may be published. The proceedings are meant to be relatively informal, but they vary a great deal in practice: anything can happen, from a confidential exchange of whispers between the child and the magistrate to a sternly formal session with child and parents stiffly at attention. The magistrates have the power to order a parent to attend with the child if they think it necessary. The child's rights to question witnesses and so forth have to be explained to him in suitable language, and his parents must be allowed to help him with his defence. In practice, juveniles are rarely legally represented in court, and a prosecution case is not often effectively challenged, so that occasionally technically innocent youngsters, especially if they are wearing the disapproved clothes of contemporary adolescent protest, risk being penalized for being at the scene of trouble when the police arrived [15]. Any attempt to make the proceedings more sophisticated or judicial, however, would be completely lost upon the majority of the delinquents. In the present writer's experience of examining many boys after their appearance in a juvenile court, few had remained calm enough to understand properly what was happening, and most were concerned only with whether they had 'got away with' probation or were to be 'sent away' [233].

The 'care, protection or control' process

Apart from hearing charges against children aged ten years or over, the juvenile courts also have to deal with children of any age who are 'in need of care, protection or control' or who are persistent truants from school. Such hearings are technically civil rather than criminal trials, and they may occur in a variety of circumstances. For instance, if it comes to the attention of the authorities (i.e. police or children's department) that a child is neglected or starving or cruelly treated or sleeping out, perhaps because a parent is alcoholic, in prison, a mental patient, a prostitute, or simply feckless and uninterested, then he may be brought to court as in need of more care and protection than his parents are providing. The parents themselves may have complained to the children's officer that their child is unruly, or sexually promiscuous or pregnant, and that they can no longer maintain proper control. A juvenile, even though not actually charged with an offence, may also be brought before the court because he or she has been involved in sexual irregularities, drunkenness, drug-taking, begging, gambling or other undesirable pursuits. The court has power to make a Fit Person Order, or an approved school committal, in all such cases. The distinction between official delinquents and children brought to court as being in need of care, protection or control is often more theoretical than practical.

In some countries the distinction between child offenders and children in need of care is not attempted, and all juvenile problem behaviour is dealt with by welfare or education departments instead of by courts of law, in which case the age of criminal responsibility and liability to criminal prosecution is not reached until around school-leaving age. This has been the accepted system in Scandinavian countries since the turn of the century [222]. Neglected, maltreated and badly behaved juveniles who cannot be handled by parents and teachers are dealt with by municipal welfare councils with power to remove a child from home and commit to foster homes or special institutions. The final outcome, therefore, is the same, the essential difference being that the decisions are taken by welfare agencies and social workers rather than by courts of law, so that the emphasis is presumably more upon dealing with a family situation and less upon fitting the punishment to the crime. The usual arguments against this type of system centre upon the risk of giving such powers to administrators, who are not subject to the same degree of public scrutiny or traditions of justice as the magistrates, and the inadvisability of contaminating the benign image of welfare workers by making them wield the big stick. Neither argument seems very cogent. It is a matter of opinion who is best qualified to make these decisions. Until a few years ago, doctors could not make compulsory admissions to mental hospitals without a magistrate's authority, but the removal of that protection hasn't led to any disaster. Probation officers have always had authority behind them, since non-cooperation on the part of their clients is a breach of the court's order, but they are not less successful than other social workers at dealing with delinquents. More to the point is the observation that juvenile courts deal with vast numbers of infractions of the law – such as travelling on buses and trains without tickets, riding bicycles without lights, pinching fruit off trees, behaving noisily in public places – which are not necessarily indicative of any need for social welfare, but are probably most effectively checked by sharp reminders, small fines, and the payment of the costs of damage [31].

Proposals for family councils and family courts

It has been proposed to introduce a Scandinavian-type system in England. In August 1965 the Home Office published the government's proposals for setting up family councils to replace the juvenile courts [131]. These would be recruited from social workers and others experienced in family problems, and they would be given similar resources for sending delinquents to detention centres or approved schools, and for arranging supervision, observation in a remand home, or the payment of compensation for damage; but they would have power to act only with the parents' concurrence. Some of the institutions would undergo transformation, at least in name, the remand homes becoming observation centres, and all the approved schools being taken over by local authorities and run in conjunction with their other residential schools for maladjusted and homeless children. The family councils would have no power to impose fines, although that relatively harmless method of expressing official disapproval has long been used by the courts in some two fifths of juvenile cases. The task of supervising young delinquents, hitherto performed by the probation officers working with juvenile courts, would be taken over by officers of the local authority children's departments. These officers, who are busy providing care and foster placements for orphans, illegitimate babies and for the children of sick or neglectful parents, might find it difficult to cope with a large influx of rebellious delinquents.

In the minority of cases where the facts of the offence are likely to be disputed by child or parent, or if the parent cannot agree with the measures proposed by the family council, the case would be referred for adjudication to a family court. One of the purposes of the family council would be to enlist the cooperation of parents in discussing how best to deal with the children, but it is uncertain how many parents would try to fight the social workers by appealing to the court. These proposals virtually abolish the distinction between children in need of care and children who commit crimes. The family councils would use the same administrative mechanism for dealing with neglected, truanting, troublesome and delinquent children. While this may be helpful in removing the stigma of a criminal record, it remains to be seen how far it will affect the keeping of statistics of juvenile crime. A stroke of the administrator's pen could abolish juvenile offences along with the juvenile courts, and, while that might look good on paper, it would hamper study and research on juvenile delinquency.

The proposed family councils and courts would cope with children up to the age of sixteen. From sixteen up to the twenty-first birthday, offenders (except in the case of very serious charges, like murder, rape or robbery) would be dealt with by a specially constituted young offenders' court, which would be required, as are the juvenile courts at present, to have regard to the welfare of the offender, not merely to punish him for the crime. The approved schools for senior boys would be taken over by the Home Office and administered together with the borstals under the title of Youth Training Centres, where the offender would be sent for six months to two years, followed by a period of compulsory after-care during which he would be liable to recall 'if he were found to be conducting himself in a way which made this course desirable in his interests'.

The supporters of these new arrangements claim that they would make way for a more therapeutic approach to children than can reasonably be expected of a juvenile court modelled after the pattern of a criminal trial and sentence. For instance, it is argued that a family council's decisions would be more flexible and more easily modified in the light of a child's reactions, or in response to changed circumstances at home, than is the case when a court has pronounced an official order. However, it must be pointed out that a reshuffling of administrative responsibilities and a renaming of institutions do not in themselves meet the greatest need, which is for more skilled workers and increased facilities for treatment. Furthermore, many children who have committed minor public nuisances and are at present dealt with by judicial warnings and fines hardly need to be discussed and processed as if they were maladjusted, and might indeed be confused and resentful at this. The welfare role envisaged for the young offenders' court seems admirable in itself, but it leads one to question why all courts cannot be required to have regard to the welfare of the unfortunates who come before them. The proposals have stimulated so much adverse comment from persons working with delinquents that perhaps the government will have second thoughts.

Penal régimes

The punitive element

In the nineteenth century, harsh measures were thought the best means of reformation. Penal régimes were frankly and unashamedly made as disagreeable and degrading as possible, with the idea of frightening off potential malefactors, and making offenders think twice before reverting to crime and risking further punishment. Convict garb, enforced silence, separate confinement, the treadmill, and the lash were means to this end.

220 The Young Offender

Strict enforcement of all these measures was strongly advocated in the *Report of the Select Committee of the House of Lords on Prison Discipline*, 1863 [137], which laid down 'hard labour, hard fare and a hard bed' as the essential ingredients of discipline. In the present century this has ceased to be the official policy of English prisons. In a stirring speech in the House of Commons in 1910, Mr Winston Churchill stated: 'The mood and temper of the public with regard to the treatment of criminals is one of the most unfailing tests of the civilization of any country.' He went on to urge upon those in charge of criminals 'tireless efforts towards the discovery of curative and regenerative processes; unfailing faith that there is a treasure, if you can only find it, in the heart of every man'. A decade later, Alexander Paterson, one of H.M. Prison Commissioners, coined the phrase that an offender comes to prison 'as a punishment, not for punishment'. Since then, the declared aim has been the training and treatment of prisoners 'to establish in them the will to lead a good and useful life on discharge, and to fit them to do so' (Prison Rules).

How far this admirable ideal comes over in practice is open to question. Very unpleasant features still exist in many prisons, particularly in the old local prisons, where everything is cramped behind the constricting walls of grim Victorian fortresses that were meant for a population half the size of what exists today. Slopping out, tobacco rationing, prison dress, limitation and censorship of letters, restricted and supervised and even caged visits, mail-bag sewing, under-paid labour, discharge with un-stamped employment cards, are all justified officially as necessary evils of security or lack of facilities, but to the outsider, and more especially to the prisoners themselves, they seem more like a continuation of the age-old policy of degradation and punishment.

Moral conviction that transgressors ought to suffer, and anxiety that unless they are made to suffer for their crimes they will not be reformed limit the extent to which the public will tolerate improved conditions in penal institutions. In so far as delinquents come from poor homes, even quite low standards of institutional comfort may exceed their customary experience. In the *Minutes of Evidence before the Select Committee of the House of Lords on the Execution of the Criminal Law*, 1847, a

witness stated, with reference to the improved treatment of boys
in prisons:

> I am prepared to say that whenever a Boy goes into prison he can
> never come out, in point of Feeling, as the same Individual again. . . .
> In Nine Cases out of Ten, he finds his personal Comfort attended to
> much better there than at home; he finds the Prison clean and airy,
> and the Labour light, and he comes out with less Disinclination to go
> there again [124].

Another witness who came before the same Committee,
Reverend Whitworth Russell, a prison inspector with twelve
years' experience, gave a similar opinion on the ineffectiveness
of imprisonment for juveniles. He said: '. . . I am confident that
in the Great Majority of Cases the Juvenile Delinquent is
rendered much worse, and much more dangerous to Society, by
Imprisonment.' Asked about the great dread of being brought
back to prison (Question 684), he replied:

> Decidedly not, after they have been in it. I have visited Prisons when
> children have been brought in for the first time, and I have seen them
> overwhelmed with Fear and Distress, clinging with instinctive dread
> even to the Officer that brought them there; and I have seen those very
> children, three or four days afterwards, laughing and playing in the
> Prison Yard with the other Convicts, and I felt then that the Dread of
> a Prison was gone from those children for ever [124].

Similar considerations arise today. In the Bow Group pamphlet
Crime in the Sixties [43], the authors refer to the argument that
pampering criminals in prison leads to an increase of crime. The
argument has particular application to open prisons, where the
régime and the surroundings are comparatively pleasant. The
authors counteract it by suggesting that 'Open prisons should
only be used for those prisoners who would otherwise be likely
to return to crime. If they are successful in this, the community
has no cause for complaint'. The implication would seem to be
that transgressors who can be dealt with harshly without risk
to the community should be made to suffer.

Prisons

Certain basic facts about the régimes inside penal institutions,
such as the numbers, qualifications and earnings of the staff, the

rules enforced, the permitted range of punishments, the nature
of the food and the sleeping accommodation, can all be gleaned
from official publications, but these dry bones need something
extra to make up a living reality. The policy pronouncements of
government agencies about penal aims and methods are of
limited help, since they are usually couched in very general terms
and employ a euphemistic style and phraseology apt to mislead
the unsophisticated. The official statement [125], with reference
to prisons, that 'Methods of training have been progressively
extended and improved, notably in the application of psychiatry
and psychology . . .' is unassailably correct, but it leaves out the
information that provisions are still so limited that not more
than a tiny fraction of the potential clients can get help from
them.

Detailed, critical appraisals of penal régimes in England are
rather rare. One reason for this is that the people best informed,
namely those who run the institutions, are traditionally pre-
cluded from free discussion and comment because they are
government servants, and because their department's affairs are
widely believed to be somehow specially protected by the
Official Secrets Acts. Quite recently, the Home Office sanctioned
publication of part of a study by two sociologists [189] of the
régime at Pentonville Prison, London. A very depressing picture
emerged, with officers disillusioned and sceptical of the value
of any attempt to reform crooks, and the prisoners themselves
resentful of the soul-destroying monotony and humiliation, and
dominated by a spirit of mistrust and non-cooperation. A more
general account of the varying conditions inside English prisons
has been published by Hugh Klare [149], Secretary of the
Howard League for Penal Reform.

For various reasons, young persons under twenty-one have
been finding their way to prison in substantial numbers. However, when the provisions of the 1961 Criminal Justice Act, s.3.,
are brought into operation, only those given long sentences of
three years or more, or those re-convicted after a previous term
in borstal and sentenced to eighteen months or more, will be
received into the prisons. Hence, in future, prisons will be
receiving only the worst of the young recidivists, and those
who have committed the most serious crimes. The conditions

prevailing in prisons will not be particularly relevant to the generality of young offenders, except in so far as they illustrate the ambivalence of purpose underlying the approach to offenders of all ages.

Detention centres

Detention centres nowadays receive more young offenders than either approved schools or borstals. Although, as is true of any penal establishment, the majority of inmates of detention centres have been sent there for thieving, those committed for crimes of violence, traffic violations, and driving away other people's vehicles are found in considerably higher proportions than among the borstal population [130]. A sample of youths aged seventeen to twenty, inmates of detention centres, were studied and interviewed by the Oxford researchers, Dunlop and McCabe [52]. For most of these youths, the energetic, organized programme, starting at 6.15 a.m., with long periods of closely supervised hard work, and the enforcement of extreme orderliness and cleanliness, with frequent changing of clothes, showers, kit inspections, floor scrubbing, and parades, came as a new experience. Some affected indifference, like the boy who commented 'It's a lot of shouting, it can't hurt you . . .', but most of them expressed resentment at the physical hardship, the prohibition of smoking, and other restrictions. However, a large number seemed to become rapidly tolerant of the routine, and even to enjoy the exercise. Loss of liberty, however, was the one aspect of their punishment which they all felt acutely. In comparison with any delay in their date of release, all other disciplinary measures were felt as minor irritants. The existence of a system of promotion to higher grades for satisfactory work and obedience, although it involved extra privileges, had not much significance to the inmates apart from its influence upon the date of release.

The nature or number of previous convictions had little bearing upon the likelihood of a youth fitting into the routine and being regarded by the staff as a good trainee. Those with a facility for physical training were at some advantage, and so were some of those with previous experience of institutional life in children's homes or approved schools. Some of the youths committed for violence were amongst the most overtly obstreperous and defiant. However, a follow-up study produced no evidence for any connexion between satisfactory behaviour inside the detention centres and the likelihood of further convictions after release. Compliance with an enforced routine has little relevance to self-control in freedom.

Contrary to what might have been expected, the bitterness against the officers running the centres which was expressed by some inmates was not shared by the majority, who, in spite of a certain distrustful reserve, were prepared to concede that the staff behaved fairly. In spite of the limitation of free conversation between inmates to short set periods, and the patrolling of dormitories, the more important human contacts were between each other rather than between offenders and staff. The leadership of the more confident and aggressive, who were sometimes the most delinquent, was shown by the rapid assumption of criminal slang and verbal bravado by the previously unsophisticated. This contamination effect is likely to become increasingly damaging if all kinds and degrees of offender continue to be mixed up together in the same detention centre. Detention centres have been criticized as retrograde institutions, because the purpose is more obviously punitive than remedial. The things one intelligent ex-detainee recalled were being stripped of clothes and possessions, ordered about senselessly, set to scrub already clean floors, paraded in the snow, and made to shave with blunt blades. He summed it up as 'three months of blind obedience in digging holes, endless P.T. and continual unreasoning deprivation', and complained that the system merely exposed the power of the law without teaching the offender how to change himself in order not to get into trouble again [204].

Judged by the re-conviction rates of those passing through detention centres (more than a half re-convicted in the three years following release) the system is not particularly successful in deterring future criminality, but then neither are the approved schools and borstals, which give more prominence to reform by education, social training, and individual attention.

Borstals

The variety of régimes

The English borstals are difficult to describe because they are so varied. Some are run on sternly authoritarian, military-style discipline, others enjoy a comparatively relaxed atmosphere with a great deal of discussion between staff and inmates. Some are built in prison-fortress style and are closed 'security' institutions, others are wide open, with youths working in the surrounding fields or even going out to employment in the neighbourhood. In methods of discipline, in the organization of work and leisure activities, in the use of incentives and grades, and in the amount of personal attention paid to inmates as individuals, borstal governors and housemasters have considerable scope for initiative. Consequently, what happens in practice, and the impact of the experience upon inmates depend a great deal on the ideas and personality of those in charge. Unfortunately, these matters elude documentation, and the late Sir Lionel Fox summed it up justly when he wrote 'To find out what is going on in a borstal in any detail, the only safe plan is to go and see' [77].

In general, borstals lay great emphasis on training in habits of steady work, and on trying to arouse interest in a job. These aims are of course particularly appropriate to the large number of incompetent and work-shy youngsters with whom they have to deal. Everyone puts in a full day's work, and the tasks provided are useful and constructive, such as building, farming, carpentry and mechanics. Trade training courses, utilizing skilled instructors and impressive workshops, are given to those sufficiently able and conscientious to follow them. Athletics, team sports, camping expeditions and similar pursuits are special features in some borstals. Classroom teaching and coaching for illiterates are also provided. Social training takes place mostly through the natural interchange between youths and staff or instructors (who are often visitors from outside) in the course of their many practical activities. Inmates have to display some willingness and effort in order to earn promotion through the various grades and secure release more quickly. Some borstals pay more attention to personal and psychological factors, and staff are encouraged to have fairly intimate talks with the youngsters about their family problems, their worries for the future, and their attitudes to crime. A few establishments have group counselling, that is discussion sessions led by a staff member at which inmates are allowed to talk more or less freely about their personal problems or their feelings towards authority. On the whole, however, the borstal tradition is based upon the assumption that, given the right mixture of practical training and authoritative persuasion, the majority of normal youngsters will fall into line. When a more individual and exploratory approach is attempted, in order to find out why some people won't or can't fit in, then the staff have to face the inevitable conflict between condemning bad conduct and understanding it. As one governor is reported to have put it: 'The degree of honesty displayed by lads in their dealings with staff has produced several problems. . . . [We are] confronted with what appears to be self-condemning statements by lads. We have had to change our methods of evaluation . . .' [127].

Before admission to any particular borstal, the trainee spends some weeks at an allocation centre, where his background history and circumstances are reviewed, his behaviour watched, and where he receives psychological tests. Finally an allocation board considers all the information and decides to which institution to send him. The decision seems to be arrived at by a kind of intuitive consensus of opinion, with certain points of reference kept in mind [190]. Age and sex, of course, are prime determinants. After that, such things as interest in a particular trade, intellectual capacity (or lack of it), danger of absconding, advisability of being near to (or far away from) visiting relatives and religious affiliations may all be taken into account. More particularly, the allocation authorities try to envisage the most suitable social climate, whether, for instance, he needs 'a framework of support and "mothering" as opposed to a more rigorous, disciplined régime'. Certain borstals are meant to cater for the older and more sophisticated types, especially those whose attitudes have hardened against authority and who would be expected to be disruptive and contaminating influences in any institution run on democratic lines. Factors which limit choice also have to be faced, for instance whether there is an appropriate vacancy, whether the available range includes any régime likely to satisfy the needs of some difficult or exceptional youth, whether a particular borstal can handle any more problem cases than it has already got, or whether the need to separate an offender from his accomplices or fellow gang-members overrides other considerations.

Coping with the more difficult cases

Borstal staffs commonly complain of the ever-increasing proportion of feckless and hopeless types whom they are obliged to receive. A recent report by an allocation centre governor describes inadequate, insecure and unstable characters, with an increasing incidence of suicidal tendency and psychiatric referrals, who drift inevitably into trouble, yet remain cynical of advice and authority, and contemptuous of legal or moral restraints [127]. It may be true that young offenders today include more psychological misfits than when thieving was more a necessity and less an expression of personality. On the other hand, it could also be that a more sophisticated scrutiny of borstal inmates is bringing about a clearer recognition of their inadequacies. The more difficult types gravitate to the recall centres, which deal with those who have offended while out on licence, and those who, on account of absconding or misconduct, have to be removed from other borstals. The Home Office reports that about one third of the youths discharged from one of these centres in 1963 were homeless [127].

In the administration of borstals, the Prison Department cannot run too far ahead of popular opinion and parliamentary comment. The 1951 *Departmental Committee to Review Punishments in Prisons and Borstal Institutions* criticized the borstal policy of leniency, appeasement and soft treatment, and advocated a tightening of discipline.

What Roger Hood [134] has called the golden age of borstals has passed. At one time they admitted only the most promising and trustworthy cases, and all the rest went to prison. Consequently, the proportion re-convicted after release was small, and so was the number of abscondings. Now that the better types get probation, while the worst types get to borstal, success rates have dwindled, abscondings increased, and optimism about the effectiveness of reformative training on liberal lines has correspondingly decreased.

The attempt to treat a larger proportion of more difficult youths under open conditions means more chance to abscond; and by stealing vehicles to make a getaway, or by breaking into houses to find food and money, absconders provoke protests by local residents, and give the whole reformative system a bad public image. On the other hand, where security precautions and discipline by brute force are found necessary right up to the moment of discharge, this is a plain indication of the failure of the ideal of training the offender to fit him for life outside. The great difficulty is that a thorough-going application of individual treatment under ideal conditions demands more in time, attention, personal skill, tolerance of disturbance, and risk-taking than state institutions, under present-day conditions, are likely to provide. Unfortunately compromise solutions sometimes get the worst of both worlds. Forgoing harsh deterrents for the sake of a benign, but not particularly effective, paternalism may suffice for the more normal personalities, but is not likely to make much impression on seriously inadequate or psychopathic types.

In a recent follow-up of the after-careers of borstal inmates, Gibbens and Prince [88] remarked upon the lack of correspondence between performance in borstals and subsequent re-convictions. This was particularly noticeable among the previously institutionalized recidivists, who knew how to toe the line and keep out of disciplinary trouble while inside, but who quickly reverted to crime on release. Another group of outward conformists with bad subsequent records was made up of intelligent but markedly neurotic or unstable lads, who were able to conceal their problems while in the protected institution environment, but who soon broke down again outside. In spite of these exceptions, there does appear to be some connexion between behaviour outside and behaviour in borstal. A. G. Rose [223], in an analysis of the files of 500 borstal inmates, found that breaches of discipline, bad work habits, and poor progress in borstal training were associated with bad previous criminal and work records, and greater liability to subsequent re-conviction. He concluded that there was probably some continuing and therefore unchanged factor of personality manifesting itself in different ways in and outside the institutions.

Approved schools

The approved schools of England, perhaps soon to change their name and become a more integral part of the welfare services, are already more fully committed to an ideology of treatment than the institutions governed by the Prison Department. They have to deal with deprived children as well as official delinquents, and to receive many youngsters whose babyish ways and lack of social sense reflect the inadequacy of their home life. Their staffs are chosen for their experience in the control and education of difficult children. Like the borstals, they have the benefit of a system whereby the boys are observed for some weeks in a classifying school before being allocated to a particular institution. While personality and disciplinary needs feature in this allocation, limiting factors, such as religious attachments or the location of vacancies, also largely determine the choice of school. Educational retardation, and potential intelligence are also taken into account, and this is important since these children are still of an age to make up for lost time, although emotional turmoil or stubborn resistance often bars the way. The classifying schools also undertake interviews with parents and inquiry into home backgrounds, so that by the time a headmaster receives the boy he is accompanied by a bulky dossier setting out his life history, present circumstances, and outstanding personality problems. Incidentally, these descriptions are interpretative as well as factual. Examples have been published by the Home Office [92]. In one of these, a boy's defensive distrust and lying was traced to resentment against an uninterested step-father and a hostile, critical mother. Such evaluations provide a useful basis from which the approved school staff can get to know their charges, but sometimes an interpretation, once on record, may be echoed uncritically by teachers and social workers ever after.

Even more than at borstals, the heads of approved schools set the tone of their establishments, and determine the relative emphasis on deportment, obedience, scholastic instruction, constructive hobbies, vocational training, athletics, contact with parents, staff conferences, psychological interpretations, and the attention given to advice from a visiting psychiatrist. The minority of schools run by local authorities, which must heed public opinion and avoid scandal or adverse publicity at all costs, are likely to select more conservative and authoritarian heads for safety's sake. Individualistic and pioneering heads are more likely to be found for schools managed by philanthropic organizations, especially if the managers include persons professionally interested in psychology or child guidance [142].

As in all institutions for offenders, a certain conflict exists between staff members committed to understanding, tolerating, and sympathizing with the deprived children, and staff members of the older tradition who prefer to stamp out bad behaviour by force, and who have little sympathy with the poor standards revealed by children of the feckless lower classes. However it is handled, the approved schools' task is an exacting one. P. D. Scott [234], in a recent review, described the grossly disordered homes from which the majority of the children have come. In his sample, seventy-seven per cent had parents who were seriously anti-social or alcoholic or markedly hostile to each other, or grossly inconsistent in the disciplining of their offspring, and these features were often associated with a history of illegitimacy and of periods with foster parents or under the care of a local authority. In these cases, little support is to be expected from the parents, either during the child's stay at school or subsequently. Should some misfortune befall an inmate, however, such parents are the first to complain vociferously in their urge to displace blame on to the school authorities. The pressure of watchfully hostile parents, press, and public can dampen reforming zeal and discourage innovation.

Cause and moral responsibility are different categories. An Institute and Chair of Criminology have recently been established in this University. It would not, I feel sure, occur to any of those engaged in investigating the causes of crime to suppose that this committed them to a denial of the moral responsibility of the criminal.

E. H. Carr, *What is History?* (The G. M. Trevelyan Lectures, Cambridge, 1961). Penguin Books (1964).

For my own part I can see no real objection to an approach to criminal behaviour which treats this as an evil thing to be eradicated by the methods that experience suggests to be most effective, and which asks no questions as to the degree of responsibility of the offender for what he has done. . . .

Barbara Wootton, *Contemporary Trends in Crime and its Treatment* (The Nineteenth Clarke Hall Lecture, 1959). London.

Protection, detection and deterrence

The variety of controls

Different ways and means of preventing delinquency or of treating established delinquents are suggested by different criminological theories. By and large, the sociological school of thought, represented by such writers as Albert Cohen, favour social reforms in preference to attempts to rectify the supposed character defects of individual delinquents. If delinquents act as they do in fulfilment of a recognized role, which is sufficiently accepted in certain sectors of society to enhance their standing among their peers, as well as to bring monetary rewards otherwise impossible for members of their class to achieve, the answer would seem to lie in reforms aimed at a more egalitarian distribution of opportunity, and a general increase in legitimate means of gratification and advancement, so that the delinquent way of life loses its attractiveness and status. On the other hand, if delinquency is conceived as a blind hitting out at society on the part of individuals who have never learned to control their primitive emotions, attention to the mental health of the community and special provisions for children deprived of normal parental care would seem to be the best approach.

In real life, the situations leading to delinquency are so complex that many different lines of attack have to be tried. While one should be able to learn something from the outcome of preventive efforts, evaluation is difficult, since any one intervention is but a drop in the ocean in relation to the total situation. However, in human affairs one has often to act in advance of scientific knowledge, and attempts to combat the delinquency problem cannot wait upon the resolution of academic controversies or the uncertain results of long-term research. Although satisfactory scientific proof may be lacking, this does not necessarily mean that no practical benefits have been derived. For example, it is a reasonable, though unprovable, assumption that relief of poverty has reduced certain kinds of theft; but even if it had not had that effect, it would have been a worthwhile social measure for many other reasons.

Early social theorists, such as Bentham and Beccaria, fastened their attention upon the legal system as the most obvious force within society guiding and controlling the range of permissible behaviour. In his influential essay *Dei Delitti e delle pene*, first published in 1764, the Marchese de Beccaria argued that social conformity would be increased if punishments were made to fit the crime, that is to say of a severity proportionate to the harm done, instead of reflecting the capriciousness of judges or the social status of the offender. He thought that too harsh a punishment for lesser crimes impaired deterrence, since nothing worse was left in reserve for dealing with the more serious crimes. All that was necessary was a punishment just sufficiently severe for it to be not worth while taking the risk for the sake of the gains ensuing from the crime in question. His ideas never had any basis in factual observation, and after nearly two centuries of tariff justice in place of arbitrary punishment crime is still with us.

Some theorists have over-emphasized the part played by the criminal law in preventing delinquency. It needs pointing out that pressure of public opinion and the general expectations of a community regarding the behaviour of its members exert a powerful controlling force. In small primitive communities lacking a formal legal code, such pressure has often sufficed to preserve a quite rigid code of behaviour, and in our own society there remain large areas of conduct which seem not to require penal sanctions. For example, in the more highly developed countries, it has lately become such a matter of shame to fall below a given standard of personal hygiene that to appear in the streets in smelling rags is a sure sign of madness or intoxication. In other areas, although legal sanctions exist in the background, the function of law seems less a matter of prescribing punishments than formulating an agreed standard for the guidance of the community. This applies to a host of welfare regulations, such as restrictions on the employment of children, compulsory insurance, control of cleanliness in selling food, and safety measures in factories. Although all these things once gave rise to bitter political controversy, for the most part reminders and inspections serve to maintain conformity, without resort to prosecutions. The existence of a delinquency problem implies a failure of the normal processes of social control, and efforts to strengthen these controls should take priority over measures for dealing with individual law-breakers.

Protective and restrictive measures

Many measures are taken to render crimes more difficult to commit, and thereby to reduce the temptation to succumb on impulse. The use of locks and bolts, safes, burglar alarms, and street lighting, and of course the patrolling policeman, are well accepted customs. Other protective devices work more indirectly. Accountancy and banking systems discourage frauds, elaborate methods of printing bank-notes prevent easy forgery, the age and test qualifications required of drivers reduce traffic crimes due to ignorance and incompetence, control of the sale of firearms and poisons reduces impulsive murders, car registrations, passports and identity cards hinder secret journeys and impede the escape of known criminals, while the banning of young people from drinking bars and the high tax on alcohol doubtless prevents some disorderly behaviour.

Some measures work on the principle of encouraging constructive social habits. The no-claim bonus scheme in car insurance rewards the safe and presumably law-abiding drivers. Compulsory weekly deductions from wages for unemployment and pension benefits protect the thriftless from periods of destitution and severe temptation.

In practice, these protective devices could be indefinitely extended, although every extension involves a certain amount of expense and inconvenience. Academics, at least, would hardly support the construction of iron grilles to guard booksellers' shelves against shop-lifters; but many might favour a plan to penalize motorists who carelessly leave an ignition key in their parked car. The central agency which checks a shopper's credit-worthiness when he wants to buy something on hire purchase is a device which not only protects the store, but also protects the improvident from their own weakness, and indirectly reduces the risk of debts and frauds. Another helpful system practised in some countries is the use of token discs in place of ready currency in public telephones or gas meters.

Many conceivable methods of protection are objectionable because they infringe civil liberties, or have other undesirable consequences. Abolition of immigration might be advocated as a means of eradicating one of the social situations leading to crime, but many people would think such a measure too drastic to be justified on these grounds. Limitation of the number of children which parents with low income may be allowed to retain could be enforced by compulsory abortions or adoptions, but the ethics of such action would be open to question.

Many possible methods of protection would be impracticable in a democratic society. Prohibition of the sale of alcohol in the United States proved virtually unenforceable owing to lack of public support. Likewise, the use of doctors and medical records to check on law-breaking is open to criticism. Most patients believe they can safely tell criminal secrets to doctors, and indeed it is often essential they should do so in such matters as abortion, venereal disease, and injuries due to personal violence, to say nothing of psychiatric conditions, in which all causes for worry or stress have to be explored. In law, though not in present custom, information concerning felonies must be reported to the police. If this was really enforced, many people might die or remain sick or infectious for fear of confiding in doctors. Such consequences could hardly be justified for the sake of exposing and punishing guilty patients and their associates. Another questionable method of protection is telephone tapping and the interception of mail, which is considered by many people too heavy a price to pay for the sake of trapping criminal conspirators. With the use of computers for searching out a particular individual, a national register of fingerprints might become practicable, although, judging by the resistance of the English public to the use of identity cards, it might not be a popular measure. Probably more people would support a proposal to amalgamate the registers of a person's birth, marriages and death, which would at least discourage bigamy.

Countries differ greatly in the extent to which they enlist the active cooperation of the public in the apprehension and punishment of offenders. Although in England and America the public have a duty to report crimes, people often prefer to look the other way for fear of becoming embroiled in inconvenient legal proceedings, and it is only in times of national crisis that citizens band together to form special police or militia units to protect law and order. In some countries, however, these arrangements are commonplace. In the Soviet Union, employees elect their own comrades' courts, which have powers to control the conduct of members of their group. These courts issue reprimands, levy fines, or request a man's demotion; furthermore, they can consider matters affecting socialist morality, even though the undesirable behaviour in question does not amount to a formal breach of the law.

Punitive deterrents

Deterrence is a topic much discussed in criminological and legal texts. It is held to operate in two ways: by teaching the caught offender that it will not pay him to offend again, and by warning off the potential offender with an example of what may happen to him if he breaks the law. Other aspects receive less attention: but the need to reinforce public morals by the proclamation of legal sanctions, the need to allow aggrieved victims to feel that their hurt has been avenged, and the need to incapacitate the worst offenders by eliminating them from society are also mentioned occasionally. Deterrence is still the chief function the judges have in mind when passing sentence.

Closely allied to the philosophy of deterrence, and equally dear to the legal mind, is the concept of criminal responsibility. This means, in effect, that any sane person should be held accountable for his own misconduct and should receive his just deserts. Once admit the idea of adjusting the punishment on utilitarian grounds, and some people will get away with too mild a punishment, and others will get too much, not for what they have actually done, but perhaps for what some psychiatrist thinks they might do in future, unless they receive appropriate 'treatment'. Curiously enough, many lawyers are content to forgo this principle in the case of juveniles and see little harm in adjusting sentences to fit the needs of the particular child, but are loath to allow the same flexibility in the case of adults. The

classical lawyer's viewpoint considers that society's best protection lies in a predictable scale of deterrents based upon the
nature of the offence and the penalty attached to it in the legal
code.

Hardly any scientific evidence is available on the effectiveness
of punitive deterrents, and discussions on the topic tend to be
abstractly philosophical and over-simplified, as if all forms of
delinquency were similarly motivated and could be similarly
controlled. The effect of punishment on the after-careers of
caught offenders might be studied by comparing groups who
have had light sentences and harsh sentences for similar offences.
So far as I know, this has not been done, but even in the unlikely
event that it could be established that some optimum level of
fine or length of imprisonment was associated with significantly
fewer re-convictions, this would tell one nothing about the
general deterrent effect. What is needed to deter an individual
from repeating his offence is unlikely to be the same as what is
needed to deter potential imitators. Exemplary sentences of long
imprisonment may be effective as a general deterrent, while
actually making the individual punished worse than before, by
unfitting him for life in freedom after release. Furthermore,
public sentiment will not now permit violent deterrents, such as
public hangings, or flogging, even if they could be proved
effective. Democratic countries have no wish to imitate the
systems of harsh, judicial coercion characteristic of dictatorships,
even though history has shown that whole populations can be
cowed into conformity by such means. Very likely, as Barbara
Wootton has suggested, some petty offences, such as wrongful
parking, in which the offender has little emotional or financial
involvement, might be reduced by increased severity of punishment. In Scandinavian countries, where driving after drinking
carries with it an automatic prison sentence, people are in fact
much more careful not to go by car to drinking parties than they
are in England or the United States, and the existence of this
legal penalty has probably contributed to their restraint. But
some difficulty arises in dealing with the more serious offences if
the big guns have already been brought out to deal with more
trivial matters. And anyway, where the stakes are high, or the
need sufficiently pressing, people will risk the most extreme

punishments. It is said that in the days when pickpockets were publicly hanged other pickpockets used to attend the executions and ply their trade among the watching crowds.

The risk of being found out

Possibly the potential offender's estimate of the risk of being caught acts as a more powerful deterrent than the severity of the punishment involved. Some work done in England by the Government Social Survey, questioning young people about their attitudes to delinquency, their own misconduct, and their anxieties about being caught and punished, seems to suggest that the unpleasantness of appearing publicly in court and the adverse reactions anticipated from family and friends loom larger in the minds of the young than the actual penalties likely to be imposed upon them.

Evidence exists that changing the likelihood of detection affects the incidence of law-breaking. Increases in crime due to reduced police supervision in times of crisis have already been commented upon.* An amusing example has been quoted by Professor J. Andenaes [8] in which a known increase in risk of detection served to deter young offenders from driving away other people's cars. At the time of the 1956 Suez petrol crisis, the Swedish government placed restrictions on the driving of private cars at weekends. This greatly increased the risk of drivers being stopped and questioned at these times. The result was a dramatic decrease in car-theft at weekends. Professor Andenaes drew the moral that 'even such a youthful and unstable group as automobile thieves react to an increase of risks when the increase is tangible enough'.

Organized, professional criminals are said to weigh up carefully the risks involved, and to avoid certain types of offence, such as shooting bank employees, because the penalties are too heavy [76]. However, such rational restraints hardly apply to impulsive crimes of violence committed in the heat of passion. In England, most murders are family affairs, and the majority of those who kill a member of their family kill themselves at the same time, so it hardly looks as if the prospect of penal sanctions has much

* See p. 52.

effect in those cases. On the other hand, the activities of young thugs are influenced by the mores of the criminal sub-culture. In England this sub-culture does not generally tolerate murderous violence, and it could be that the older, professional criminals, who have been rationally deterred from carrying firearms, may have helped to set the tone in this respect.

Welfare

Crime prevention may also be sought by more positive social measures, intended to relieve people of the necessity to obtain their ends illegitimately. A classic example is National Assistance and old-age pensions, which should remove the need for anyone to steal to eat. This represents but one of a host of sensible welfare measures which operate on the general principle of attacking the social evils which provoke offences. Such schemes have a long history, and in a changing and developing society the scope for them is constantly enlarging. In the nineteenth century, the realization that intolerable physical conditions of filth, pestilence and overcrowding provided breeding grounds for immorality and crime led to the establishment of state-financed systems of public health, sanitation and housing for the poor. In England, reformers like Lord Shaftesbury and Edwin Chadwick, who sat together on the first Board of Health, brought moral fervour to bear on drains and refuse disposal. The latter's *Report on the Sanitary Condition of the Labouring Population*, 1842, by drawing attention to the degrading conditions of the urban poor, and the inevitable effects on the health and character of their children, gave considerable impetus to the social welfare movement [283].

In modern times, a multitude of services for promoting the health and wellbeing of children are taken for granted. All births have to be reported immediately, and in England local authorities are empowered to send health visitors to private homes to see that babies are being properly cared for. At a later stage, children come under the surveillance of schools, and school medical services. The children's departments of each local authority watch over the whole, providing residential homes and other services for children whose parents are prevented by illness or other circumstances from giving adequate care. They also have the power, subject to court orders, to remove children forcibly from parents considered cruel, immoral or inadequate. By recent legislation,* they are required to seek out and advise parents of children who appear to be at risk of becoming delinquent.

In addition to the services which see to it that the elementary physical and moral needs of children are being met in their homes, the school and youth services outside provide essential training in literacy, in technical knowledge, and in social skills, without which no young person can fit in successfully with the requirements of modern society. Parent-teacher associations, the youth employment service, Sunday schools, Scouts, youth clubs, organized sports, to say nothing of the commercial enterprises which supply young people with meeting places, hobbies, pop music, public entertainments, motor scooters and interesting clothes, all help to lessen the incidence of disgruntled misfits and unemployables, and to combat idleness and boredom, and hence presumably contribute something to the prevention and control of delinquency. Criminologists, of necessity, concentrate upon the failures, and upon measures for improvement, but it is easy to forget how much advance has already been accomplished in a short time, and how much worse the situation would be without the existing services.

Naturally, no amount of welfare will provide an insurance against all forms of delinquency. However, there is little fear of reaching the point where further extension of welfare would bring little return, for the amount invested is always restricted by economic, political and moral considerations. Aid to the improvident, and to the actual or potential delinquent, is still limited by the fear that too lavish a provision for the undeserving might lower the incentive for the average man to work hard and stay honest. The wish to prevent wrongdoers escaping punishment sometimes stands in the way of effective counter-measures against particular abuses. For instance, one might expect to decrease the incidence of blackmail by giving immunity from prosecution to victims prepared to collaborate with the police in producing evidence to convict the blackmailers; but that would mean that the victim's crimes (most often deviant sexual misconduct) would go unpunished. In England, addicts can be

* Children and Young Persons Act, 1963, s.1.

given controlled supplies of their drug by doctors, but in the
United States this is unlawful, and widely regarded as reprehensible, since it would mean allowing a forbidden gratification
without penalty. This situation not only forces American addicts
into worse crimes in their efforts to get money to pay the high
price of smuggled drugs, it also profits the illicit narcotic traders,
who are thus encouraged to push their drugs upon still more
young people, so that they become 'hooked' and swell the
numbers dependent upon the racketeers. The evils attendant
upon self-attempted or back-street criminal abortions could be
largely prevented if both girls and boys accepted, understood and
had ready access to contraceptives, and if abortions could be
performed lawfully in hospitals on social as well as medical
grounds. In some countries, such as Canada, the official attitude
finds either of these measures morally and legally intolerable. The
fact is that once one leaves the abstract question of cause and
examines the ramifications of crime prevention, one is immediately confronted by a host of unresolved social issues
affecting everyday habits and beliefs.

The more potent schemes of prevention, especially those which
involve intervention in the affairs of the adult community,
naturally arouse the most opposition. Another limiting factor
is the unfortunate side effect whereby more social action on one
front usually means less action in some other direction. If too
much money gets spent on education, there is less for pensions.
If too much attention is given to helping the lame ducks to
achieve a minimum standard of proficiency, there is risk of
neglecting to draw out the potential talents of the gifted minority
who might become valuable leaders and innovators.

Education

Improved teaching methods

Recent developments in prevention consist for the most part of
attempts to make the welfare services more effective. The basic
aims are to reduce the level of conflict and maladjustment in the
population at large, and to provide special attention or help for
those groups who, as a result of personal or economic handicaps,

are specially vulnerable to delinquent temptations. In conformity with the view that delinquency arises from a multiplicity of interacting factors, the attack has to be mounted along a wide front, but the schools are perhaps better situated than any other service to bring influence to bear upon young people.

In the deliberations of the United Nations Congress on the Prevention of Crime [264] the role of education was given special prominence. It was pointed out that all kinds of improvements in educational methods have relevance, since they help to draw a larger proportion of pupils into effective participation in school life, and hence to reduce the numbers of the discontented and potentially delinquent. For instance, the identification of children with obscure disabilities of perception which interfere with reading, and the development of techniques to overcome this successfully bring in some pupils previously considered ineducable. The fostering of a democratic classroom atmosphere, in which children are helped to assume a rational attitude to their own moral and social responsibilities, the use of television and other aids for enhancing the interest and impact of what is taught, and the adjustment of the curriculum to suit the interests and social circumstances of the children in particular areas: all these help in overcoming the apathy and antagonism of the more difficult and socially alienated pupils. Schools which put too exclusive an emphasis on traditional academic subjects, neglect practical and manual activities, and fail to use models, films, drawing and other non-verbal methods of communication, aggravate the inferiority of the socially deprived, whose handicaps are generally most severe in reading and verbal facility. An understanding of the sort of jobs people do in trade and in the community services is more helpful to the practical minded youngster than learning scraps of a foreign language. The use of teaching machines and programmed learning allows the retarded pupil to proceed at his own pace without public exposure of his mistakes. Home visits by teachers enlist the interest and co-operation of apathetic parents. The promotion of hobby groups and discussion groups, the organization of holiday camps with additional instruction, the recruitment of teachers with special experience in handling lower-class children, the provision of expert counsellors for helping the teaching staff to cope with problem cases and the provision of pre-school nurseries for preparing small children to take part in classes have all been tried [103]. In Stockholm a practical enterprise of special relevance to delinquency prevention is the system of instructing schoolchildren in the functions of the police so as to counteract prejudice against the forces of law and order. Policemen come into the schools to talk about their jobs, and visits to police stations are arranged.

Concentration on the poor risks

Many schemes concentrate upon the children from poorer homes, since they supply so many of the scholastic failures and official delinquents. Methods have been introduced to try to combat the generally low motivation, poor concentration and social ineptitude prevalent among these children. If left to their own devices, such children become a nuisance in class, arouse the teacher's antagonism, and gradually fall further and further behind both academically and socially [48]. These school misfits are apt to seek in truancy, and in the thrills of delinquency, some compensation for their inability to compete in more acceptable ways. Teachers are usually able to identify such trouble-makers more easily than they can do anything to improve them. Since they are so unattractive and uncouth, at least on middle-class standards, teachers have to guard against showing contempt or class prejudice. Being aware of their inferiority, these children are on the look-out for slights and insinuations, and anything of this sort alienates them still more.

Some of the most determined attacks on the problem have been made in the United States as part of the national campaign against poverty and racial discrimination. The poorer and more delinquent-prone segment of the American school population is glaringly obvious, since most of the children in question are of distinctive ethnic background, that is Negro, Puerto-Rican, Mexican – anything other than the dominant white, protestant group to which most middle-class Americans belong. It has been proved that the poor performance of these under-privileged children is partly the result of educators accepting the low standard as inevitable, and failing to draw out such potential as exists.

In New York, the 'Higher Horizons Program' set out to give a community of under-privileged and retarded schoolchildren a vigorous educational campaign, which included exposure to music and cultural activities, remedial coaching for individuals, and much proselytizing among parents. Ambition was aroused so that the children began to aim for vocational and scholastic goals previously regarded as unrealistic. The outcome was a phenomenal increase in the pupils' attainments. The demonstration that poorer children perform better if they are stimulated more, or placed among better-class children of higher standards has led to another New York enterprise, a drive to break down the segregation of the worst pupils in the worst schools. Children are collected by bus and transported to schools in other areas where the population is more mixed and they can have the benefit of being among more civilized class-mates [239].

Educating the community

Naturally there are severe limits to what such schemes can accomplish. However enlightening the school day, the children have to go back to their homes at the end of it, and if the contrast between what they have learned at school and what they experience at home is too great, that in itself can be a source of misery and conflict. Where racial and economic handicaps have deadened the interests, ambitions and morals of the parents, the home situation will always be a hindrance to a child's social and academic progress. Forcing such children into open competition with those from better backgrounds may sometimes produce so much stress that learning is worse blocked than before. An alternative scheme, also tried in New York, consists of all-day Neighbourhood Schools in which activities continue after the normal school hours, drawing in parents and others for meetings and discussions on local issues. In this way, the educational programme seeks to influence children, their parents, and the community, all at the same time.

Schemes for extending services from the schools into the community, for organizing leisure time, for help in finding jobs, and for bringing in parents, have also been tried. In New York, the Columbia School of Social Work is associated with one of the most ambitious programmes of this kind. It goes under the stirring title of Mobilization for Youth Incorporated. The 1965 synopsis lists experiments with over fifty different methods of approach. These include special teaching techniques for use with discouraged and undisciplined children, the provision of facilities and helpers to encourage the completion of homework, vacation schools using unconventional instructional materials, and non-punitive counsellors for tracking down and helping absentees from school. Other projects are concerned with extra-curricular instruction to improve employment prospects. Youngsters who have left school with no marketable skills are given aptitude tests and then introduced to schemes devised for coaching backward pupils in the specific tasks they might be called upon to carry out when they join offices or factories. One scheme goes so far as to set up actual work-places, repair garages, offices and so forth, where candidates can receive realistic training on the job. Another project concentrates on youngsters who have appeared before a juvenile court, arranging visits to their homes, and giving advice to their families on how to make the best use of the numerous social agencies available to them. Another project provides legal aid, teaching unsophisticated people how to exert their citizens' rights when in conflict with landlords, police, courts or welfare departments. Another organizes disgruntled young people into social action groups, diverting their attention from futile acts of rebellion to more constructive forms of democratic protests, such as forming committees, holding meetings, sending deputations to speak to officials, and producing pamphlets.

Capturing the audience

Bringing in the 'unclubbable' types

One of the greatest difficulties in operating schemes for delinquency prevention is that the boys who are most in need of help are hardest to reach. The wilder and more undisciplined boys are often uninterested in or ineligible for the clubs and activities arranged by voluntary and religious organizations, or else they are ousted from the clubs because they are too destructive or too great a nuisance. One trouble has been that official youth activities have perhaps tended to be rather too tame and over-organized to appeal to the dare-devil propensities of some of these youths. An effort to rectify this has been made in the Outward Bound courses which provide more adventurous expeditions and sports activities. At the same time, the Duke of Edinburgh Award scheme gives recognition to achievements in these activities, rewarding, for example, skills in rescue work. Numbers of boys from approved schools and borstals have been encouraged to join in these schemes, with promising results.

Unfortunately, a minority of socially inept and hostile youths is inevitably left out of any scheme which suits the normal youngster. Since it is from this hard core that recidivist delinquents are likely to be recruited, ways and means have been sought for making contact with them and trying to draw them into schemes for their social betterment. The social case-worker approach, based on the psychotherapeutic model, in which one waits for the client to give voice to his problem, simply doesn't work with youths who don't acknowledge that they have any personal problem, and who think that their troubles are all the fault of other people. More active or aggressive methods of approach have had to be used, and in effect some social workers have completely reversed their technique and become what amounts to missionaries trying to sell unpopular ideas to a resistant clientele.

In recent years so much has been reported along these lines that it is difficult to select any one example, but perhaps the activities of the Harvard team led by Ralph Schwitzgebel [231] will serve the purpose. He recruited clients by accosting likely-looking youths in the less pleasant parts of Boston and offering to pay them to come to his laboratory and talk into a tape-recorder. He was open with them about the general purpose, which was to help students of delinquency, although at first some of his clients thought that there must be more to it, and that they were actually being taken along for some dishonest or immoral purpose. He generally invited the youth to bring along a friend to look over the set-up, and gave them time to think over the proposition before deciding; a strategy opposite to that of the common con man, who tries to force an immediate commitment.

The talks into the recorder led gradually to the youths confiding in the researchers and participating in therapeutic discussions of their problems. At first they were encouraged to expound their own views on social questions, and to participate in philosophical discussions on delinquent conduct, before working round to a more personal angle. It was considered that having to reflect about such questions might in itself lead to more restraint in their behaviour.

The scheme depended upon continued regular attendance, and since the boys who took part were the sort who were unused to thinking ahead and keeping regular appointments they had to be trained in this by means of higher fees for prompt appearance, and by such powerful reminders as being collected by a large car with a pretty girl inside. They were also paid for carrying out practical tasks which were devised as a subtle and indirect means of controlling their conduct. For example, some of them were required to keep diagrammatic charts of their own behaviour, others were loaned cine-cameras for recording the activities of their gangs. In order to encourage the acquisition of driving licences, so that boys could borrow cars legitimately instead of stealing them, one of the tasks set and successfully completed was the revision and clarification of a driving instruction manual.

This particular programme of delinquency prevention included a follow-up of the subsequent convictions of the 'treated' group, and of a matched control group of similar delinquents who had not had the same attention. The numbers involved were small, but the experimenters calculated that the re-conviction rates of the boys taking part was significantly less than that of the control group, and also less than would be expected on the basis of the re-conviction rates of other samples of delinquents in Boston.

Street-corner research

The scheme just described concentrated on developing techniques for inveigling delinquents into attending what was in essence a slightly disguised treatment centre. Other workers have adopted the alternative strategy of going out to meet delinquents, and potential delinquents, on their own ground, making friends with them, even joining up with their gangs, in the hope that by infiltration from the inside they might subvert the influence of the more anti-social leaders, and persuade others into a frame of mind in which cooperation with social agencies becomes feasible. As the Roman Catholics found with their worker priests, social participation carries with it special dangers. Sometimes it becomes doubtful which side is doing the converting. If the 'detached worker', as he is called, becomes too much identified with the gang and its problems he may take their side against authority. Conflict may arise if the police come to feel that gangs are being stimulated and given added status by having a 'detached worker' allocated to them, or that the worker is forgetting his duty as a citizen when he fails to warn the police when he knows a crime is being planned, or that the worker is repeating damaging allegations about improper police methods.

Whatever may be the true extent of the detached workers' effect, or lack of effect, upon the incidence of delinquency, they have at least provided a rich source of descriptive material on life in the delinquent sub-culture. Mary Morse [191] has reported on a series of experiments in which young workers were sent out in different parts of England to try to make contact with young people who were not attached to any official youth organization, with a view to finding out how the existing facilities might be adapted to bring in these drifting isolates. Not all the groups studied were made up of potential delinquents, but one in particular, described as the Lymport coffee-bar youths, consisted mostly of delinquents who came from one of the poorer and drearier areas of the town. In that area, the police were treated with suspicion, even by adults, and certain offences, such as shop-lifting, were widely regarded as normal and justified. The young woman worker got to know the youths by dint of taking a job as a waitress in their favourite coffee bar. Although she did all she could to conceal her true purpose, she was regarded as an oddity, and was teased on account of her educated accent, and was even suspected by some of being a student observer, but in spite of all that she was sufficiently taken into their confidence to be able to make some astute comments on their attitudes and mode of life.

The group centred around a few popular and spirited young men who were unquestionably established delinquents. The loose collection of their friends and acquaintances who met in the coffee bar provided a source of ever-ready accomplices for planned house-breaking and similar activities. Most of them came from large, poor families, characterized by broken homes, marital infidelity, promiscuity and alcoholism. Once they had left school, their parents generally left them to get on with their own affairs, until such time as they provoked trouble with the police, when they would be threatened with being turned out of the house. Convictions, followed by incarceration in penal institutions, finally brought about the dissolution of the clique. Although some of these boys made occasional use of boxing or swimming facilities, formal attachments to youth clubs were avoided. Most of them claimed to see money-making as the chief goal of life, and they were both envious and suspicious of persons of substance. Their fantasies were of the get-rich-quick variety. Money was a perpetual problem, for though many were capable of earning high wages, this was offset by reckless drinking and spending at weekends, and in some cases by work-shyness or inability to stick at a job for any length of time. Indeed it was noticeable that in spite of high wages some youths got bored after their first few years experience of dead-end and uninteresting jobs, and joined the ranks of layabouts. At times the local pawn-shop housed most of their clothes. Drunkenness, bravado in the face of threatened imprisonment, and delinquent escapades were all part and parcel of their image of manhood.

Perhaps the most important lesson to come out of these studies was that the supposedly unreachable youngsters were in fact approachable given an initially uncritical, undemanding and sympathetic approach on the worker's part. The obvious short-coming of most youth organizations was in expecting too much of these young people too soon. No change is to be expected in morals or behaviour until a close and special contact has been built up with some responsible worker who can bridge the gap between disgruntled youth and uncomprehending authority. In the worst areas, such as Lymport, special clubs are needed if the unattached are to be catered for at all, for their behaviour would quickly ruin any normal club. A second point which emerged, none the less important for being trite and unexciting, was the need to tackle a constellation of social and personal factors simultaneously. The youth with a grievance based upon parental rejection or neglect was very likely also to be frustrated at work by the preferential treatment and apprenticeships awarded to those with a better education than himself. He was also likely to spend his leisure among those with similar problems and disillusionments, and so to have his anti-social attitudes continually reinforced.

Middle-class deviants

A further and rather more novel conclusion emerged as a result of studying a variety of groups and areas, namely that delinquent groups may show quite different kinds of social disturbance calling for different measures of prevention. Whereas the tribulations of the Lymport youths were exactly as described in all the texts on deprived delinquents, a more middle-class group of unattached young people, residing in the coastal resort of Seaport, presented a new set of backgrounds and problems. This group was studied by a young man who took a flat in the neighbourhood, patronized the coffee bar where they met, made friends with them, joined in their parties, and helped organize a drama group which became a focal meeting point. The members of this group came from relatively affluent homes, and their parents were mostly people who had made money and got ahead, at least economically, though not necessarily in social acceptance. The youngsters had commonly been to grammar schools or technical colleges. They were an unstable lot, with a poor showing in educational or vocational accomplishment. Although their aspirations were towards highly paid positions, such as actors or successful writers, they were incapable of sustained effort, and most of them had failed to get very far in the educational system and were drifting discontentedly and aimlessly from one job to another. It seemed that many had lacked warmth or consistent support from their preoccupied parents, and had become embittered by their failure to fulfil their own and their parents' ambitions for further social and educational advancement. Their unsettled and rebellious behaviour went beyond the limits of normal adolescence. They not only rejected parental injunctions and affected to despise the trappings of conventional respectability, they were contemptuous of other teenage groups as well. They hated the 'hearties', who offended by adopting conventional enthusiasms (the pipe-smoking young conservatives), and also the 'thicks', the tough working-class types of lesser education and cruder tastes. Their own preferences were for middle-class luxuries without middle-class effort. They liked to cadge lifts and favours, to use trains and visit cinemas without paying, and their favourite recreation was going to private teenage parties where sexual licence, rowdyism, heavy drinking, and sometimes illicit drugs, could all be indulged. They avoided youth clubs, which they considered dull and generally unsympathetic.

The companionship and mutual support of a group of fellow rebels and extremists helped to cover their individual insecurities and fear of commitment. Although some among them were officially convicted delinquents, this was less common than among the Lymport youths. Their illicit activities tended more towards getting away with something when the opportunity presented than to planning the old-fashioned crimes which so often lead to swift arrest. Under the influence of the social worker's prodding they succeeded in putting on a theatrical play, and this success, unexpected either by themselves or by their disillusioned parents, seemed to bolster their self-confidence and make them a little more amenable to normal society.

Evaluation of schemes for delinquency prevention

Helping potential delinquents

Social measures which impinge upon the whole community are very difficult to assess, because there can be no control group of untreated cases for comparison. If increasing welfare activity in the field of housing and education is followed by a decrease in juvenile delinquency, this is not necessarily a matter of cause and effect, since the statistics are subject to continuous and largely unexplained changes independent of any programme of prevention. However, where particular neighbourhoods are saturated with delinquency-prevention activities, as in the 67-block slum area of Manhattan covered by the Mobilization for Youth scheme, it should be possible in time to get a rough idea by comparing changes in the delinquency rates in the experimental area with changes in other similar neighbourhoods over the same period. But such evaluations will always be rather crude. For one thing, varying public interest and police activity affect the statistics, and this process may be considerably enhanced by the publicity attached to preventive programmes.

Programmes of treatment for individuals, which are directed at selected persons identified as potential delinquents, are in principle easier to evaluate, since there remains a body of un-treated cases for comparison. Since most such programmes have given disappointing results when subjected to statistical analysis, one must be clear that it is one particular type of prevention only that is being evaluated.

One of the best-known campaigns of this kind, which included a built-in system of evaluation, was the Cambridge–Somerville Youth Study.* Some 250 boys of average age eleven years, each one matched with a 'control' boy of similar age, social class, intelligence and high delinquency potential (as assessed impres-sionistically by teachers and social workers), were given the benefit of a fairly intensive and long-term programme of social treatment. Each boy was allotted a big brother or counsellor who was supposed to offer active advice and help. In point of fact, the counsellors succeeded in bringing most of the boys into contact with Scouts, Y.M.C.A., or other youth organizations, more than half of the boys received special scholastic tutoring, and a third had the benefit of direct counselling or psychotherapy for per-sonal problems. Owing to wartime disruptions and other causes, the programme was not as consistently intensive as had been intended originally, but it was certainly far more than would have been got routinely from the educational and welfare services, which was all that the 'control' boys received. When the results were analysed, comparing the delinquency records of both groups over the next seventeen years, it was found that the treated group had just as many convictions as the untreated group, and that both the numbers and types of crimes were similar in the two groups [164]. A further comparison, to see if

* See pp. 28, 71, 110, 161.

those who had had more frequent contacts with counsellors did any better, likewise yielded no significant difference, although a dozen boys who received very intensive treatment did rather better than a dozen carefully matched controls.

Disappointing results

The disappointing outcome of the Cambridge–Somerville project has been experienced in other studies also. Two American psychiatrists, E. F. Hodges and C. D. Tait [123], have published the results of a similar project, begun in 1954, centred on the Second Police Precinct in Washington, an area which at that time included about seven per cent of the population of the District of Columbia, while contributing about eighteen per cent of the recorded crimes and sixteen per cent of the juvenile court cases. It was in fact a slum area characterized by low income, overcrowding, and dilapidated housing. Children from two elementary schools in the area served as subjects; 179 were referred for help on account of difficult behaviour at school, and of these seventy-three were considered to be potential delinquents in need of treatment. Of these thirty-seven received treatment, while the other half were left untreated for comparison. The majority of both the treated and untreated groups consisted of Negro boys. The chief service received by the treated group consisted of social casework, under the guidance of psychoanalytically trained psychiatrists, to the extent of about a dozen interviews with each mother, and a dozen interviews with each child, spread over a period of one to two years in most cases. The treatment was unsolicited by the families concerned, and their failure to keep appointments was a main cause of irregularity in number and frequency of interviews. In the course of time, the parents became less cooperative or receptive to the social workers, and the parents of children who became delinquent were significantly less often cooperative than the rest. This resistance to treatment appeared to stem from the mothers' handicaps of poverty, hours of work outside the home and limited intelligence.

Followed up eight years later, sixty-nine per cent of the treated children and sixty-three per cent of the untreated children had become official delinquents. Further comparisons of the treated

and untreated groups on the basis of their delinquency potential
as assessed by the Glueck prediction system* suggested that, if
anything, the treatment group had started off in a slightly
favoured position, with a slightly smaller antecedent likelihood
of delinquency. This only served to emphasize the apparent
failure of the traditional treatment approach as a means of
preventing delinquency.†

Yet another study on similar lines with a similar result was
reported by some investigators working for the New York City
Youth Board [45]. They assembled two samples of potentially
delinquent schoolboys, each consisting of twenty-two boys,
matched for probability of delinquency on the Glueck system, as
well as for age, intelligence level, and ethnic group. Agreement
was reached with a child guidance clinic to undertake treatment
for all boys in the first of these samples, with a view to lessening
their delinquent tendencies. In fact, all but two of these treated
boys were in contact with the clinic for at least thirty months,
and two thirds for over four years. The other group of twenty-
two boys received no treatment. Some ten years later the
delinquency records of the two groups were compared, and
exactly the same number (ten) official delinquents were found in
both the treated and untreated groups. As the authors put it in a
mild under-statement, the result offered no encouragement for
the hope that child guidance therapy is effective in materially
reducing the incidence of delinquency among a population of
predisposed boys.

Another and larger-scale project was carried out with problem
pupils at a New York high school in an attempt to demonstrate
the effect of group discussions and individual counselling by the
skilled professional caseworkers of a Youth Counselling Service
in preventing delinquency and promoting social adjustment
among teenage girls [177]. Some four hundred pupils were identified as potential problems on the basis of previous school reports.
Such points as indiscipline in class, defiance, quarrelsomeness,
tempers, dishonesty, unexplained absences, failure to perform
up to the level of individual intelligence, moodiness and nervous
habits were taken as indications of potential disturbance. Between

* See p. 165.
† But see p. 285.

a quarter and a third of the girl-pupil population were considered potential problems. The selection must have been valid, since records collected over subsequent years showed that the group identified as potential problems were consistently poorer in performance and social adjustment than the rest of the girls.

The main experiment consisted in picking at random a half of the potential problem girls, submitting these to a special treatment programme by the Youth Counselling Service, and then following the progress of the treated and untreated groups. Progress was assessed in various ways, by academic performance and conduct marks; by teachers' reports of work traits and character; by histories of truancy, of leaving school without graduation, of illegitimate pregnancy, of contacts with police or courts; and by self-rating questionnaires of social attitudes. On none of these criteria did the treated group appear different from the untreated group to any significant degree. And yet the treated group had been exposed to all the traditional resources of the casework approach. Individual therapy was attempted with 125 girls. Of these, a small minority proved unapproachable, owing to parental refusal of visits, running away, or premature removal from school. About a half of the girls failed to develop any very close involvement in the treatment, although many of them were seen a dozen or more times by the caseworker. The parents of these girls were usually uninterested or antagonistic in the face of the Youth Service's attempts to help. They included some of the most disturbed cases from the worst backgrounds. The group treatment programme fared better in securing and maintaining eager participation. Generally, both clients and caseworkers felt that the discussions, which concentrated on the difficulties and uncertainties of adolescence, had been of benefit in fostering confidence and social maturity. Nevertheless, judged by concrete results, the whole programme of preventive treatment was sadly ineffective.

Reasons for failure

One is forced to conclude from these studies that the commonly accepted treatments of individuals are not very useful in preventing delinquency. The conclusion is highly unpalatable to

social caseworkers and child guidance therapists, whose minis-
trations are made to seem futile. It also seems to imply that
commonly held assumptions about the psychological determinants of delinquency, if not altogether mistaken, are of small value
in the development of practical remedies. However, at the risk
of appearing credulous, or of indulging in special pleading, it is
necessary to point out that psychological treatment is not being
given a fair trial unless it is firstly intensive and secondly
applied to properly selected cases. Psychoanalytic literature,
from which case-workers have taken their theoretical framework,
emphasizes that successful therapeutic effects generally occur
only after a long and intensive relationship between client and
analyst. It is on the special quality of this relationship, and its
power to affect all other relationships into which the patient may
enter, that psychoanalysis depends. Indeed it could hardly be
otherwise if the treatment is successfully to counteract habits
conditioned by a lifetime of past experience plus the continued
pressures of events outside the analytic hour. In practice, most
clinic psychotherapy and social work based on the analytic
model falls far short of this ideal; superficial contacts of thirty
minutes or less once a fortnight being much more typical than
the long and almost daily interviews associated with classic
psychoanalysis. This could be one reason for the ineffectiveness
of treatments as currently practised, but if so it is hard to see
what to do about it, except perhaps to concentrate attention on
a few at the expense of the many. Another and more promising
possibility is that the conventional psychological treatment
approach works with delinquents who have psychological disorders, but has a negligible or even harmful effect upon the
majority, whose behaviour represents a natural response to social
pressures. Finally, it could be that the individual approach
commonly fails because those in greatest need are unapproachable by traditional clinic methods. These suggestions are taken
up more fully in the next chapter which deals with treatments for
established delinquents.

I

11 The Treatment of Apprehended Delinquents

The possibility of analytic influence rests upon quite definite preconditions. . . . Where these are lacking – as in the case of children, of juvenile delinquents, and, as a rule, of impulsive criminals – something other than analysis must be employed. . . .

Sigmund Freud in a foreword to *Wayward Youth* by August Aichhorn (1925). (First English edition, Imago, 1951.)

We have no reason to consider the staff of the School Medical Service or of the Psychiatric Department of the hospitals or even the Child Guidance Clinic personnel so outstandingly successful in the treatment of young delinquents that we should all bow down in front of them in reverential awe!

J. B. Mays, *Sociological Review Monographs*, No. 9 (1965). Keele. p. 196.

From psychotherapy to therapeutic community

Resistance to traditional psychotherapy

Unlike the preventive social measures described in the last chapter, which apply to all and sundry, the attempt to treat apprehended delinquents rests on the assumption that they have something wrong with them, unless, of course, the word treatment is being used as a euphemism for detention in custody. In practice, most youngsters who get as far as being committed to approved schools do show signs of individual maladjustment, mostly in the form of some degree of anti-social or psychopathic distortion of character. The old-fashioned medicine for such bad characters is stiff, reformatory discipline; but psychoanalytic theories suggest that an opposite approach might be more effective.

Traditional psychoanalysis requires the client to ponder aloud upon his deepest feelings and motives, while the therapist prompts him if the flow stops or lapses into triviality. Now and then the therapist may interject challenging interpretations, but mostly the client has to work things out for himself, since self-realization is the essence of the process. This method, or modifications of it, was developed for the treatment of educated, middle-class anxiety neurotics. They cooperate readily, because their tensions impel them to unburden themselves, and they generally have an aptitude for introspection and verbalization. The typical delinquent character type seldom takes kindly to this procedure. By temperament and social background he is inclined to put his feelings into action rather than words, and to have little capacity for abstraction or introspection. Furthermore, on the surface at least, delinquent characters are often slap-happy, extraverted persons; their worries, if any, are not about themselves, but about externals, like what punishment they may get, or what injustices they have experienced. In classical psychoanalysis, the patient is told: 'The problem is in you, and you can solve it if you want.' If the patient doesn't turn up, or doesn't talk, that is 'resistance', a sign that he doesn't want to change. On this criterion, one would have to give up as untreatable the many delinquents who say: 'There's nothing wrong with me, I don't know why they sent me here.' This impasse goes a long way towards explaining the ineffectiveness of the efforts of clinics to change delinquents by traditional methods of individual psychotherapy. The old model doesn't fit, since the delinquent's conflict is with society not within himself, and the therapist's language and way of thinking are incomprehensible to him.

Reality therapy and group therapy

One way of adapting the treatment to suit the delinquent is for the therapist to become more active and directive, to confront the patient forcibly with the disasters his transgressions are likely to bring upon him, to hold up a metaphorical mirror to show him just where and how he goes off the rails. Schmideberg [227] has called this 'reality therapy'. Instead of waiting expectantly for the patient to work things out he is shown firmly, consistently and repeatedly the limits within which he must learn to live. Such treatment has something in common with plain old-fashioned moral training, except that the appeal is to the realities of the social situation rather than to an abstract religious ethic. In the hands of a skilled psychotherapist, who avoids personal recrimination or blame, and who understands the difficulty the delinquent finds learning to control his reactions, this can be a more powerful weapon than the conventional homily.

Another way to appeal to the delinquent's sense of realities is by conducting psychotherapy in a group setting: half a dozen or more patients meeting together with the therapist to discuss their life histories and problems. This technique, like psychoanalysis, developed as a method of treating neurotics, but it has a wider application. Some people are unable to look inwards and see themselves as others see them, but they can nevertheless observe and interpret other people's motives and behaviour quite astutely. In a therapeutic group they can see and learn from others with similar difficulties. Since they import into the group their own habitual patterns of reaction in social situations, they can also learn from the comments of their fellow members the sort of impact their behaviour produces. Clinical impressions suggest that the group experience makes a more vivid impression upon some delinquent characters than any amount of abstract discussion at individual interviews.

The therapeutic community

Daily life within a small community can be arranged like a therapeutic group, in which the participants can learn slowly, and profit from their mistakes, without too much harm to themselves or others. This is the ideal of the therapeutic community, and attempts have been made to organize reformatory institutions on this basis. Since the delinquent must learn through experience with other people, especially people of greater maturity than himself, his contacts with the staff of the institution have to be informal, and the general atmosphere needs to be friendly and intimate, in fact as close as possible to that of a healthy family, which is the natural setting for social learning. Too much regimentation, red tape, or the giving of peremptory orders merely strengthen the barrier of dislike and distrust with which the delinquent fends off the demands of authority; so the institution needs to be run on democratic lines, the inmates being given as much personal responsibility as they can cope with, being drawn into the process of rule making and enforcement, and being given ample opportunity for free discussion of public grievances and personal problems. Since the experience of cooperation in worthwhile enterprises develops social skills and social confidence, inmates need plenty of scope for self-expression in constructive and vocational activities. For some delinquents the experience of living for a time under such conditions may suffice to produce a beneficial change of attitude; for others it provides a necessary background support without which they could not be reached by individual treatment. The therapeutic community does not consist in any single method or programme so much as in a guiding philosophy according to which the facilitation of educative social interaction is an essential preliminary to psychological change.

The ideas and practices referred to are not really new, although the name for them has been taken up in a big way in recent penological writing. They first came to the fore in an educational context, notably in progressive boarding schools and in reform schools for wayward juveniles.

Early examples of therapeutic schools

Long before psychological theory lent support to such endeavours, humanitarian and religious motives inspired the foundation of homes for young delinquents where they might be trained and looked after in a manner approximating to the care provided by normal parents. A very early example was the school for depraved children at Neuhoff, Switzerland, founded in 1775 by Pestalozzi, whose name is remembered today in the international villages for refugee children. A pioneer of the use of small family groups living in separate units or cottages was J.H.Wichern, who opened the Rauhe Haus, near Hamburg, in 1833. The pattern was followed on a larger scale by the French judge F. A. De Metz in the Colonie Agricole at Mettrai, which began in 1840 and had considerable influence on the organization of other reformatories. Mary Carpenter [27] described Mettrai enthusiastically in terms which suggest an extraordinarily modern system. The boys were divided in separate houses, each under the care of its own housemaster and his assistants, so that they met together in the larger community only during work and recreations. Corporal punishment was forbidden, prison walls dispensed with, and discipline kept through the masters' constant association with their charges. The school also had what would nowadays be called a system of after-care. Jobs were found for the boys on leaving, and each was allocated a 'patron' for advice and supervision. Only a small percentage relapsed into crime. Another successful school was the reformatory at Saltley, near Birmingham, begun in 1853, where the superintendent, John Ellis, a former shoe-maker and a remarkable character, set up a system of self-government under which he cooperated with a committee of the boys in formulating and enforcing democratic rules. As so often happens, the venture passed into oblivion with the charismatic character who had sustained it.

Since then, other schools in different parts of the world have come and gone, each one in large measure repeating the experience of its predecessors, occasionally quite independently and in ignorance of what had gone before. Thus, at the turn of the century, William George set up a school in New York State, known as the Junior Republic, because it took as model the United States constitution, and had the boys form themselves into self-governing committees to learn in practice the arts and rewards of good citizenship. A follower of George, Homer Lane, came to England and set up in Dorset the Little Commonwealth, where children were made to work out their own system of self-government, and to form themselves into groups for discussion and mutual help. In Russia, in the aftermath of the Bolshevik revolution, the appearance of roving bands of homeless young thieves and robbers led to the establishment of colonies for juveniles, organized by the pioneer Anton Makarenko. He was another to make full and successful use of the democratic approach, self-helping groups and informal discussions. The more recent examples in England and America are too numerous to mention. Significantly enough, several have come to an end through withdrawal of support by the responsible authorities [141; 243; 284].

For many reasons the ideal of the therapeutic community is difficult to translate into practice. One source of difficulty is the annoyance aroused in some administrators when the clear and orderly appearance of a respectable institution is sacrificed to the psychological needs of turbulent youth. The whole approach makes great demands upon the staff, who have to come off their pedestals and tolerate familiarity and personal criticism from uncongenial and frequently hostile inmates. It calls for personal qualities of democratic leadership in the staff, otherwise the relaxation of authoritarian control may lead to unhelpful chaos and confusion, or perhaps give a chance to the worst characters to bully and tyrannize the rest. The ideals are more readily put over in small groups, in which the individual enthusiast can exert a personal influence on all concerned, than in large institutions which have a way of encouraging bureaucracy and social distance. Perhaps just because they are so exacting, these ideals often get watered down and forgotten, only to be rediscovered and propagated again under another name by some new enthusiast of the next generation.

Mental-hospital experience

The idea of a therapeutic community has taken root most firmly in the mental hospitals. These institutions have many problems in common with penal establishments; both are dealing with deviant behaviour, both are trying to persuade their inmates into conformity. The old-fashioned hospital operated a severely authoritarian and custodial régime. Although fetters and whips went out long ago, locked wards, barred windows, padded cells, and hefty male nurses for the disturbed sections were nevertheless much in evidence until recently, as was a heavy emphasis upon the chain of command, with the patients at the lowest point of the pecking order. Under these conditions, some patients lost all initiative and lapsed into hopeless apathy. Others reacted with violence to the restraints that were meant to subdue them [99]. In the last twenty years, a great change has come about. Now the hospitals are proud of their open doors, and most patients come and go as they please without physical or legal restraint. Instead of being shut away or put to bed, patients are given responsibilities to the limits of their capacity, and encouraged to take part in work and social activities as well as in discussion groups with doctors and nurses. Admittedly, the use of new tranquillizing drugs has helped the process along, but even so it is clear that many patients were in the past restricted unnecessarily and to their detriment, and that much difficult and erratic behaviour can be kept in check by the influence of a favourable environment [37].

In England, the psychiatrist Maxwell Jones was one of the leading pioneers of the therapeutic community ideal. He provided a link between hospital and penal practice by developing an 'open' unit at Belmont Hospital (now the Henderson Hospital), which specialized in treating psychopathic and neurotic offenders. This is a largely self-governing patient community with group psychotherapy and communal work activities the main treatment resource.

Therapeutic communities in action

Aichhorn's school

The therapeutic community approach has also been tried in reformatory school projects for ordinary young delinquents who have not been diagnosed as neurotic or psychiatric cases. Three examples may be mentioned by way of illustration. The first was an experiment by an Austrian, A. Aichhorn [2], which has become a classic of penology and education. The second was a recent experiment in the rehabilitation of homeless borstal boys inaugurated by Frank Foster, then Director of Borstal After Care, and carried out with the help of Dr D. Miller, a practising psychoanalyst in London [180]. The last example, from the United States, was an instance of the failure of a would-be therapeutic community, as recorded by a participant sociological observer, H. W. Polsky [208].

Aichhorn began his experiment just after the First World War when he was put in charge of a residential institution for delinquent boys at Oberhollabrun. He had had long experience as a school-teacher, and an organizer of settlements for boys. He brought to his new task a burning conviction that the bad behaviour and character deformities of most delinquents were due to lack of consistent love and care during the formative years of childhood; that their aggressive and provocative attitudes represented their way of fighting back against a world which they had come to perceive as hostile and rejecting. He believed that continued punishment and coercion could only make them that much readier to take revenge upon society after release, and that the only hope of reclaiming them was to satisfy their frustrated craving for affection by an initial policy of unconditional acceptance, which could be followed later by a very gradual and tolerant programme of training to enable them to meet the demands of normal society. His ideas and the practices he introduced were the result of intuitive understanding, but when he became familiar with psychoanalytic theory he was able to interpret and explain his work in those terms.

In the management of reformatories he advocated breaking down inmates into small groups, with members not too diverse in character. As for the environment, he wrote: 'we felt intuitively that above all we must see that the boys and girls from fourteen to eighteen had a good time ... an environment must be created in which they could feel comfortable' [3]. He deprecated the kind of establishment in which rows of beds were ranked like soldiers, not an inch out of line, with covers folded precisely at right angles. Such meticulous conformity, difficult enough for the normal child to attain, could only be achieved among dis-social children by brute force, and would disappear once that force was left behind. He found that a policy of studied tolerance, in which the staff allowed the youngsters to be as rude and provocative as they pleased, without retaliation, generally paid off in time. In the past, the children's chronic sense of grievance had always been confirmed by automatic punishment, but now, once they realized that the expected reaction was no longer forthcoming, they experienced an upsurge of confusing emotion which shattered their cold and sullen defensiveness, brought out their yearnings for human attachments, and laid them open to influence by friendly members of staff.

Aichhorn's faith in this non-punitive approach led him to apply it even to those difficult cases whose quarrelsomeness and defiance reached such extremes that they were not tolerated by their fellow delinquents. A dozen such boys, every one of whom had been brought up without affection in a broken or disharmonious home, were placed together and left to their own devices, staff members intervening only when necessary to prevent injury. Opportunities for play and interesting occupation were provided, but not obligatory. Before long the furniture and windows were all broken, the place was a shambles, and boys were taking their food in corners, like animals, rather than sit together at the meal-table. Still Aichhorn persisted, feeling that once their aggression had reached a certain pitch it would expend itself and be replaced by other feelings. And so it turned out. After their outbursts had subsided, or become less frequent, they began to form attachments to the staff, and developed as much dependency and jealousy of each other as one might have expected from nursery children. They were then moved to fresh quarters, which they did not break up, and the slow process of training these over-sensitive and childish youngsters could begin. Aichhorn was aware that at this stage, in the slogan of a later exponent of the reformative art, Bruno Bettelheim, *love is not enough*. Once the emotional ice had broken, and the youngsters had become amenable to influence, the staff had to apply gradually measured doses of frustration, discipline and restriction so as to train their charges to meet the demands of normal life. The therapeutic community provided an environment in which emotional ties could develop, and in which the youngsters could find comfort and support while being tamed and broken in to social control.

Limitations of the treatment

The ideal therapeutic community varies with the needs of the particular group under care. Aichhorn knew the foolishness of applying to everyone methods devised for the established delinquent character. A normal, well-socialized youngster does not need to be handled like a baby who hasn't yet learned to control his tantrums and elementary hate reactions, and the boy who merely joins in with illegal escapades because that is expected behaviour among his group does not need to be treated as if he had some serious defect of personality. On the other hand, although a great many apparently impossibly psychopathic youngsters will form a therapeutic attachment in time, given sufficient patient endurance on the part of the staff, a minority will always remain unamenable and require a different approach. The policy of patient expectancy assumes that a normal potential exists, despite the present distorted reactions, but in cases of brain damage or defect, for instance, this may not be the case. So-called autistic children, who seem incapable of perceiving the world around them sufficiently clearly to respond realistically, and who remain wrapped up in their own imaginings, would hardly be aroused by the sort of approach that works with ordinary children. After serious brain injuries, if certain areas are affected, some unfortunate people become emotional zombies whose feelings lack the intensity or the discrimination necessary for any great attachments. In rare cases, some severely psychopathic youngsters, especially those of the coldly withdrawn passive type, who may be intellectually dull as well, give a rather similar impression. Sometimes these characters have come from apparently normal homes. Although it is difficult to prove, it could be that some of them are suffering from a congenital brain defect which makes them unresponsive to normal socializing influences. If so, they are unlikely to be much improved by placement in a therapeutic environment suited to more normally constituted youngsters.

The Northways Home

Derek Miller, whose treatment project took place some quarter of a century after Aichhorn's, and was inspired by a more sophisticated level of psychoanalytic theory, came to many of the same practical conclusions as had earlier exponents of liberal reformatory régimes. Like Aichhorn, he emphasized the need to have a group of compatible and not too abnormal individuals. He selected his delinquents so that all of them were working-class youths from socially deprived backgrounds, but he would include only those of about average intelligence, and he would not admit those whose behaviour disturbance was so great as to presuppose some form of madness or brain damage, or to require hospital treatment. All of them were at least potentially capable of forming reasonable human relationships.

The essence of the treatment, as in other therapeutic communities, was to provide a situation in which the delinquent felt loved and understood, in which relationships could develop, in which the more destructive expressions of aggression were controlled, while at the same time the basic need of youth to be moderately defiant and assertive of masculinity was allowed for, and in which a gradual assumption of normal responsibilities was helped along by personal attention, advice, discussion and interpretation as occasion arose.

The clients in fact consisted of young men aged seventeen to twenty released on licence from borstals, and with no parental home to which they could return. They were seen by the psychiatrist while on leave from their institutions, shortly before release, and if considered suitable they were invited to visit the house, Northways, and offered a place there. Acceptance was voluntary, but the great majority came gladly. They were recidivist delinquents, with an average of four previous convictions, and an average of nine years spent in institutions by each boy.

The whole scheme was on a small scale, twenty-one youths being dealt with over a two-year period, with perhaps only half that number living in the house at any one time. A woman warden, a male assistant, and the visiting psychiatrist acted as therapists. Discussion sessions with the boys were held weekly by the psychiatrist. No topics were banned, and such difficulties as those due to epidemics of stealing in the home were openly discussed. At first the boys showed their distrust by making superficially obsequious and compliant noises, while concealing their true thoughts. Boys out of a job might leave the house at the usual time so as not to have to admit the fact. However, as time went on, the boys lost some of their distrust, they no longer needed to test the staff's sincerity by provocative actions, and as the atmosphere settled down it became possible for boys to spend more of their energy helping each other instead of fighting. In fact, the project demonstrated yet again that seemingly unapproachable and unresponsive characters can be brought into a therapeutic relationship given patience and restraint on the part of the staff, and a willingness to make allowances for the limitations and peculiarities of their charges.

One feature of these youths which had to be understood was their inability to express their feelings except by impulsive action. For example, following the arrest of one of their members the discussion group pointedly steered clear of reference to what had happened. Instead, they fell to grumbling about the uselessness of discussions, and started quarrelling and fighting. After the therapist had pointed out that they must be very worried about the arrested boy, they quietened down and were able to talk sadly about the situation. But in order to intervene at all effectively, the therapist had to be able to perceive the emotional pressures behind the boys' behaviour. Their demands upon the staff were enormous and childishly irrational, they competed for attention, they resented the staff attending to their own family concerns or having time off, they fantasied the psychiatrist as an enormously affluent person who could be asked for anything, and they tried to set one staff member against another.

While allowing a great deal more licence than is customary in institutions, the psychiatrist kept firmly to certain rules and limits, which the boys could not exceed if they wished to stay in the house. For example, if stealing from outsiders was reported or detected, he would report it to the police, and he would not allow them to shock the woman warden with crude sex talk or gestures. He would not intervene to protect the boys from the natural social consequences of bad behaviour, or from normal social responsibilities (such as reporting to the borstal after-care officers), since the object of the exercise was to help them to confront reality. Likewise, the conditions of the borstal licence and of their financial contribution to their stay in the house were used to circumvent deliberate unemployment, and the existence of trustees who would not permit rowdyism or nuisance to neighbours was exploited to reinforce the realities of the situation. A special effort was made to keep the boys' concerns and aspirations directed towards jobs, interests and friends outside, so that the training process would help them to integrate with the normal community instead of becoming dependent upon institutional life. The psychiatrist was also firm about stating when a boy had progressed sufficiently to make arrangements for leaving, and would not allow himself to be dissuaded from this decision by a flare-up of misconduct meant to demonstrate a need for further protection.

Within these wide limits the boys had freedom to express themselves and get in and out of difficulties. They had door keys to come and go as they wished, although they were expected to notify the warden if they intended to stay out for the night. Some care was taken not to make demands upon them that would be considered inappropriate for young men of their age and class; so washing up and feminine domestic tasks were done for them, but they had to work to help pay for it. Such demands as the boys were asked to meet were quite enough to reveal their social ineptitude in numerous ways, and to provide material for discussion and guidance. They were ignorant and confused about tax forms, unemployment benefit, National Health registration, and hire purchase charges. For want of initiative an inordinate proportion of their leisure time was spent watching television, and they talked about tidying up the garden without ever getting round to it. At work, they slacked off when unsupervised, but resented being ordered about. Their difficulties showed up particularly in their relations with girl-friends, whom they treated with extreme inconsiderateness, while at the same time making jealously possessive demands. Some of the boys were sexually very promiscuous, as if to repair their wounded masculinity, while others were fearful of intercourse.

The differences between Northways and ordinary penal treatment

Unlike the older treatment experiments, which traditionally relied upon clinical impressions to substantiate the value of the work, this project did include a control, a group of homeless borstal boys matched with the Northways inmates for age, intelligence and average number of previous convictions and time spent in institutions. The control group received only the usual borstal after-care services. The after-careers of the Northways boys, as regards re-conviction, settled marriages and employment records, were consistently better than the control group, although the numbers were too small for satisfactory statistical demonstration. There was also the complicating factor that the good offices of the Northways staff probably got their boys more consideration at the hands of employers, after-care officers, etc., so the whole of any good effect could not necessarily be attributed to the therapeutic experience itself.

One can see how difficult it would be to reproduce fully in a big institution the conditions exemplified by the Northways project. Sheer size would preclude the enormous amount of time and attention given to each boy, and administrative considerations would hamper flexibility. For example, Miller comments that in spite of effort and good will, the borstals could not provide discharged boys with a suit of clothes in a style they could wear without embarrassment. Similarly, the vocational training they had received in institutions did not prepare the boys for conditions in industry outside, and some of them had come away with silly notions of the extent of their skill or what they could earn in a normal labour market. On the psychological side, while some institutions subscribe to the therapeutic community theory, inadequate practice, with staffs not fully trained for the task, can bring a potentially effective technique into serious disrepute. An essential ingredient in all psychological treatment is a close and continued relationship between the therapist and his clients. In the special case of delinquents in custody the time of release into the world outside represents the most critical period, when they stand in greatest need of the help and support of their therapist. Unfortunately, in conventional penal institutions inmates are generally passed on to different after-care authorities the moment they leave.

Cottage Six

The next example is instructive because it shows how an attempt to produce a therapeutic community may fail despite the presence of a trained professional staff fully committed to putting it into practice. H. W. Polsky studied the work of Hollymeade, an American residential school for Jewish problem children, half of whom were sent by the courts. The school was committed to a therapeutic community ideal, and was an open institution, in so far as there was no enclosing security fence, although patrolling custodial officers were employed to try to prevent abscondings. Inmates were allocated to different residential cottages according to sex, age, social class and the nature of their delinquency. Cottage Six housed twenty of the older, tougher boys, placed under the care of a married couple, the house parents, who lived in the building. The boys attended school classes within the grounds, and also paid regular visits to a social caseworker for individual psychotherapy. Their progress with the caseworker was supervised by the staff psychiatrists. These interviews constituted the major therapeutic effort and the chief point of contact between the boys and the clinical staff. However, the professional clinical workers left the institution each evening and weekend, and so for the greater part of the time the boys were left with only the cottage parents. These were working-class people with no professional training, who were separated from the treatment staff by a considerable gulf of status, knowledge and function. This flaw in the system enabled the small cottage group to build up an inmate tradition at odds with the official values of the institution.

Inside the cottage, the stronger and more aggressive boys

boasted of their delinquency, bullied the weaker or more timorous, and established a pecking order by the use of threatening gestures, incessant comments of an insulting or teasing kind, and occasional beatings. The cottage parents unwittingly colluded in this anti-social behaviour by favouring the more aggressive boys because they were helpful in keeping order within the house. They also shared the aggressive delinquent's dislike and contempt for the weak and snivelling, the 'queers' and the 'bush boys'. Queers were the softer or more timorous types who were the butt of teasing and insinuations about being homosexual. Bush boys were weaklings who bitterly resented their low status and tried to make up for it by futile bickering and tantrums among themselves. In one striking incident a low-status boy turned on his tormentor in a violent assault, was beaten up by the others for his pains, and then transferred to a state mental hospital because his behaviour was so disruptive. In this sub-culture, newcomers were soon pressed into a professed admiration for delinquent skills, for the forbidden pursuit of the girls who inhabited neighbouring cottages, for success in 'sliming out' of classroom attendance, and for ability to manipulate and bully people, since all these things were synonymous with respect and privilege in the cottage environment. Boys who were taking their casework treatment seriously never referred to it in the cottage. Sometimes they kept themselves a little aloof, though apparently falling in with the mood and attitudes of the prevailing culture. The habit of protecting inner feelings by superficial conformity can work two ways, by playing bad to please peers, or by playing good to please authorities. Private talks with individual boys showed that some were less committed to the cottage values than appeared from their bravado in public.

The experience of Hollymeade shows how important it is to the proper functioning of a therapeutic community that the staff should not be divided against themselves, and that everyone should have a role in the treatment effort. The system whereby a professional staff of psychologists and social workers undertakes treatment, while the non-professional custodial staff looks after discipline and locking up, is quite inimical to the therapeutic community ideal. Within the staff hierarchy, the expert therapist's duty is to teach others to help him rather than to keep his own special relationship with inmates sacrosanct. As with many other requirements, this comes easier in institutions that are not too large.

Behaviour therapy

This is the name given to a series of techniques based upon the theories of learning and conditioning as exemplified in the writings of behaviouristic psychologists such as H. J. Eysenck.* Basically, they consist of training by a manipulation of rewarding and punishing stimuli. In a sense, all forms of education and child training do just this, but the experimental psychologists maintain that in ordinary life rewards and punishments are not applied sufficiently consistently or quickly to produce the best effect, and punishments are often unnecessarily severe and protracted.

In experiments with animals, situations can be rigged quite simply. Choosing the right path (literally) can be rewarded with food, or taking the wrong path can be punished with an electric shock, so that one can work out the optimum timing and severity of punishment, or the relative effectiveness of punishment or reward. Human behaviour is so much more complicated and difficult to keep under surveillance that results are less clear-cut, but similar general principles are believed to hold true.

Learning by 'conditioned avoidance' of unpleasant stimuli has already been mentioned.† This is the basis of aversion treatment, a method that has long been in use for alcoholics. The favourite tipple is given, followed at once by some unpleasant stimulus, usually an injection of emetic, although electric shocks or even a whip would presumably work just as well. The process is repeated again and again until the patient is too exhausted for it to be continued safely. After a few weeks' rest, he goes through the course again. Provided the timing of the stimuli is right, an automatic aversion reaction sets in, and the patient can't stand the thought or taste of alcohol, at least for the time being. The same technique has been used with sexual deviants, by first showing them pictures to evoke their illicit desires, and then

* See p. 137.
† See p. 140.

administering a shock or emetic to build up an aversion [78]. The temptation to commit forms of crime, such as burglary or violent robbery, is not so easily aroused to order, so aversion treatment has hardly been used in any systematic·way for the generality of delinquents [110]. Moreover, aversion is less effective where the situation and the response are not very clear-cut and specific. It might discourage particular acts, like taking money from shop tills, without having much effect upon deceit and dishonesty in other situations.

The use of automatic rewards for correct behaviour (operant conditioning) has been tried, using money or gift tokens as the easiest means of quick gratification. Burchard and Tyler [25] claim to have produced remarkable improvement in the behaviour of a delinquent boy in a reform school by this means, when conventional methods of punishment had failed. In animal experiments in which food is offered to those who respond correctly, the gratification is more powerful and immediate, since they are starved for some time beforehand. The same effect can be obtained in humans by first placing them in a situation of discomfort, and then offering relief as a reward. A technique for the purpose has been described by a Canadian psychiatrist, P. M. Middleton [178], formerly consultant to a penitentiary. The discomfort is produced by injection of a paralysing drug, succinyl choline, which arrests breathing and produces asphyxia. The relief consists of whiffs of oxygen under pressure, given with an anaesthetic machine. Under these circumstances, delayed reward amounts to a quite impressive punishment, as the subject becomes asphyxiated. One drawback of the technique is the subject's inability to behave either correctly or incorrectly, since he is paralysed. This is overcome by the use of a pressure cuff around one arm to stop the drug reaching one hand. The subject, who is otherwise completely immobile, can use this hand to signal to the therapist. In treating a young delinquent, the therapist asks him to imagine himself reacting correctly to imagined situations, such as telling a friend who proposes to break into a shop that the idea is stupid. When he has the idea clearly in mind, he signals and gets the rewarding whiff of oxygen.

The techniques of behaviour therapy are anathema to some therapists because it seems like manipulating people against their will. A natural extension of behaviouristic principles could lead to brain-washing, with drugs given to increase conditionability or suggestibility, and a sophisticated alternation of torture and kindness used to batter down resistance. On the other hand, in extreme cases, where the actual alternative is fifteen years' preventive detention, or frequent condemnation to bread and water and solitary confinement, who is to say that a short spell of brain-washing might not be more humane – if only it worked.

Demonstrating results

Comparing re-conviction rates

The effectiveness of various methods of disposal of offenders in the penal system is hard to assess, since persons awarded different sentences for similar offences are not necessarily comparable. Moreover, when attempts have been made to examine approximately comparable offenders undergoing different penal régimes, the long-term outcome has usually been found much the same in both cases. Cynics can argue, therefore, that it makes no appreciable difference to re-convictions what sentence the courts decide upon.

An example of somewhat disappointing findings in relation to the effectiveness of more progressive penal measures is a research by Sir George Benson [17], who used the Mannheim–Wilkins prediction score* to identify comparable groups of young offenders who had been awarded sentences of borstal training and imprisonment respectively. He found no difference in outcome. More recently, Charlotte Banks [14], who analysed the re-convictions of samples of youths passing through prisons, borstals and detention centres, concluded that the important factor determining future outcome was the number of previous convictions. The type of penal institution to which a boy was sent appeared to have little influence.

In their 1964 handbook on sentencing for the use of the courts, the Home Office [132] tried to assess the effectiveness of different sentences by first calculating 'expected' re-conviction rates, taking into account age, class of offence and number of

* See p. 164.

previous convictions. Adjusting the 'expected' rates to 100 for arithmetical simplicity, it was found that, of a sample of juveniles convicted in the London Metropolitan Police District, first offenders discharged or fined had an actual re-conviction rate considerably lower than the expected figure of 100 (rates of 87 and 72 respectively), whereas those committed to approved schools had a re-conviction rate of 149, considerably higher than expectation. Similarly, among young first offenders of seventeen to twenty-one years of age, those discharged or fined did considerably better than expectation (rates of 89 and 75 respectively), whereas those given custodial sentences did worse, with a rate of 150.* The contrasts were much less striking, however, in the case of adult offenders, or offenders of any age who had been convicted previously.

Random allocation to different régimes

The figures just quoted must be treated with reserve, since the courts doubtless took into account when sentencing many factors of behaviour and social background not allowed for in these comparisons. Nevertheless, as far as they go, the figures do lend support to the many observers who claim that a young offender's first experience of penal custody is likely to have a bad effect upon him as an individual, and to render him more liable to re-conviction.

In theory, it should not be difficult to test scientifically the reformative effect of different methods of dealing with offenders who have been caught, since one has a ready-made criterion for comparison in the statistics of re-convictions following release. All one needs to do is to allocate a group of offenders at random between the different methods of disposal, and then wait to see if those awarded any particular punishment or treatment are less often re-convicted. Unfortunately, although many authoritative persons will fully admit in abstract discussion that they have no idea what works best, when it comes to making practical decisions about real people they are unable to leave matters entirely to chance. The Prison Department has power to send offenders to

---

* These conclusions were only tentative, however, since for some age groups the calculations were based upon small numbers.

open or closed prisons or borstals, but their decisions have to take into account escape risks, the number of vacant places, and whether a potential inmate will cause trouble in an open institution. The courts have power to choose between fine, probation and confinement, but in so far as they must appear fair and just they cannot do this completely at random. One way out of the impasse is to make a random choice within specified limits. For instance, magistrates could be asked to select some offenders deserving of confinement, but not so bad that probation was out of the question, and then to allow a flip of the coin to decide in which cases to allow the more lenient course.

So far as I know nothing of this kind has been done by any English courts. Some American investigators have been able to compare the outcomes of different disposals of juvenile offenders determined by a judge in Utah, who used random numbers to make the selection [59; 60]. Originally, the pool of eligible delinquents was meant to consist of relatively serious offenders, who might be committed to reform school, awarded probation, or given probation with the addition of intensive psychological counselling and social work. However, Judge Paxman, the enlightened lawyer who collaborated in the scheme, found too few cases suitable for committal, so the random choice had soon to be reduced to one of probation or probation plus counselling. This was a pity, since the greatest difference seemed to be in the boys sent to institutions, who fared worse than the rest. However, there was also a slight difference between the other two groups, in that the boys who got special attention were less often re-convicted.

Matched offenders on probation and in prison

Another method of evaluating different disposals makes use of the arbitrary element already present in these decisions. Since magistrates vary considerably in the severity of their sentences [133], and the penal authorities often distribute similar offenders between institutions operating different régimes, it is possible to collect matching groups of similar offenders who have had different treatments and to compare the results. One such comparison, which was a model of carefulness and clarity, was made by L.T.Wilkins [281] when he was at the Home Office Research Unit. He assembled matching pairs of offenders, the members of each pair being of the same age and sex, convicted of the same kind of offence, and having the same number of charges and offences taken into consideration and the same number of previous convictions. In each pair, one had been sentenced to imprisonment and the other put on probation. The big question was whether the probationers fared better or worse than the prisoners. The answer was that no significant difference in re-conviction rates was detectable.

Had this experiment produced a different result, favouring one form of treatment over the other, it could have been argued that the matching was imperfect. The weak point in all such experiments is that the matching process cannot take into account all of the factors which may have relevance. Supposing, for instance, that offenders who are polite in court have better prospects of freedom from future convictions, and also better chances of being awarded probation. This would mean that probationers would have a better record on follow-up because magistrates had selected the better types in the first place. Since politeness in court would not be visible in official records, it could not be taken into account in the matching process.

'Open' and 'closed' borstals

In a well-known English study of borstal boys, Mannheim and Wilkins [169] compared the outcome of two groups of institutions, the 'open' and 'closed' borstals. Generally speaking, the former are somewhat more relaxed in atmosphere, and the inmates are given more personal responsibility, while the latter have a stricter discipline, and opportunities for self-expression and non-conformity are fewer. The technique of comparison was different, though similar in fundamental principle. The investigators used extensive data on borstal boys to construct prediction tables indicating probability of re-conviction on release in any individual case. These were based on a few points in the boy's official record which experience had demonstrated to be highly correlated with subsequent re-conviction. The tables provided a basis for calculating the expected frequency of future convictions allowing for the proportions of good and bad risks in any particular group of borstal boys. The expected re-convictions of groups of boys, allocated to open and closed borstals respectively, could then be compared with their actual re-convictions in order to see if these different treatments resulted in any significant deviation from the expected outcome. The investigators concluded that open borstals had a better success rate than closed borstals, even after all possible allowances had been made for the fact that the youths sent to open borstals were better risks. Those who believe that the more relaxed and liberal training régimes are not only kinder and pleasanter but also more effective can take some comfort from this result. But of course, as in the comparisons by matching methods, the possibility lurks in the background that some relevant factors omitted from the expectancy calculations may account for the differing re-conviction rates rather than the treatment itself.

Reasons for negative results

Uncertainty of interpretation hardly arises in many comparisons of penal treatments, since the statistical results often show no significant differences. Wilkins's comparison of sentences of probation and imprisonment was a case in point. One can interpret such negative results in several ways. Nigel Walker [272] points out that perhaps penal measures are for most offenders interchangeable, so that those who would be discouraged from repetition of offences by imprisonment could be equally discouraged by a fine. This explanation is supported by the fact that re-conviction rates are so much more closely associated with the type of offence, the number of previous convictions, and the age of the offender than they are with the nature or severity of the sentence awarded.

Another interpretation is that all the existing penal treatments are equally futile, or at least negligible in their effects compared with the other pressures that determine an offender's future behaviour. Another and more likely explanation is that the concepts of 'offender' and of 'treatment' are too vague and all-embracing to be workable. Different kinds of offenders, like different types of sick persons, might benefit from different treatments. Furthermore, the official label covers a wide range of actual treatment experiences. Probation can mean anything from cursory visits to intensive psychological probing, depending upon the competence and commitments of the officer in charge. In short, the apparent ineffectiveness of penal measures might be the fault of applying ill defined treatments indiscriminately to all and sundry.

Varying effectiveness according to type of offender

It has already been indicated in a previous chapter* that delinquents fall into groups of contrasting psychological make-up and differing treatment needs. This was neatly demonstrated at an American naval establishment, Camp Elliott, San Diego, in what has become a classic experiment in the treatment of delinquents by Grant and Grant [106]. The investigators had previously developed a system of classifying the personality of an offender according to what they called his level of maturity development, which is manifest in his manner of handling personal relationships. At the lowest level, 1, analogous to that of a small baby, other people are scarcely envisaged as separate entities. At level 2, other people are perceived as suppliers or withholders of his personal wants, but of no interest in themselves. At level 3, they are seen as objects which can be manipulated for his own purposes, but he still has little appreciation of others as individuals with thoughts and feelings in their own right. At level 4, he has developed a primitive conscience, and is capable of experiencing guilt, inferiority and admiration, but at this stage he has an undiscriminating black-and-white image of right and wrong derived from a crude perception of the feelings of parents and others. He is thus prone to neurotic conflict between his natural impulses and his unrealistic conscience. At level 5, he becomes more perceptive and flexible and can feel sympathy with others.

This classification has much in common with the stages of moral development described by Peck and Havinghurst [201], and still earlier by Piaget [205].† However, the point of interest

* See p. 173.
† See p. 180.

for the moment is that the Grants reported that delinquents of relatively high maturity level (4 or more) responded better to a psychological counselling approach the more intensively it was applied, whereas with increasingly intensive treatment those of less mature personality did worse and worse. (The criterion of success in this experiment was satisfactory return to military duties.) The implication would seem to be that, in order to benefit from treatment involving discussion and exploration of motives, the offender must have reached a certain maturity level, otherwise the therapeutic effort may make him worse rather than better.

Confirmation of this view was obtained in another Californian project, the Pilot Intensive Counselling Organization, known for short as the P.I.C.O. experiment [1]. Juvenile delinquents in an institution were divided prospectively into two groups considered likely to be 'amenable' or 'non-amenable' to treatment. The former group displayed more anxiety and readiness to accept help, and had a higher level of verbal intelligence than the latter. All offenders, regardless of their prospects, were then allocated at random for either intensive counselling or else for the ordinary institutional régime. Success was judged by frequency of arrests and subsequent penal confinements during a follow-up of several years after release. The amenables did better with counselling than without, but the non-amenables who got counselling did distinctly worse than those dealt with in a more traditional manner. Similar results were obtained when the same experiment was repeated in a second institution.

Since the Grants' pioneer experiment, the maturity scale classification has been used in a number of experiments, mostly in California, as a means of testing the value of different kinds of treatment régimes for different types of delinquents. The chief drawback of the classification has been that it is based upon interpretations of the offender's responses in the course of lengthy interviews, and of course skills and attitudes of the interviewer affect the reliability of the assessment. However, psychologists have now devised questionnaire style tests which appear to do the same job and to produce substantially similar results without the complicating factor of interviewer bias [105].

An evaluation of the usefulness of the maturity level classification in practice is now being made in the Community Treatment Project of the California Youth Authority [275]. Excluding a minority of serious offenders considered ineligible, a group of juveniles, sufficiently seriously delinquent to have been committed to the Youth Authority, were allocated at random either to the Authority's traditional institutional programme or to an experimental programme of Community Treatment. The average age of the offenders was fifteen years, and those sent to the Community Project were each placed under the supervision of an agent responsible for carrying out treatment. The agents had an average case load of only eight to ten delinquents each, and could therefore afford to give every one a lot of attention. Treatment was varied according to individual needs as gauged by maturity level, and ranged from temporary confinement, surveillance and firm discipline, or foster-home placement, through guided group activities to individual counselling and psychotherapy.

Failures over a span of fifteen months following release or termination of special treatment (revocation of parole or recommitment by the courts being counted as failure) were distinctly more frequent among the ordinary penal group than among the community treatment group – forty-eight per cent compared with twenty-nine per cent. Comparison of responses on the California Psychological Inventory before and after treatment by the two groups showed that the experimental subjects had more frequently changed towards a better social adjustment than had the control subjects. This kind of research represents a substantial step in refining both treatment method and evaluation to a point where statistical demonstration of effectiveness becomes a feasible proposition.

12 Some Cautionary Afterthoughts

Our state of ignorance

When I was writing this book, a list of questions was sent to me from a student struggling to write an essay on juvenile delinquency and wanting some short authoritative answers. 'Why is there an increase in delinquency?' 'Does it run in families?' 'Why is it so much more marked in boys?' 'How widespread is the gang system, and are most gangs delinquent?' 'Are delinquents usually characterized by variability of mood or lack of concentration?'

When I look back on these elementary questions, it occurs to me how disappointed this student and other readers may be to find so many of these basic issues discussed, and so few clear-cut answers provided. In truth, the subject of delinquency bristles with unanswerable questions. The more one sees of it, the less one sees through it. Delinquency, like ill health, consists of a vast conglomeration of different phenomena, and no simple explanation or cure will be found to fit more than a small segment of the whole. The problems are so many-sided, so changeable, and so complex in all their social and psychological ramifications that we have hardly got to the stage of stating the issues coherently, let alone resolving them.

The topics covered in this book were selected because they represent some of the traditional preoccupations of criminologists, and hence a body of research and literature exists upon which to draw. A great many important topics have been left out simply because of the lack of relevant facts or research findings. For instance, in the recently publicized episodes of rowdyism at seaside resorts, or the epidemic of telephone smashing, or the consumption of intoxicating drugs, one would like to know if these are the work of the traditional thieving delinquents, or if they herald the appearance of new types of offender as well as new types of offence. In view of the criticisms made about over-large school classes and lack of control by teachers, one would like to know how much difference it makes to the risks of becoming delinquent which school a boy attends. Many people would like to know about the effect, if any, of television and the mass-media, but a learned committee now looking into this question finds it easier to list the investigations that need to be carried out than to reach decisive opinions. Even on the more traditional research topics, such as the social-class distribution of delinquents or the true amount of the increase in youthful law-breaking, the available evidence, although voluminous, is often conflicting and inconclusive.

There are many reasons for our continued state of ignorance or uncertainty about the basic facts of the situation. Delinquent acts are secret and shaming, and investigators can more easily persuade people to confide their private sex lives than to give a truthful account of their crimes. Parents, education authorities and politicians are all sensitive about the topic, and sometimes give more lip-service than active support to research, especially when research threatens to invade privacy or reveal an unpalatable state of affairs. The officials who deal with apprehended delinquents, the police, the magistrates, and the staffs of penal establishments, have, on the whole, contributed comparatively little to the published research findings. Maybe they don't consider it their job, or maybe they are too preoccupied with routine matters to spare the time for surveys; but efficient commercial organizations would never allow far-reaching executive decisions to be made without collecting all the available information. The Home Office *Criminal Statistics* and *Supplementary Statistics* do, of course, provide, an invaluable guide, but how much more useful they would be if the obsessive head-counting gave way sometimes to an analysis of representative samples of police records. This would give more information on the social backgrounds of offenders, their companions in crime, and the nature and circumstances of their misdeeds than whole text-books of criminology. The enormous numbers of social and psychological examinations carried out by the Prison Department at remand centres and borstal allocation centres could be used much more for producing published findings on the characteristics of offenders.

One difficulty is that the enforced reticence of public servants acts as a brake, and not all that is known is necessarily published. Government agencies do carry out research for their own purposes. A most valuable study of the self-reported delinquencies and social attitudes of a national sample of youths has been carried out by the Central Office of Information. One hopes a published report will be forthcoming.

The phenomena of youthful crime

In spite of the uncertain state of empirical evidence, some attempt has been made in this book to look for general patterns in contemporary English delinquency that might help to elucidate its origins or to decide treatment strategy. To this end, numerous exceptions and anomalous minority groups have been neglected, so any generalizations one makes are sure to arouse controversy and be fraught with difficulties and reservations. Nevertheless, it may be worth while to recapitulate some of the tentative suggestions that have emerged.

Criminal statistics are dominated by their largest category, the offences against property, and generalizations about delinquents as a whole really refer to thieves. Regardless of age, most first offenders are not re-convicted, and the minority of young offenders who are convicted repeatedly nevertheless have a strong tendency to cease being convicted in their early twenties. Hence, as far as records of convictions go, it would appear that delinquent habits are for the most part only very sporadic, and that the great majority of young people grow out of them. The long-term criminal career is a statistical freak in comparison with commonplace delinquency of an occasional and not very serious kind. In spite of the publicity given to atrocious or brutal crimes, the fact is that the great majority of the offences committed by young persons are not very serious, not carefully planned or premeditated, and not part of a professional commitment to crime.

The opinion that most convicted youths are ordinary youngsters who are not going to become recidivists is supported by the results of surveys of self-reported delinquency. The findings suggest that many of those brought before the courts are no different in behaviour or social attitude from their peers, who have committed just as many delinquent acts, but without being caught. With these points in mind, it is not surprising to find that the general run of young offenders brought to court are mentally and physically fit, and come from backgrounds typical of the social class to which they belong. Since so many delinquents are quite ordinary youngsters, it is reasonable to suppose that their behaviour represents the normal response of their age group to everyday circumstances. Hence the plausibility of explanations for the increase in convictions which lay emphasis on the increased exposure of the younger generation to opportunities and temptations. In other words, simple things like the increase in unguarded cars and other property, and increased leisure and freedom, which enable adolescents to wander about and get into mischief, may have more to do with the bulk of the delinquency statistics than maternal deprivation or personal maladjustment or the supposed deterioration in moral standards or family stability.

In any case, no one really knows how much of the increase in convictions, especially for minor offences, is due to the authorities becoming more determined and more effective in their attack on adolescent misbehaviour. The reservoir of unreported offences is always enormous, and the harder the authorities work on it, the more they will dredge up.

It is only when one begins to isolate from the general mass the hard core of highly persistent delinquents with repeated convictions that a group emerges with noticeable social and psychological peculiarities. The characteristic social background of persistent delinquents (low class, low income, educational backwardness, broken home, over-large family, child neglect, poor neighbourhood) has been described *ad nauseam*. Wherever this cluster of social deprivations is prominent, the delinquency rate is very high. This seems to apply just as much today, when the deprivation consists of relative poverty and social ostracism, as it did when poverty meant rags and near-starvation. But social deprivation alone, although it remains the most readily identifiable factor in persistent delinquency, fails to account for the increasing numbers of offenders who come from more affluent homes.

Among those convicted of sexual crimes, or serious crimes of personal violence, there is a smaller proportion of youthful offenders than among persons convicted of larceny or breaking-in. Sexually deviant activities in particular bring adults to court more often than youths. In the criminal histories of persons convicted of crimes of violence or sex, convictions for property offences often occur as well. Nevertheless, many sex offenders are timorous, inhibited neurotic types, quite different from the ordinary boisterous young delinquent. Others suffer from subnormality or social clumsiness, handicaps which frustrate their efforts to obtain permitted sexual outlets. Likewise, among seriously violent offenders, some are much more seriously maladjusted and anti-social than the general run of ordinary offenders. Drug-takers, on the other hand, are not necessarily anti-social at all in other respects. Although addiction may lead weak characters into crimes and other disasters, many young people participate in the craze for trying out prohibited drugs without coming to serious harm.

Delinquency theories

According to one point of view, there is nothing very special to explain. Occasional acts of defiance or rebellion are, and always have been, normal features of the transition from youthful exuberance to manly restraint. The phenomenon has become more noticeable merely because the enormous size, and the complex and impersonal organization, of modern communities make them more vulnerable to youthful disruptions. The more unattended cars are left about, the more plastic telephones are waiting to be prised open, the easier it becomes for youths to travel and congregate at popular weekend resorts, the greater the scope for nuisance. Adults naturally react less tolerantly, and prosecutions spiral upwards.

The behaviour of the hard core of persistent offenders cannot be so easily dismissed. It appears to be both different in origin and more serious in effect. The offenders involved have a high incidence of broken homes, educational failures, and neglected or erratic upbringing. Sociological theories interpret their behaviour as a natural reaction, on the part of the less privileged and the less well endowed, to the frustrations they experience in their unsuccessful attempts to get on and get ahead in the modern rat race. The theories differ in emphasis more than in

fundamentals. The earlier writers, such as Thrasher and Sutherland, emphasized the effect of bad example, and the ease with
which criminal habits could be learned by youngsters in the
slums. Later theorists, like Merton and Cohen, emphasized the
factor of social injustice. Lower-class boys were said to turn sour
and rebellious because they were being made to conform to
middle-class rules, and jump through middle-class hoops, without benefit of middle-class rewards.

Psychologists, and especially psychoanalysts, stress the
characteristics of delinquents as individuals. They suggest that
insufficiency of love or of consistency in infant care is liable to
induce a permanent distortion of personality which paves the
way for delinquency in later years. The sociological and psychological views do not altogether conflict, since most of the features
of upbringing which the analysts find damaging (such as neglect
or rejection of children, erratic training, and separations at
critical phases of development) are just those features which the
sociologists find most prevalent in the socially deprived segments
of the community. But even though the general incidence of
family disturbance reflects social forces, the analysts believe that
it is the level of disturbance in his own family which affects most
the individual youngster. This is particularly obvious among
youths from materially secure homes who have nevertheless
become delinquent.

Modern sociologists take into account these psychological
ideas. L. Yablonsky argues that the kind of gang or sub-culture to
which a youth is drawn depends on his style of upbringing. If he
has been moulded into a disgruntled, suspicious psychopathic
personality, he will find himself at home only among gangs of
similar aggressive-minded misfits. When stable working-class
communities developed an ethos all their own, and poverty was
no disgrace, the effects on developing youth were less damaging
than in social situations in which the lowest social grades are
largely made up of families who have drifted downwards on
account of social incompetence, and whose child-rearing practices
are therefore particularly unsatisfactory.

The classification of offenders into 'types' helps to coordinate
the rival claims of psychological and social determinants. Large
numbers of sporadic offenders are 'normal' persons behaving

no differently from other persons in their social setting. Many persistent delinquents are anti-social characters, persons who have been damaged by social and family adversities. They are too aggressive, suspicious and impulsive to adjust to the ways of normal groups, although some may be 'pseudo-socialized' to the extent of being able to fit in with a gang of similar misfits. The disturbance is a matter of degree, and if very marked tends to be called psychopathic, although this does not mean it is irrevocable. Finally, a small minority of persistent delinquents are maladjusted in a different sense, being inhibited, conflict-ridden types analogous to the classic anxiety neurotic.

Research has gone some way towards confirming, by means of social surveys, testing techniques and clinical assessments, that many persistent delinquents really do display demonstrable psychopathic traits, such as impulsiveness, inability to postpone gratifications, lack of concern for others, and so on. There is also similar evidence for the existence of the sub-group of predominantly neurotic offenders. Some of the research on these lines has been concerned with traits believed to be largely inherited, such as body-build and motor coordination, both of which are demonstrably connected with the likelihood of becoming delinquent. Such research is a far cry from the nineteenth-century preoccupation with inborn moral degeneracy, but nevertheless the findings bring a sharp reminder that some of the individual characteristics which favour delinquent reactions may be due to biological differences as well as upbringing and other environmental influences. Many people, though disposed to accept biological factors as an explanation of the contrasts between male and female criminal propensities, maintain a somewhat illogical resistance to the idea that such factors may have a wider influence. Evidence from electro-encephalographic studies and other sources strongly suggests that subtle forms of brain damage, even though not always manifest in paralysis or other gross physical symptoms, may handicap an individual's chances of social adjustment. If combined with unfavourable social influences, these physical factors may contribute to very serious forms of psychopathy and criminal behaviour.

In short, in explaining persistent delinquency, as with all unusual behaviour patterns, one has to take into account a great variety of factors: social, individual, biological and environmental. The simple answer is a myth.

Delinquency prevention and treatment

Reliable information about the phenomena of delinquency may be hard to come by; but facts about remedies and their effectiveness are still more scarce. As Grygier put it:

> The field of penology has been full of good intentions and false hopes. We have built penitentiaries and expected people to repent; we have assumed that juvenile delinquents need training and will receive it, naturally, from 'training schools' . . . Only recently have we begun to have second thoughts on these matters and to take first steps in checking our preconceived notions in controlled experiments . . . [109].

Resistance to systematic experiment and assessment on the part of sentencers and penal administrators largely accounts for the sad fact that few data are available on the response of comparable groups of delinquents to different punishments or training methods. Such elementary comparisons as have been made generally suggest that one kind of disposal is as good, or as bad, as another.

There are some obvious reasons why present penal methods may not be very effective. The bold, pioneer treatment endeavours of men like A. Aichhorn, who appeared to enjoy some measure of success, are infernally difficult to put over in government institutions, where treatment needs must be watered down to meet the exigencies of economy, uniformity, public opinion, and the attitudes of custodial staff. Even in the most progressive of open borstals, where a great deal of time and effort is spent talking with boys and looking into family problems, an inmate may find himself 'sentenced' to an extra month for slipping out an extra letter to his mother beyond the stipulated ration. While group discussions and a therapeutic community atmosphere have seemed effective in intensive, psychiatrically directed projects like that of Dr Miller, their worth depends upon great perseverance in establishing and maintaining close relationships with difficult characters. The task of alleviating serious social handicaps and character defects calls for much more sophisticated techniques of educational and psychological training than are generally available in most penal establishments. Institutions are too often run to suit the least disturbed, who are capable of responding favourably to ordinary methods, whereas of course it is the worst cases who should get the best attention.

At present, one of the most obvious shortcomings of the institutional treatment of persistent offenders, especially where it concerns the rehabilitation of the more severely maladjusted, is the necessity for transfer of care at the moment of discharge, when the offender stands most in need of the help and support of the caseworker who knows him. Another difficulty is the large number of employment prospects automatically closed to young men who have been in borstals. The armed services, who used to take them, no longer do so, and many other official bodies have similar policies. This kind of discrimination means that society as a whole has little faith in the reformative effect of penal treatment, and little sense of obligation to try to make a place for anyone marked out as an official delinquent. For the small minority whose personality defects are too severe to respond to any such methods, or who have medical or psychiatric disorders in addition, professional medical care in specialist hospital units is badly needed, and the health service should provide the facilities. At present, the courts all too often commit youths to borstals, knowing them to be too grossly disturbed to benefit from a régime designed for normal boys, simply because no suitable place can be found for them in hospitals. In spite of the provisions for compulsory hospital treatment for psychopaths under the Mental Health Act, 1959, doctors have a regrettable propensity to reject offenders of all ages if their defects are too troublesome or apparently unchangeable, and to cast them out of medical care into penal custody, as once lepers were cast untreated into colonies. Only in this instance the incurables don't languish and die; after their 'time' is done they return as harmful as ever.

Such contradictions highlight the ambivalence of purpose of present-day penal institutions, which in turn reflect the conflict of ideas in society as a whole. Another difficulty which besets our state institutions is the wide range of problems and types of person that they have to deal with. American research suggests that the kind of régime best suited to one type of personality, or one level of maturity, may be positively harmful to another. The present methods of sentencing offenders make no allowance for this sort of thing. If the present proposals for setting up welfare boards, in the shape of family tribunals, for dealing with juvenile delinquents leads to greater discrimination in disposal, and a willingness to experiment and to check results, it would indeed be a great advance.

In discussing treatment or training in custody, which is regrettably necessary for some persistent delinquents, one must remember that this applies to a minority only, and is not the answer to the great bulk of sporadic offenders who appear once or twice at court and never again. The general high level of delinquency convictions is largely kept up by provocations, opportunities and temptations acting upon the youthful population as a whole. Hence, preventive action, in the form of protective and detective devices to reduce opportunities, and social welfare to reduce temptations, are much more likely to lower the general delinquency rate than a proliferation of custodial establishments. Furthermore, attention to the rudiments of child care and mental health might forestall the development of some of those warped and aggressive characters from whom persistent delinquents are so often recruited.

For the majority of first offenders, sharp reminders that they have transgressed the limits of tolerable conduct are often all that is needed, and measures involving removal from a normal environment and segregation among established social deviants should be avoided as far as possible. Occasionally, the fact of coming to court will bring to light circumstances requiring the attention of the welfare services, and the opportunity to help should not be missed. One of the advantages of having a probation officer concerned in such cases is that he should know the right source of help, whether it be legal advice, psychiatry, National Assistance or Alcoholics Anonymous. Unfortunately, in practice the services needed are not always readily available or easy to call upon where the problem concerns an offender.

Nobody expects any one explanation or treatment method to solve all health problems. Advocates of a single cure-all for delinquency, whether it be harsher punishment or more child guidance, are equally unrealistic. An unremitting attack on a wide front, using different methods for different problems, holds out the best hope for progress. Above all, social and penal measures, which seek to change behaviour, should be securely based upon rational inquiry into the causal factors involved, and should include objective assessment of the results of different courses of action.

List of References

303

Unless otherwise stated, books are published in London.

1 cited on p. 284 Adams, S. (1962). 'The P.I.C.O. Project', in Johnston, N. B., et al., The Sociology of Crime and Delinquency, pp. 213–24. New York, J. Wiley.

2 267 Aichhorn, A. (1925). Wayward Youth. (1st English edition Imago, 1951.)

3 268 Aichhorn, A. (1925). op. cit., p. 149.

4 158 Ainsworth, M. D. Salter (1965). 'Further research into the adverse effects of maternal deprivation', in Bowlby, J., Child Care and the Growth of Love, 1965 edition. Penguin Books.

5 59 Akers, R. L. (1964). 'Socio-economic status and delinquent behaviour'. Journal of Research in Crime and Delinquency, 1, 38–46.

6 152 Alexander, F., and Staub, H. (1956). The Criminal, the Judge and the Public: A Psychological Analysis. Glencoe, Ill., Free Press.

7 120 Alström, C. H. (1950). 'A study of epilepsy in its clinical, social and genetic aspects'. Acta Psychiatrica, Suppl. 63. Copenhagen.

8 239 Andenaes, J. (1965). 'Punishment and the problem of general prevention'. Fifth International Congress of Criminology. Montreal.

9 112 Anderson, J. W. (1958). 'Recidivism, intelligence and social class'. British Journal of Delinquency, 8, 294–7.

10 138 Anthony, H. Sylvia (1959). 'Association between psychomotor behaviour and delinquency'. Nature, 183, 343–4.

11 170 Argyle, M. (1961). 'A new approach to the classification of delinquents with implications for treatment'. California Board of Corrections, Monograph No. 2, 15–26.

12 62 Bagot, J. H. (1941). Juvenile Delinquency. Jonathan Cape.

13 20, 23 Banks, Charlotte (1962). 'Violence'. *The Howard Journal*, 9, 1–13.

14 278 Banks, Charlotte (1964). 'Reconviction of young offenders'. *Current Legal Problems*, Vol. 17. Stevens & Sons.

15 70, 72, 215 Banks, Charlotte (1965). 'Boys in detention centres', in Banks, C., and Broadhurst, P. L. (eds.), *Studies in Psychology*. London University Press.

16 195 Bender, L. (1965). 'Offender and offended children', in Slovenko, R. (ed.), *Sexual Behaviour and the Law*. Springfield, Ill., C. Thomas.

17 278 Benson, G. (1959). 'Prediction methods and young prisoners'. *British Journal of Delinquency*, 9, 192–9.

18 202 Berkowitz, L. (1962). *Aggression*. New York, McGraw-Hill.

19 187 Bewley, T. (1965). 'Heroin addiction in the United Kingdom (1954–1964)'. *British Medical Journal*, 2, 1284–6.

20 86 Bloch, H., and Niederhoffer, A. (1958). *The Gang : A Study in Adolescent Behaviour*. New York, Philosophical Library.

21 92 Boruda, D. J. (1961). 'Prediction and selection of delinquents', in *Juvenile Delinquency Facts and Facets*, No. 17. U.S. Children's Bureau.

22 27 Bovet, L. (1951). *Psychiatric Aspects of Juvenile Delinquency*. W.H.O. Monograph No. 1.

23 157 Bowlby, J. (1946). *Forty-four Juvenile Thieves*. Baillière, Tindall & Cox.

24 157 Bowlby, J. (1953 etc.). *Child Care and the Growth of Love*. Penguin Books.

25 277 Burchard, J., and Tyler, V. (1965). 'The modification of delinquent behaviour through operant conditioning'. *Behaviour Research and Therapy*, 2, 245–50.

26 62, 72, 110, 118 Burt, C. (1925). *The Young Delinquent* (4th edition 1944). London University Press.

27 208, 264 Carpenter, Mary (1851). *Reformatory Schools for the Children of the Perishing and Dangerous Classes and for Juvenile Offenders*.

28 70   Carr-Saunders, A. M., *et al.* (1942). *Young Offenders*. Cambridge University Press.

29 190   Casriel, D. (1963). *So Fair a House: The Story of Synanon*. New York, Prentice-Hall.

30 112   Castell, J. H. F., and Mittler, P. J. (1965). 'Intelligence of patients in sub-normality hospitals'. *British Journal of Psychiatry*, *3*, 219–25.

31 217   Cavenagh, W. E., and Sparks, R. F. (1965). 'Out of Court?'. *New Society*, 15 July.

32 117   Charles, D. C. (1953). 'Ability and accomplishment of persons earlier judged mentally deficient'. *Genetic Psychological Monographs*, *47*, 3–71.

33 187   Chein, I., *et al.* (1964). *Narcotics, Delinquency and Social Policy*. Tavistock Publications.

34 132   Chess, S., *et al.* (1960). 'Implications of a longitudinal study of child development'. *American Journal of Psychiatry*, *117*, 434–41.

35 40   Christie, Nils, *et al.* (1965). 'A study of self-reported crime'. *Scandinavian Studies in Criminology*, *1*, 86–116.

36 27   Christie, Nils (1960). *Unge Norske Lovertredere*. Oslo.

37 266   Clark, D. H. (1965). 'The Therapeutic Community – concept, practice and future'. *British Journal of Psychiatry*, *111*, 947–54.

38 114   Clarke, A. D. B., and Clarke, A. M. (1954). 'Cognitive changes in the feeble-minded'. *British Journal of Psychology*, *45*, 173–9.

39 18   Clifford, W. (1965). 'Problems in criminological research in Africa south of the Sahara'. *International Review of Criminal Policy*, *23*, 11–17.

40 93   Cloward, R. A., and Ohlin, L. E. (1961). *Delinquency and Opportunity: A Theory of Delinquent Gangs*. Glencoe, Ill., Free Press.

41 89   Cohen, A. K. (1955). *Delinquent Boys: The Culture of the Gang*. Glencoe, Ill., Free Press.

42 188   Connell, P. H. (1965). 'The assessment and treatment of adolescent drug takers'. *Proceedings of the Leeds Symposium on Behavioural Disorders*. Dagenham, May & Baker.

43 221   Cooper, Beryl, and Nicholas, G. (1963). *Crime in the Sixties*, p. 29. Bow Group.

44 115   Craft, M. J. (1959). 'Personality disorder and dullness'. *Lancet*, 25 April, 856–8.

45 255   Craig, Maude M., and Furst, P. W. (1965). 'What happens after treatment'. *Social Service Review*, *39*, 165–71.

46 207   Cristoph, J. B. (1962). *Capital Punishment and British Politics*. Allen & Unwin.

47 121   Douglas, J. W. B. (1960). '"Premature" children at primary schools'. *British Medical Journal*, *1*, 1008–13.

48 244   Douglas, J. W. B. (1964). *The Home and the School*. MacGibbon & Kee.

49 161   Douglas, J. W. B., and Blomfield, J. M. (1958). *Children Under Five : the Results of a National Survey*. Allen & Unwin.

50 120   Drillien, C. M. (1964). *The Growth and Development of the Prematurely Born Infant*. E. & S. Livingstone.

51 208   Du Cane, E. F. (1885). *The Punishment and Prevention of Crime*, p. 200.

52 223   Dunlop, A. B., and McCabe, S. (1965). *Young Men in Detention Centres*. Routledge.

53 115   East, W. Norwood, *et al.* (1942). *The Adolescent Criminal*. Churchill.

54 63   East, W. Norwood, *et al.* (1942). op. cit., Tables 63 and 64.

55 123   Ehrlich, S. K., and Keogh, R. P. (1956). 'The psychopath in a mental institution'. *Archives of Neurological Psychiatry*, *76*, 286–95.

56 58, 110, 118 Eilenberg, M. D. (1961). 'Remand home boys: 1930–1955'. *British Journal of Criminology*, *2*, 111.

57 122   Ellingson, R. J. (1954). 'The incidence of EEG abnormality among patients with mental disorders of apparently non-organic origin: a critical review'. *American Journal of Psychiatry*, *111*, 263–75.

58 40   Elmhorn, K. (1965). 'Study in self-reported delinquency among school-children in Stockholm'. *Scandinavian Studies in Criminology*, *1*, 117–46.

59	280	Empey, L. T., *et al.* (1961). 'The Provo Experiment in delinquency rehabilitation'. *American Sociological Review*, *26*, 679–96.
60	280	Empey, L. T., *et al.* (1964). 'The Provo Experiment'. *California Board of Corrections*, Monograph No. 4.
61	198	Epps, Phyllis (1951). '300 female delinquents in borstal'. *British Journal of Delinquency*, *1*, 187–97.
62	41	Erickson, M. L., and Empey, L. T. (1963). 'Court records, undetected delinquency and decision making'. *Journal of Criminal Law, Criminology and Police Science*, *54*, 456–69.
63	147, 171	Eron, L. D., *et al.* (1963). 'Social class, parental punishment for aggression and child aggression'. *Child Development*, *34*, 849–67.
64	137, 144	Eysenck, H. J. (1964). *Crime and Personality*. Routledge.
65	141	Eysenck, H. J. (1964). op. cit., p. 117.
66	146	Eysenck, H. J. (1964). op. cit., p. 160.
67	143	Eysenck, H. J. (1959). 'The inheritance and nature of extraversion', in Halmos, P., and Iliffe, A. H. (eds.), *Readings in General Psychology*. Routledge.
68	143	Eysenck, H. J., *et al.* (1960). *Behaviour Therapy and the Neuroses*. Oxford, Pergamon.
69	58, 118	Ferguson, T. (1952). *The Young Delinquent in his Social Setting*. Oxford University Press.
70	72	Ferguson, T. (1952). op. cit., p. 22.
71	73	Ferguson, T. (1952). op. cit., p. 21.
72	26	Ferguson, T., and Cunnison, J. (1956). *In Their Early Twenties: A Study of Glasgow Youth*, Table 24, p. 76. Oxford University Press.
73	107	Ferrero, G. L. (1911). *Criminal Man: According to the Classification of Cesare Lombroso*.
74	94	Fletcher, C. (1964). 'Beat and gangs on Merseyside'. *New Society*, 20 February.
75	36	Fletcher, R. (1962). *The Family and Marriage in Britain*. Penguin Books.
76	239	Fordham, Peta (1965). *The Robbers' Tale*. Hodder & Stoughton.

77   207, 225   Fox, L. W. (1952). *The English Prison and Borstal System*. Routledge.

78   277   Freund, K. (1960). 'Some problems in the treatment of homosexuality', in Eysenck, H. J. (ed.), *Behaviour Therapy and the Neuroses*. Oxford, Pergamon.

79   151   Friedlander, Kate (1947). *Psycho-analytic Approach to Juvenile Delinquency*. Kegan Paul.

80   97   Fyvel, T..R. (1961). *The Insecure Offenders*. Chatto & Windus; Penguin Books (1963, revised).

81   197, 198   Gibbens, T. C. N. (1958). 'Psychiatry in remand homes for wayward girls'. *Actes du cinquième congrès international de défense sociale*, pp. 579–88. Stockholm.

82   58, 115, 119, 138, 169   Gibbens, T. C. N. (1963). *Psychiatric Studies of Borstal Lads*. Maudsley Monographs No. 11. Oxford University Press.

83   56   Gibbens, T. C. N. (1963). op. cit., p. 62.

84   70, 72   Gibbens, T. C. N. (1963). op. cit., p. 69.

85   203   Gibbens, T. C. N. (1963). op. cit., p. 17.

86   123   Gibbens, T. C. N., et al. (1959). 'A follow-up study of criminal psychopaths'. *Journal of Mental Science*, *105*, 108–15.

87   195   Gibbens, T. C. N., and Prince, Joyce E. (1963). *Child Victims of Sex Offences*. I.S.T.D.

88   26, 228   Gibbens, T. C. N., and Prince, Joyce E. (1965). 'The results of borstal training', in Halmos, P. (ed.), *Sociological Review Monograph*, No. 9. Keele.

89   122   Gibbs, F. A., and Bagchi, B. K. (1945). 'Electroencephalographic study of criminals'. *American Journal of Psychiatry*, *102*, 294–8.

90   138   Gibson, H. B. (1964). 'The Spiral Maze: a psychomotor test with implications for the study of delinquency'. *British Journal of Psychology*, *54*, 219–25.

91   11   Giles, F. T. (1959). *The Child and the Law*. Penguin Books.

92   70, 229   Gittins, J. (1952). *Approved School Boys*. H.M.S.O.

| 93 | 63 | Glaser, D., and Rice, K. (1959). 'Crime, age, and employment'. *American Sociological Review*, *24*, 679–86. |

94 166   Glueck, Eleanor T. (1964). 'Identification of potential delinquents at 2–3 years of age'. *International Journal of Social Psychiatry*, *12*, 5–16.

95 72, 118, 165   Glueck, S., and Glueck, E. T. (1950). *Unravelling Juvenile Delinquency*. New York, The Commonwealth Fund.

96 28   Glueck, S., and Glueck, E. T. (1940). *Juvenile Delinquents Grown Up*. New York, The Commonwealth Fund.

97 126   Glueck, S., and Glueck, E. T. (1956). *Physique and Delinquency*. New York, Harper.

98 165   Glueck, S., and Glueck, E. T. (1964). *Ventures in Criminology*. Tavistock Publications.

99 266   Goffman, E. (1961). *Asylums*. New York, Doubleday Anchor.

100 57   Gold, M. (1963). *Status Forces in Delinquent Boys*. Ann Arbor, Michigan University Press.

101 59   Gold, M. (1963). op. cit., p. 173.

102 158   Goldfarb, W. (1943). 'Infant rearing and problem behaviour'. *American Journal of Orthopsychiatry*, *13*, 249–65.

103 244   Gordon, E. W. (1965). 'A review of programs of compensatory education'. *American Journal of Orthopsychiatry*, *35*, 640–51.

104 108   Goring, C. (1913). *The English Convict*. H.M.S.O.

105 284   Gottfredson, D. M., and Kelley, B. B. (1963). 'Interpersonal maturity measurement by the California Psychological Inventory'. *Institute for the Study of Crime and Delinquency*, *Report 1*. California.

106 283   Grant, J. D., and Grant, M. Q. (1959). 'A group dynamics approach to the treatment of nonconformists in the navy'. *Annals of the American Academy of Political and Social Science*, *322*, 126–35.

107 38   Grimble, A. (1965). 'Morality and venereal disease'. *Excerpta Criminologica*, *5*, 383–406.

108 65   Grunhut, M. (1956). *Juvenile Offenders Before the Courts*. Oxford, Clarendon Press.

109 296   Grygier, T. (1965). In *Criminology in Transition*. Tavistock Publications.

110 277   Gwynne Jones, H. (1965). 'Behaviour and aversion therapy in the treatment of delinquency'. *British Journal of Criminology*, 5, 355–65.

111 204   Halloran, J. D. (1964). *The Effects of Mass Communication*. Leicester, University Press.

112 29   Hammond, W. H., and Chayen, E. (1963). *Persistent Criminals*, p. 26. H.M.S.O.

113 159   Harlow, H. F. (1961). 'The development of affectional pattern of infant monkeys', in Foss, B. (ed.), *Determinants of Infant Behaviour*. Methuen.

114 159   Harlow, H. F., and Harlow, M. (1962). 'Social deprivation in monkeys'. *Scientific American*, 207, 136–46.

115 43   Hartshorne, H., and May, M. A. (1928). *Studies in Deceit*. New York, Macmillan.

116 46   Hartshorne, H., and May, M. A. (1932). *Studies in the Organization of Character*. New York, Macmillan.

117 145, 170   Hathaway, S. R., and Monachesi, E. D. (1956). 'The M.M.P.I. in the study of juvenile delinquents', in Rose, A. M., *Mental Health and Mental Disorder*. Routledge.

118 169   Hathaway, S. R., and Monachesi, E. D. (1953). *Analysing and Predicting Juvenile Delinquency with the M.M.P.I.* Minneapolis, Minnesota, University Press.

119 53   Havard, J. D. J. (1960). *The Detection of Secret Homicide*, pp. 51–60. Macmillan.

120 173   Hewitt, L. E., and Jenkins, R. L. (1946). *Fundamental Patterns of Maladjustment*. Michigan, State of Illinois, D. H. Green.

121 122   Hill, D., and Pond, D. A. (1952). 'Reflections on 100 capital cases submitted to electro-encephalography'. *Journal of Mental Science*, 98, 23–43.

122 68   Hirsch, C. A. (1953). 'La criminalité des

Nord-Africains en France'. *Revue internationale de criminologie,* 298–302.

123 254   Hodges, E. F., and Tait, C. D. (1965). 'A follow up study of potential delinquents'. *American Journal of Psychiatry, 120,* 449–53.

124 221   Home Office (1847). *Reports of Committees,* Vol. VII (3), pp. 297, 79.

125 222   Home Office (1959). *Penal Practice in a Changing Society,* Cmnd 645. H.M.S.O.

126 211   Home Office (1960). *Prisons and Borstals: Statement of Policy and Practice* (4th edition), p. 57. H.M.S.O.

127 226, 227   Home Office (1964). *Prisons and Borstals 1963,* Cmnd 2381, pp. 26, 29, 33. H.M.S.O.

128 214   Home Office (1966). *Criminal Statistics, England and Wales, 1965,* Cmnd 3037, pp. xxiii, xxvi. H.M.S.O.

129 192   Home Office (1966). *Criminal Statistics, England and Wales, 1965,* Cmnd 3037, paragraph 14, p. xiii; Table IV (a), p. 188. H.M.S.O.

130 223   Home Office (1965). *Prisons and Borstals, 1963, Statistical Tables,* Cmnd 2630, Tables D.9 and D.15. H.M.S.O.

131 217   Home Office (1965). *The Child, the Family and the Young Offender,* Cmnd 2742. H.M.S.O.

132 24, 211, 278   Home Office (1964). *The Sentence of the Court.* H.M.S.O.

133 280   Hood, R. (1962). *Sentencing in Magistrates' Courts.* Stevens & Sons.

134 227   Hood, R. (1965). *Borstal Reassessed.* Heinemann.

135 108   Hooton, E. A. (1939). *The American Criminal: An Anthropological Study.* Cambridge, Mass., Harvard University Press.

136 61   House of Commons (1817). *Second Report of the House of Commons Committee on the State of the Police in the Metropolis.*

137 220   House of Lords (1863). *Report of the Select Committee of the House of Lords on Prison Discipline.*

138   52   Hurwitz, S. (1952). *Criminology*, p. 393. Copenhagen and London, Allen & Unwin.

139   67   Jones, Howard (1956). *Crime and the Penal System*. University Tutorial Press.

140   66   Jones, Howard (1958). 'Approaches to an ecological study'. *British Journal of Delinquency*, *8*, 277–93.

141   265   Jones, Howard (1960). *Reluctant Rebels*. Tavistock Publications.

142   230   Jones, Howard (1965). 'The approved school: a theoretical model', in Halmos, P. (ed.), *Sociological Review Monographs*, No. 9. Keele.

143   143   Jung, C. G. (1923). *Psychological Types*.

144   54   Jungk, R. (1961). *Children of the Ashes* (trans.). Heinemann; Penguin Books (1963).

145   130   Kallman, F. J. (1938). *The Genetics of Schizophrenia*. New York, Augustin.

146   190   Kessel, N., and Walton, H. (1965). *Alcoholism*. Penguin Books.

147   52   Kinberg, O. (1935). *Basic Problems of Criminology*, pp. 130–36. Copenhagen, Levin and Munksgaard.

148   193   Kinsey, A. C., *et al.* (1948). *Sexual Behavior in the Human Male*. Philadelphia, Saunders.

149   222   Klare, H. J. (1962). *Anatomy of Prison*. Penguin Books.

150   180   Kohlberg, L. (1964). 'The development of moral character', in Hoffman, M. L., *et al.* (eds.), *Child Development*, Vol. 1. New York, Russell Sage Foundation.

151   169   Kvaraceus, W. C. (1961). 'Forecasting delinquency'. *Exceptional Children*, *27*, 429–35.

152   160   Lewis, Hilda (1954). *Deprived Children*. Oxford University Press.

153   119   Lewison, E. (1965). 'An experiment in facial reconstructive surgery in a prison population'. *Canadian Medical Association Journal*, *92*, 251–4.

154   160   Little, A. (1965). 'Parental deprivation, separation and crime'. *British Journal of Criminology*, *5*, 419–30.

155   144   Little, A. (1963). 'Professor Eysenck's theory of crime: an empirical test on adolescent

offenders'. *British Journal of Criminology*, 4, 152–63.

156 19   Little, A. (1965). 'The increase in crime 1952–1962: an empirical analysis on adolescent offenders'. *British Journal of Criminology*, 5, 77–82.

157 56   Little, W. R., and Ntsekhe, V. R. (1959). 'Social class background of young offenders from London'. *British Journal of Delinquency*, 10, 130–35.

158 147, 171   Loban, W. (1953). 'A study of social sensitivity among adolescents'. *Journal of Educational Psychology*, 44, 102–12.

159 122   Loomis, S. Dale (1965). 'EEG abnormalities as a correlate of behaviour in adolescent male delinquents'. *American Journal of Psychiatry*, 121, 1003–6.

160 18   Lunden, W. A. (1961). *Statistics on Delinquency*. Iowa, State University Press.

161 211   McClintock, F. H. (1961). *Attendance Centres*. Macmillan.

162 74, 201   McClintock, F. H. (1963). *Crimes of Violence*. Macmillan.

163 23   McClintock, F. H. (1963). op. cit., Appendix XI.

164 27, 71, 110, 118, 161, 253   McCord, W., and McCord, Joan (1959). *Origins of Crime*. New York, Columbia University Press.

165 18   McQueen, A. J. (1960). 'A comparative perspective on juvenile delinquency', in *Delinquency, Patterns, Causes, Cures*. Ann Arbor, University of Michigan.

166 67   Mannheim, H. (1965). *Comparative Criminology*. Routledge.

167 57   Mannheim, H., Spencer, J., and Lynch, G. (1957). 'Magisterial policy in the London juvenile courts'. *British Journal of Delinquency*, 8, 13–33.

168 25, 164   Mannheim, H., and Wilkins, L. T. (1955). *Prediction Methods in Relation to Borstal Training*. H.M.S.O.

169 281   Mannheim, H., and Wilkins, L. T. (1955). op. cit., Table 54.

170 112   Marcus, B. (1956). 'Intelligence, criminality and the expectation of recidivism'. *British Journal of Delinquency*, *6*, 147–51.

171 202   Martin, J. M. (1961). *Juvenile Vandalism*. Springfield, Ill., C. Thomas.

172 95   Matza, D. (1964). *Delinquency and Drift*. New York, J. Wiley.

173 39   Mays, J. B. (1954). *Growing Up in the City*, p. 25. Liverpool, University Press.

174 37   Mays, J. B. (1963). *Crime and the Social Structure*. Faber.

175 213   Mays, J. B. (1965). 'The Liverpool Police Juvenile Liaison Officer Scheme', in Halmos, P. (ed.), *Sociological Review Monographs*, No. 9, Keele.

176 88   Merton, R. K. (1957). *Social Theory and Social Structure*. Glencoe, Ill., Free Press.

177 255   Meyer, H. J., Bargatta, E. F., and Jones, W. C. (1965). *Girls at Vocational High*. New York, Russell Sage Foundation.

178 277   Middleton, P. M. (1964). 'Motor deprivation or paralysed awareness in the treatment of delinquency'. Paper read at the International Congress of Social Psychiatry, London.

179 54   Milgram, S. (1965). 'Some conditions of obedience and disobedience to authority'. *Human Relations*, *18*, 57–76.

180 267   Miller, D. (1964). *Growth to Freedom*. Tavistock Publications.

181 91   Miller, W. B. (1958). 'Lower class culture as a generating milieu of gang delinquency'. *Journal of Social Issues*, *14*, 5–19.

182 188   Ministry of Health (1965). *Drug Addiction: The Second Report of the Interdepartmental Committee*. H.M.S.O.

183 195   Mohr, J. W., Turner, R. E., and Jerry, M. B. (1964). *Pedophilia and Exhibitionism*. Toronto, University Press.

184 71   Monahan, T. P. (1957). 'Family status and the delinquent child: a re-appraisal and some new findings'. *Social Forces*, *35*, 250–59.

185 203   Morris, H. H., *et al.* (1956). 'Aggressive

behaviour disorders of childhood'. *American Journal of Psychiatry*, *112*, 991–7.

186 197   Morris, Ruth R. (1964). 'Female delinquency and relational problems'. *Social Forces*, *43*, 82–9.

187 66   Morris, T. P. (1957). *The Criminal Area*. Routledge.

188 56   Morris, T. P. (1957). op. cit., p. 166.

189 222   Morris, T. P., and Morris, Pauline (1963). *Pentonville*. Routledge.

190 226   Morrison, R. L. (1957). 'Borstal allocation'. *British Journal of Delinquency*, *8*, 95–105.

191 249   Morse, Mary (1965). *The Unattached*. Penguin Books.

192 38   Morton, R. S. (1966). *Venereal Diseases*. Penguin Books.

193 67, 69   Moses, Earl R. (1947). 'Differentials in crime rates between negroes and whites'. *American Sociological Review*, *12*, 411–20.

194 167   Mulligan, D. G., Douglas, J. W. B., Hammond, W. A., and Tizard, J. (1963). 'Delinquency'. *Proceedings of the Royal Society of Medicine*, *56*, 1083–4.

195 40   Murphy, F. J., *et al.* (1946). 'The incidence of hidden delinquency'. *American Journal of Orthopsychiatry*, *16*, 686–96.

196 111   Naar, R. (1965). 'A note on the intelligence of delinquents'. *British Journal of Criminology*, *5*, 82–5.

197 160   Naess, S. (1959). 'Mother–child separation and delinquency'. *British Journal of Delinquency*, *10*, 22–35.

198 119   Ogden, D. A. (1959). 'Use of surgical rehabilitation in young delinquents'. *British Medical Journal*, *2*, 432–4.

199 198   O'Kelly, Elizabeth (1955). 'Delinquent girls and their parents'. *British Journal of Educational Psychology*, *28*, 59–66.

200 126   Parnell, R. W. (1958). *Behaviour and Physique*, p. 61. Arnold.

201 180, 283   Peck, P. F., and Havinghurst, R. J. (1960). *The Psychology of Character Development*. New York, J. Wiley.

202   115   Penrose, L. S. (1964). *The Biology of Mental Defect* (3rd edition), p. 44. Sidgwick & Jackson.

203   172   Peterson, D. R., and Quay, H. C. (1961). 'Personality factors related to juvenile delinquency'. *Child Development, 32,* 355–72.

204   224   Pharoah, N. (1963). 'The long blunt shock'. *New Society,* 26 September.

205   179, 283   Piaget, J. (1932). *The Moral Judgment of the Child* (trans. M. Gabain). Routledge.

206   52   Pinatel, Jean (1963). *Criminologie,* p. 108. Paris, Dalloz.

207   197   Pollak, O. L. (1950). *The Criminality of Women.* Philadelphia, Pennsylvania State University Press.

208   267   Polsky, H. W. (1962). *Cottage Six: The Social System of Delinquent Boys in Residential Treatment.* New York, Russell Sage Foundation.

209   121   Pond, D. A. (1961). 'Psychiatric aspects of epileptic and brain-damaged children'. *British Medical Journal, 2,* 1377–88, 1454–9.

210   40   Porterfield, A. L. (1946). *Youth in Trouble.* Fort Worth, Texas.

211   111   Prentice, N. M., and Kelly, F. J. (1963). 'Intelligence and delinquency: a reconsideration'. *Journal of Social Psychology, 60,* 327–37.

212   19   Prys Williams, G. (1962). *Patterns of Teenage Delinquency,* p. 19. Christian Economic and Social Research Foundation.

213   173   Quay, H. C. (1964). 'Personality dimensions in delinquent males as inferred from the factor analysis of behaviour ratings'. *Journal of Research in Crime and Delinquency, 1,* 33–7.

214   207   Radzinowicz, L. (1948). *A History of the English Criminal Law,* Vol. 1, pp. 14, 523. Stevens & Sons.

215   19   Radzinowicz, L. (1966). *Ideology and Crime.* Heinemann.

216   78   Radzinowicz, L. (1966). op. cit., p. 99.

217   194   Radzinowicz, L., ed. (1957). *Sexual Offences.* Macmillan.

218 169   Reiss, A. J. (1951). 'Delinquency as the failure of personal and social controls'. *American
Sociological Review*, *15*, 196–207.

219 175   Reiss, A. J. (1952). 'Social correlates of
psychological types of delinquency'. *Ameri-
can Sociological Review*, *17*, 710–18.

220 34   *Report of the Commissioner of Police of the
Metropolis for the year 1932*, Cmnd 4294,
p. 16.

221 33   *Report of the Committee of the Society for
the Improvement of Prison Discipline and for
the Improvement of Offenders* (1818), pp. 11,
13.

222 216   Romander, H. (1965). *The Child Welfare
Act of Sweden*. Stockholm, Ministry of
Justice.

223 56, 70, 228 Rose, A. G. (1954). *Five Hundred Borstal
Boys*. Oxford, Blackwell.

224 207   Rose, (A.) G. (1961). *The Struggle for Penal
Reform*. Stevens & Sons.

225 116   Rudolf, G. de M. (1961). 'Crime amongst
the unsupervised mentally sub-normal'.
Medical Press, *245*, 466–72.

226 69   Savitz, L. (1962). 'Delinquency and migra-
tion', in Wolfgang, M. E., *et al.* (eds.), *The
Sociology of Crime and Delinquency*. New
York, J. Wiley.

227 262   Schmideberg, Melita (1960). 'Making the
patient aware'. *Crime and Delinquency*, *6*,
255–61.

228 38, 192   Schofield, M. (1965). *The Sexual Behaviour
of Young People*, pp. 88–9. Longmans.

229 195   Schofield, M. (1965). *Sociological Aspects of
Homosexuality*, p. 154. Longmans.

230 170   Schuessler, K. F., *et al.* (1950). 'Personality
characteristics of criminals'. *American Journal
of Sociology*, *55*, 476–84.

231 247   Schwitzgebel, R. (1964). *Streetcorner Research*. Cambridge, Mass., Harvard Univer-
sity Press.

232 94   Scott, P. D. (1956). 'Gangs and delinquent
groups in London'. *British Journal of Delinquency*, *7*, 4–26.

233 215   Scott, P. D. (1959). 'Juvenile courts: the juvenile's point of view'. *British Journal of Delinquency*, 9, 200–209.

234 20, 26, 36, 230   Scott, P. D. (1964). 'Approved school success rates'. *British Journal of Criminology*, 4, 525–56.

235 188   Scott, P. D., and Willcox, D. R. C. (1965). 'Delinquency and amphetamines'. *British Journal of Psychiatry*, 111, 865–75.

236 171   Sears, R. R., MacCoby, E. E., and Levin, H. (1957). *Patterns of Child Rearing*. New York, Row, Peterson & Co.

237 35   Sellin, Thorsten, and Wolfgang, Marvin E. (1964). *The Measurement of Delinquency*. New York, J. Wiley.

238 65   Shaw, R. Clifford, and McKay, Henry D. (1942). *Juvenile Delinquency and Urban Areas*. Chicago, University Press.

239 245   Sheldon, E. B., and Glazier, R. A. (1965). *Pupils and Schools in New York City*. New York, Russell Sage Foundation.

240 124   Sheldon, W. H., et al. (1949). *Varieties of Delinquent Youth*. New York, Harper.

241 126   Sheldon, W. H., et al. (1949). op. cit., p. 836.

242 131   Shields, J. (1962). *Monozygotic Twins*. Oxford University Press.

243 265   Shields, R. W. (1962). *A Cure of Delinquents*. Heinemann.

244 41, 59   Short, J. F., and Nye, F. I. (1958). 'Extent of unrecorded juvenile delinquency'. *Journal of Criminal Law, Criminology and Police Science*, 49, 296–302.

245 170   Silver, A. W. (1963). 'TAT and M.M.P.I. psychopath deviant scale differences between delinquent and non-delinquent adolescents'. *Journal of Consulting Psychology*, 27, 370.

246 185   Sington, D., ed. (1965). *Psycho-social Aspects of Drug-Taking* (Proceedings of Conference at University College, London), p. 40. Oxford, Pergamon.

247 188   Sington, D., ed. (1965). op. cit., p. 39.

248 131   Slater, E. T. O. (1953). *Psychotic and Neurotic Illnesses in Twins*. H.M.S.O.

249 75   Sprott, W. J. H. (1954). *The Social Background of Delinquency.* Nottingham, University Press.

250 113   Stein, Z., and Susser, M. (1960). 'Families of dull children'. *Journal of Mental Science, 106,* 1296–319.

251 73   Sterne, R. S. (1964). *Delinquent Conduct and Broken Homes.* New Haven, Conn., College and University Press.

252 119   Stott, D. H. (1962). 'Evidence for a congenital factor in maladjustment and delinquency'. *American Journal of Psychiatry, 118,* 781–94.

253 168   Stott, D. H. (1963). *The Social Adjustment of Children.* London University Press.

254 168   Stott, D. H. (1964). 'Sociological and psychological explanations of delinquency'. *International Journal of Social Psychiatry* (Congress edition, No. 4), 35–43.

255 131   Stumpfl, F. (1936). *Die Ursprünge des Verbrechens dargestellt am Lebenslauf von Zwillingen.* Leipzig.

256 194   Sturup, G. K. (1960). 'Sex offenses: the Scandinavian experience'. *Law and Contemporary Problems, 25,* 361–75.

257 68   Sutherland, Edwin H., and Cressey, Donald R. (1955). *Principles of Criminology* (5th edition, revised). Chicago, Lippincott.

258 54   Sutherland, Edwin H., and Cressey, Donald R. (1955). op. cit., p. 163.

259 86   Tannenbaum, F. (1938). *Crime and the Community.* New York, Columbia University Press.

260 85   Thrasher, F. M. (1927). *The Gang.* Chicago, University Press.

261 141   Trasler, G. B. (1962). *The Explanation of Criminality.* Routledge.

262 73   Trenaman, J. (1952). *Out of Step.* Methuen.
263 70   Trenaman, J. (1952). op. cit., p. 195.
264 243   United Nations (1965). 'Social forces and the prevention of criminality'. *Third Congress on the Prevention of Crime and the Treatment of Offenders.* Stockholm.

265 59 Vaz, E. W. (1966). 'Self-reported juvenile delinquency and socio-economic status'. *Canadian Journal of Corrections, 8*, 20–27.

266 111 Vernon, P. E. (1965). 'Environmental handicaps and intellectual development'. *British Journal of Educational Psychology, 35*, 1–22.

267 166 Voss, H. L. (1963). 'The predictive efficiency of the Glueck Social Prediction Scale'. *Journal of Criminal Law, Criminology and Police Science, 54*, 421–30.

268 67, 207 Walker, N. (1965). *Crime and Punishment in Britain.* Edinburgh, University Press.

269 99 Walker, N. (1965). op. cit., p. 103.

270 116 Walker, N. (1965). op. cit., p. 59.

271 196 Walker, N. (1965). op. cit., Table 34, p. 296.

272 282 Walker, N. (1965). op. cit., p. 257.

273 40 Wallerstein, J. S., and Wyle, C. J. (1947). 'Our law-abiding law-breakers'. *Probation, 25*, 107–12.

274 160 Wardle, C. J. (1961). 'Two generations of broken homes in the genesis of conduct and behaviour disorders in children'. *British Medical Journal,* 5 August, 349.

275 285 Warren, M. Q., and Palmer, T. B. (1965). 'Community Treatment Project. Fourth progress report'. *California Youth Authority, CTP Research Report,* No. 6.

276 29, 129, 146 West, D. J. (1963). *The Habitual Prisoner.* Macmillan.

277 22 West, D. J. (1965). *Murder followed by Suicide.* Heinemann.

278 34 Whitaker, Ben (1964). *The Police.* Penguin Books.

279 86 Whyte, W. F. (1943). *Street Corner Society: The Social Structure of an Italian Slum.* Chicago, University Press.

280 117 Wildenskov, H. O. T. (1962). 'A long-term follow-up of subnormals originally exhibiting severe behaviour disorders or criminality'. *Proceedings of the London 1960 Conference on the Scientific Study of Mental Deficiency,* 217–22. Dagenham, May & Baker.

281 281 Wilkins, L. T. (1958). 'A small comparative

study of the results of probation'. *British Journal of Delinquency*, 8, 201–9.

282 24, 91   Wilkins, L. T. (1964). *Social Deviance.* Tavistock Publications.

283 240   Williams, E. N. (1965). *A Documentary History of England*, Vol. 2. Penguin Books.

284 265   Wills, W. D. (1964). *Homer Lane: A Biography.* Allen & Unwin.

285 204   Wilson, B. R. (1961). 'Mass media and the public attitude to crime'. *Criminal Law Review*, 376–84.

286 100   Wilson, B. R. (1965). *The Social Context of the Youth Problem*, Thirteenth Charles Russell Memorial Lecture. 17 Bedford Square, London W.C.1.

287 77   Wilson, Harriet C. (1962). *Delinquency and Child Neglect.* Allen & Unwin.

288 201   Wolfgang, M. E., and Ferracuti, F. (1964). 'Violent aggressive behaviour as a socio-psychological phenomenon'. *International Journal of Social Psychiatry* (Congress edition, No. 4).

289 109   Woodward, Mary (1955). *Low Intelligence and Delinquency.* I.S.T.D.

290 33   Worsley, Henry (1849). *Juvenile Depravity.* Charles Gilpin.

291 62   Worsley, Henry (1849). op. cit., pp. 90, 246.

292 92   Yablonsky, L. (1962). *The Violent Gang.* New York and London, Macmillan.

293 37   Young, M., and Willmott, P. (1957). *Family and Kinship in East London.* Routledge; Penguin Books (1962).

Indexes

General Index

Abortion, 242
'Acting out', 152–3
Addiction, 185–91, 241–2
Age: and crime incidence, 14–16, 29; and legal process, 11, 208–18; and re-conviction rate, 24–5, 291; and type of crime, 20–22, 30, 200, 217, 291
Aggression, release of, 52, 54–5, 189
Aggressive social work, 247
Aggressiveness, 76, 122–3, 147, 150–51, 167, 171, 174–5, 188–9, 201, 203, 224, 267–8, 271, 275. *See also* Violence.
Alcohol, 191. *See also* Drinking offences.
Alcoholics Anonymous, 190, 298
Allocation centres, 226
Animals, deprived, 158–9
Anomie, 87–9
Anti-social characters, 149–50, 171, 173–6, 189. *See also* Psychopaths.
Approved schools, 201, 209, 211, 218, 247
Aspiration level, 59, 245
Attendance centres, 211–12

Behaviour therapy, 276–8
Borstals, 25, 58, 164, 210, 225–9, 247, 273, 281–2, 297
Boston, 28, 52, 126
Brain damage, 117, 120–23, 269
Broken homes, 54, 61, 69–73, 142, 157–62, 227, 268, 270

Californian treatment research, 283–5
Cambridge–Somerville Youth Study, 27, 40, 71, 110, 161, 253–4
'Care, protection or control' process, 12, 199, 216–19
Casework, 217, 252–4, 255–7, 264, 274, 280, 284–5, 298
Chicago, 65, 86, 93, 100, 144, 175
Child guidance, 28, 214, 254–6
Child rearing, 37, 46, 76–7, 100, 142, 147, 151, 216, 294. *See also* Maternal care.
Children: murders of, 52–3, 78; sex assaults on, 194–5
Children's Acts, 34, 209, 241
Civil process. *See* 'Care, protection or control' process.
Civil rights, 215, 236, 246
Classification, 173–82, 283–5
Clubs, 246–7, 249–50
Comparative studies, 14, 17–18, 53, 98, 187
Conditioning, 139–42, 146, 276–8
Conformity, 83–4, 140, 234
Conscience, theory of, 140, 179–82
Convictions: incidence of, 13, 19, 21, 34, 77, 161–2, 192, 200; increases in, 22–4, 33–5, 47; non–indictable, 16–17. *See also* Criminal statistics; Re-conviction rates.
Corporal punishment, 209, 211, 264
Cottage Six, 274–6

Courts, reports for, 214
Crime: definition of, 12, 83; index of, 35, 41; unrecorded, 34, 39–42; wave of, 33–4, 47. See also Convictions.
Criminal Justice Acts, 11, 210, 211, 212, 222
Criminal Record Office, 129
Criminal responsibility, 11, 237
Criminal statistics, 13–16, 19, 21, 29, 34, 192, 200, 213–14, 290, 291; foreign, 17–18; validity of, 34–6. See also Convictions.
Criminal type inborn, 106–9, 129–33
Crowther Report, 97

'Dark figure', 34, 39–42
Denmark, 18, 52, 117, 194. See also Scandinavia.
Deprivation in infancy, 114–15, 158–9
Detection, 52, 235–6, 239
Detention centres, 72, 211, 223–4
Deterrence: punitive, 233–5, 237–40, 298; protective, 235–7, 298
Differential association, 84–5, 87
Disabilities, 118–21. See also Brain damage.
Divorce, 36–7, 47, 71–3, 75
Drinking offences, 22, 33, 34, 66, 120, 142, 164, 186, 187, 189–90, 191, 203
Drug addiction, 185–91, 241–2

Ecological studies, 64–9. See also Neighbourhood influences.
Economic factors, 61–4, 74, 77–8
Education Act (1944), 12
Education, remedial, 225, 243–6
Educational experiments, 242–6
Educational retardation, 46, 57–9, 97–8, 111–12. See also Intelligence.

Electro-encephalograph (E.E.G.), 122–4, 295
Epilepsy, 120–22, 186
Extraversion, 142–6, 261

Familial crime incidence, 129
Family backgrounds, 74–9, 114–15. See also Broken homes; Child rearing; Maternal care.
Family courts, 217–19
Family: multiple problems in, 130; size of, 73–7
Female delinquency, 15, 22, 45, 196–200, 201
Fines, 212, 279
First offenders, 19, 42, 194, 279
Fit Person Orders, 209, 216
Flint Youth Study, 57, 59, 197
Follow-up studies, 20, 27–9, 71–2, 110, 117, 145, 160–62, 168, 169, 194, 248, 254–6, 273
Frustration intolerance, 149, 202

Gangs, 54, 85–7, 89–90, 94–5, 100, 165, 187, 202, 249–52, 294
Gibson maze, 138
Glueck prediction system, 165–7
Group therapy, 255, 262
Guilt, neurotic, 152

Hanging, 207
Henderson Hospital, 266
Hereditary factor, 129–33
Heroin addiction, 185–8
Hiroshima, 52, 54
Home Office: addict register, 187; classification of offences, 12; committee on children, 16; Prison Department, 211, 229, 279–80, 290; research, 24–5, 29, 278–9, 281. See also Criminal statistics; Family courts.
Homeless delinquents, 54, 61, 227, 270

Homosexuality, 34–5, 41, 192–3, 195–6, 275
Honesty tests, 42–6
Hooliganism, 23–4, 30, 33, 202, 289
Howard League, 222

Imprinting, 158
Incentives to good behaviour, 235, 248, 277
Insanity, 124. *See also* Mental Health Act.
Intelligence: of offenders, 109–17; and type of crime, 111–12, 116–17
Introversion, 143

Juvenile courts, 17, 28, 214, 218, 280

Legal representation, 215
Liverpool, 39, 62, 65, 94, 213

Maladjustment, measurement of, 119, 120, 167–9, 172–3, 175, 181, 283–4
Maternal care, 161–2, 165, 166, 254
Maternal deprivation, 157–62
Maturity levels, 180–82, 283–5
Marijuana, 185–6, 188
Mental Health Act, 112, 191, 297
Mental hospitals, 217, 266, 297
Mentally abnormal offenders, 122–4. *See also* Neurosis.
Mentally subnormal offenders, 115–17
Mesomorphy, 124–8, 138, 143, 145
Middle–class delinquents, 40, 44, 83, 100, 201, 251–2
Minnesota Multiphasic Personality Inventory, 145, 169–70

Mobilization for Youth Inc., 246, 253
Moral defectives, 106–7. *See also* Psychopaths.
Moral deterioration, 36–9
Moral development, 178–82
Moral instruction, effect of, 45–6
Moscow, 98
Murder, 22, 52–3, 78, 122, 239

Neighbourhood influences, 39, 55, 64–7, 77, 100, 175, 245
Neurosis, and delinquency, 144–5, 148–9, 152–4, 167, 172–6
New York City Youth Board, 255
Northways Home, 270–74
Norway. *See* Scandinavia.

Offences: indictable, 12–13; non-indictable, 16–17. *See also* Convictions; Crime; Sex offences; Violence.
Official Secrets Act, 222
Open prisons and borstals, 221, 281–2
Opportunity for crime, 44, 52–5, 78, 93
Orphans. *See* Broken homes.
Outward Bound courses, 247

Paedophiles, 194–6
Parental behaviour. *See* Child rearing; Maternal care.
Parental illness, 77
Parkhurst Prison, 208–9
Pavlovian theory, 141
Penal system, 207–30, 296–8; history of, 207–11
Pentonville survey, 222
Personality deviation. *See* Antisocial characters; Psychopaths.
Personality tests, 137–47, 166, 169–73, 182, 284, 285

Pestalozzi School, 264
Physical disabilities, 118–21
Physique and delinquency, 124–8, 138, 143, 145
Police: cautions, 213; effects of absence of, 52; juvenile liaison schemes, 213, 244; prosecution policy, 34–5, 213
Porteus maze, 137–8
Poverty, 61–4, 74, 77–8
Predicting delinquency, 139, 158 ff., 163–7
Premature birth, 120, 121
Prevention, 48, 233–7, 298; by community services, 240–46; by detached workers, 246–52; by treating potential offenders, 252–7
Prisons, 61, 208, 221–3
Probation, 212, 217, 283, 298; results of, 281
Promiscuity, 38, 198–200, 216, 273
Prosecution policy, 34–5, 213
Psychoanalytic theory, 147–54, 261–2
Psychomotor performance, 137–9, 171
Psychopaths, 117, 122–3, 130, 142, 144, 150–51, 170–71, 174–5, 176–7, 266, 269; compulsory treatment of, 191, 297

Race, 52, 67–9, 97, 201, 244
Random allocation to treatments, 279–80
Reality, training for, 210, 213, 225, 241, 246, 262, 272
Recidivists, 29, 41–2, 46, 48, 270–72, 292
Re-conviction rates, 24–9, 72, 160, 194, 224, 278–9, 281–2
Religion, 28, 74, 208, 249

Remand homes, 58, 112, 118, 198, 211, 214–15, 217
Restrictive measures, 235–7
Retreatism, 88, 93
Revolutions, 52
Ritualism, 89

Scandinavia, 17–18, 27, 52, 117, 194, 216, 244
Schools: behaviour in, 58–9, 139, 167–9, 171, 255; delinquency rates in, 66
Self-reported delinquency, 39–42, 291
Sentences, 207 ff., 213–14, 279; effects of, 278–9, 280–81
Separation from parents, 71–3, 157–62
Sex offences, 23, 41, 64, 116, 147, 192–6, 198–9
Sex of offenders, 15, 45
Sexual behaviour, 38
Shop-lifters, 196–7, 211
Situational crime, 44, 52–5, 78, 93
Social class, 40, 44, 46, 56–7, 59–60, 65–6, 77–9, 89, 100, 201, 251–2
Social handicap, 28, 56–9, 62, 65–8, 74–9, 88–9, 97–8, 111–15, 244, 292
Social policy. *See* Deterrence; Prevention.
Social protest, 87–91
Socialized delinquents, 174, 175, 177
Stigmata of criminality, 106–8, 128
Sub-culture of delinquency, 89–94, 96, 100–101, 187, 250, 294
Super-ego, 149–50, 171
Sweden. *See* Scandinavia.
Synanon, 190

Television, 204
Theories of delinquency, 87–98, 99–101, 137–54, 293–6
Tolerance, need for, 91–2
Training delinquents, 210, 213, 225, 241, 246, 262, 272
Treatment: by anti-convulsant drugs, 123; by conditioning, 276–8; by cosmetic surgery, 119; by group methods, 255, 262–3; by psychotherapy, 261–2; by therapeutic community, 263–76; continuity, 297; for potential delinquents, 252–7; results, 252–7, 278–85, 298. *See also* Prevention.
Truants, 58, 168, 213
Twins, studies of, 130–32

Unemployment, 63–4, 77
Urban delinquency, 65, 91, 113

Vandalism, 202, 289
Venereal disease, 38, 47, 198
Violence: abnormal, 117, 120, 122, 188–9; and immigration, 68; nature of, 23–4, 53, 200–204, 239; statistics of, 20–21, 64, 200

Welfare agency jurisdiction, 199, 215–17
Welfare programmes, 240–46

Youth culture, 38–40, 88, 91, 95–6, 100–101, 250
Youth organizations, 241, 246–7, 250, 253

Index of Persons

Aichhorn, A., 267–70, 296
Ainsworth, Mary, 158
Akers, R. L., 59
Alexander, Franz, 152, 153, 172
Alström, C. H., 120
Andenaes, J., 239
Anderson, J. W., 112
Anthony, H. Sylvia, 138
Argyle, M., 170–72
Avison, N. H., 19

Bagot, J. H., 62
Banks, Charlotte, 20, 70, 72, 278
Beccaria, Marchese de, 234
Benson, Sir George, 278
Bentham, J., 234
Bettelheim, Bruno, 269
Bloch, H., 86
Boruda, D. J., 92
Bovet, L., 27
Bow Group, 221
Bowlby, John, 157
Burchard, J., 277
Burt, Sir Cyril, 72, 110, 118

Capper, John, 208
Carpenter, Mary, 208, 264
Carr-Saunders, A. M., 70
Chadwick, Edwin, 240
Charles, D. C., 117
Christie, Nils, 27, 40, 54
Churchill, Sir Winston, 220
Clarke, A. D. B., 114
Cloward, R. A., 93
Cohen, Albert K., 89–91, 98, 232, 294
Craft, Michael, 115

Cressey, Donald R., 54, 68, 170

Dickens, Charles, 208
Douglas, J. W. B., 72, 121, 160–61, 167
Drillien, C. M., 120
Du Cane, Sir Edmund, 208
Dunlop, Anne B., 223
Durkheim, E., 83, 87–8

East, Sir Norwood, 63
Eilenberg, M. D., 58, 118
Ellis, John, 264
Elmhorn, Kerstin, 40
Epps, Phyllis, 198
Erickson, M. L., 41
Eysenck, H. J., 137, 139, 141–2, 144, 145–6, 276

Ferguson, T., 26, 58, 72, 73, 74, 118
Ferracuti, F., 201
Foster, Frank, 267
Fox, Sir Lionel, 225
Freud, Sigmund, 148, 152
Friedlander, Kate, 151, 174
Fyvel, T. R., 97, 98

George, William, 265
Gibbens, T. C. N., 26, 56, 58, 70, 72, 115, 119, 123, 138, 169, 197, 198, 203, 228
Gibbs, F. A., 122
Gibson, H. B., 138
Gittins, J., 70
Glaser, D., 63

Glueck, S. and E. T., 28, 72, 118, 126–7, 165–6
Goddard, H. H., 109
Goldfarb, W., 158, 159
Golding, William, 54
Goring, Charles, 108
Grant, J. D. and M. Q., 283–4
Grunhut, Max, 65
Grygier, T., 296

Harlow, H. F., 159
Hartshorne, H., 43, 46, 60, 179
Hathaway, S. R., 145, 166, 169, 170
Havinghurst, R. J., 180, 283
Hewitt, L. E., 173, 175
Hill, Dennis, 122
Hirsch, C. A., 68
Hodges, E. F., 254
Hood, Roger, 227
Hooton, E. A., 108
Hurwitz, S., 52

Jenkins, R. L., 173, 175
Jones, Maxwell, 266
Jung, Carl, 142
Jungk, Robert, 54

Kallmann, Franz, 130
Kinsey, A. C., 193
Klare, Hugh, 222
Kohlberg, Lawrence, 180
Kranz, H., 131
Kretchmer, E., 124, 125
Kvaraceus, W. C., 166, 169

Lane, Homer, 265
Lange, J., 131
Lewis, Hilda, 160
Linken, Arnold, 188
Little, Alan, 19, 144, 160
Little, W. R., 56
Loban, W., 171

Lombroso, Cesare, 106–8, 128
Loomis, S. D., 122

McCabe, S., 223
McClintock, F. H., 23–4, 74, 201
McCord, W. and J., 27, 71, 110, 118, 161
Maliphant, Rodney, 65
Mannheim, H., 25, 57, 70, 164, 278, 281
Makarenko, Anton, 265
Marcus, B., 112
Martin, J. M., 202
Matza, D., 95–6
May, M. A., 43, 46, 60, 179
Mays, J. B., 37, 39
Merton, R. K., 88–9, 90, 93, 294
Metz, F. A. De, 264
Middleton, P. M., 277
Milgram, Stanley, 54
Miller, Derek, 267, 270–74, 296
Miller, W. B., 91
Mohr, J. W., 195
Monachesi, E. D., 145, 166, 169, 170
Monahan, T. P., 71
Morris, H. H., 203
Morris, Ruth, 197
Morris, T. P., 56, 66
Morse, Mary, 249
Moses, Earl R., 67, 69

Naess, S., 160
Ntsekhe, V. R., 56
Nye, F. I., 41, 42, 59

Ogden, D. A., 119
Ohlin, L. E., 93
O'Kelly, Elizabeth, 198

Parnell, R. W., 126
Paterson, Alexander, 220
Paxman, Judge, 280

Peck, P. F., 180–82, 283
Peterson, D. R., 172–3
Piaget, J., 179–80, 283
Pinatel, J., 52
Pollak, O. L., 197
Polsky, H. W., 267, 274–6
Pond, D. A., 121, 122
Porterfield, A. L., 40
Porteus, S. D., 137–8
Power, Michael, 17, 66
Prince, Joyce, 228
Prys Williams, G., 19

Quay, H. C., 172–3

Radzinowicz, Leon, 78
Reiss, A. J., 169, 175
Rice, K., 63
Romilly, Samuel, 207
Rose, A. Gordon, 56, 70, 228
Rose, G. N. C., 19
Rudolf, G. de M., 116
Russell, Rev. Whitworth, 221

Savitz, L., 69
Schmideberg, M., 262
Schofield, Michael, 38, 192, 195
Schuessler, K. F., 170
Schwitzgebel, Ralph, 247
Scott, P. D., 26, 36, 94, 188, 230
Sellin, Thorsten, 35–6
Shaftesbury, Lord, 240
Shaw, Clifford, 65
Sheldon, W. H., 124–6, 128
Short, J. F., 41, 42, 59
Sillitoe, Alan, 98
Slater, E. T. O., 131
Solomon, R. L., 141

Sprott, W. J. H., 75, 78
Stein, Z., 113
Stott, D. H., 119, 120, 168
Stumpfl, F., 131
Sturup, G. K., 194
Susser, M., 113
Sutherland, E. H., 54, 68, 84–5, 87, 294

Tait, C. D., 254
Tannenbaum, F., 86
Thrasher, F. M., 85, 93, 294
Trasler, Gordon, 141
Trenaman, J., 70, 73, 74
Tyler, V., 277

Vaz, E. W., 59
Vernon, P. E., 111

Walker, Nigel, 99, 116, 196, 282
Wallerstein, J. S., 40
Warburton, F., 144
Wardle, C. J., 160
Whitaker, Ben, 34
Whyte, W. F., 86, 93
Wichern, J. H., 264
Wilkins, L. T., 24, 25, 91, 164, 278, 281
Wilson, B. R., 100–101
Wilson, G., 106
Wilson, Harriet, 77, 78
Wolfgang, Marvin, 35–6, 201
Woodward, Mary, 109
Wootton, Barbara, 158, 238
Worsley, Henry, 62
Wyle, C. J., 40

Yablonsky, Lewis. 92–3, 100, 294